Memory-Based Parsing

Natural Language Processing

Volume 7

Memory-Based Parsing
by Sandra Kübler

Memory-Based Parsing

Sandra Kübler

Eberhard Karls Universität Tübingen

John Benjamins Publishing Company

Amsterdam / Philadelphia

∞™ The paper used in this publication meets the minimum requirements of American National Standard for Information Sciences – Permanence of Paper for Printed Library Materials, ANSI Z39.48-1984.

For my parents

Library of Congress Cataloging-in-Publication Data

Sandra Kübler

Memory-based parsing / Sandra Kübler.

p. cm. (Natural Language Processing, ISSN 1567–8202 ; v. 7)

Includes bibliographical references and index.

1. Computational linguistics. 2. Parsing (Computer grammar)

P98.5.P38 K83 2004

410/.285 22 2004052954

ISBN 90 272 4991 1 (Eur.) / 1 58811 590 9 (US) (Hb; alk. paper)

John Benjamins Publishing Co. · P.O. Box 36224 · 1020 ME Amsterdam · The Netherlands

John Benjamins North America · P.O. Box 27519 · Philadelphia PA 19118-0519 · USA

CONTENTS

Chapter 1
Introduction

In this chapter, we will give an overview of the two concepts that are central to this book: parsing and machine learning. We will conclude this chapter with an outline of the book.

1.1 Parsing

Syntactic parsing has long been one of the central tasks in the field of Natural Language Processing (NLP). The term *parsing* has been used in different scientific disciplines such as NLP, cognitive psychology, and compiler construction, and is generally used as a basic concept which does not require a definition or a description. In all fields, the general concept describes an algorithm or an application of such an algorithm (as a computer program or in the human mind) that is capable of examining an input for correctness with reference to a specific grammar and assigning a structural description to the input. But even within the field of NLP, there is no agreement concerning the content of these structural descriptions.

The Oxford Companion to the English Language (McArthur, 1992) defines parsing as:

> (1) Analyzing a sentence into its constituents, identifying in greater or less detail the syntactic relations and parts of speech.
> (2) Describing a word in a sentence, identifying its part of speech, inflectional form, and syntactic function.

This definition clearly attributes parsing to the field of syntactic analysis. There are, however, approaches to parsing that have a semantic interpretation of the input as their aim. Another possible type of structure would be text or discourse structure. In this and the following chapters, we will restrict our discussion of parsing to parsing as it is used in NLP, and more specifically to the field of syntactic analysis. We will use *parsing* and *syntactic parsing* as synonyms since syntactic analysis is the major area of application for the parsers described here.

A parser can generally be separated into two major parts: the parsing algorithm and thc data (i.c. grammar, lcxicon, ctc.). A parsing algorithm is generally independent of the grammar but not of the expressive power of the grammar. The higher the grammar is in the Chomsky Hierarchy (regular, context-free, context-sensitive, or unrestricted rewrite grammars), the more complex the parsing algorithm needs to be. Research in NLP can be grouped into two main areas: parsing based on finite-state (regular) grammars or standard context-free grammars, with the aim of broad data coverage, and parsing based on more powerful grammar formalisms such as Lexical-Functional Grammar (LFG) (Kaplan & Bresnan, 1982), Tree-Adjoining Grammar (TAG) (Joshi, 1987) or Head-Driven Phrase Structure Grammar (HPSG) (Pollard & Sag, 1994), which provide an in-depth analysis of narrowly defined sets of data. Until recently, the linguistic knowledge encoded in these various grammar formalisms was in the form of hand-crafted grammatical rules and principles. The language model used by such approaches is a discrete model, i.e. the task of the parser is to decide on the correctness of a sentence and on the analyses, both with regard to a specific grammar. Manual creation of grammars though, is a very time-consuming task. This problem is well known in NLP as the *knowledge acquisition bottleneck*. In order to overcome this problem, *data-driven* approaches to parsing were developed. Data-driven models accept the linguistic information as given in an already annotated training corpus. Such parsers concentrate on methods of extracting the necessary information from these annotations, generally in form of rules and probabilities. These two paradigms of discrete and data-driven approaches, however, only present two extreme positions; there exist many parsers which incorporate features of both paradigms.

The main problem that occurs in parsing is *syntactic ambiguity*. Given a grammar of non-trivial size and a sentence, there generally exist several possible analyses concerning the attachment of phrases. In sentence (1), for example, the German noun phrase "die Woche" is morphologically ambiguous between nominative and accusative case. Thus, this noun phrase could potentially function as the subject, the direct (accusative) object, or a bare-NP verbal modifier. The two prepositional phrases are ambiguous between modifying the verb or the immediately preceding noun phrase.

(1) ansonsten bin ich die Woche in Dresden zum Kongreß
apart from that am I the week in Dresden to a conference
'apart from that I am in Dresden that week for a conference'

The two paradigms incorporate different strategies of treating such ambiguities. Parsing with hand-crafted rules and discrete language models lists all possible analyses; it has no means to rank these readings by preference. For this reason, the main task in improving these types of parsing approaches concerns the reduction of such ambiguities in the grammar by relying on linguistic knowledge such as subcategorization information and selectional restrictions. Knowledge of the morphological analysis of the phrase in combination with subject-verb agreement would exclude the subject reading for the noun phrase "diese Woche", and subcategorization information would also exclude the direct object reading for this noun phrase. Data-driven approaches, such as parsers based on probabilistic context-free grammars, on the other hand, select a preferred reading from the list of analyses. Preferences are learned from annotated texts of a specific domain in the form of probabilities. These parsers can therefore adapt to different domains as well as to different text types. If such a parser was trained on the domain of the arrangement of business appointments and of travel scheduling, the rule probabilities should reflect that, in this domain, the analysis of "diese Woche" as a verbal modifier is associated with the highest probability.

The two paradigms, parsing with hand-crafted grammars and data-driven parsing, also differ in terms of the coverage of grammars. Parsers that are based on hand-crafted grammars concentrate on very detailed analyses of specific phenomena in language. In contrast, data-driven approaches have broad data coverage and robustness as their goal, aiming at assigning at least one analysis to any input sentence, even if such an analysis requires rules of very low probabilities.

As described above, data-driven parsing approaches extract regularities of language data in form of probabilities from training material. Since most of these parsers belong to the category of supervised learning methods (cf. the next section for a definition of supervised machine learning), they require syntactically annotated texts (treebanks) from which they can learn these regularities. The calculated probabilities, however, can only be reliable if they are based on a certain number of occurrences of a phenomenon and so the treebanks need to be rather extensive. At present, a generally accepted size for treebanks is in the order of 1 000 000 words. As the manual or semi-automatic annotation of syntactic structures is very labor-intensive, this size is dictated more by the availability of resources than by the actual needs of data-driven parsers. Extracting the necessary information from these treebanks is not a trivial task: the extraction algorithm needs to be able to find regularities which cover not only the data in the training set but also unseen events. For this task, *machine learning* techniques are generally used. Machine learning will be introduced in the following section.

In this book, we will concentrate on data driven approaches to parsing with the aim of broad coverage. More specifically, we will concentrate on approaches which are based on the machine learning paradigm of *memory-based learning* (cf. next section). A machine learning component extracts the intended structures from an annotated corpus so that during the actual parsing, decisions can be made based on a comparison with the training data. The different approaches presented in later chapters differ in the types of information extracted from the training data as well as in the generalizations made from the original trees.

Since only supervised approaches will be described, a treebank for training is indespensable. For most approaches, one of two treebanks was used: the Penn treebank (Marcus et al., 1993, 1994) for English and the TüBa-D/S treebank (Stegmann et al., 2000) for German.

The Penn treebank is a syntactically annotated corpus in the domain of financial news. It has become a standard in the evaluation of parsers for English, thus ensuring a comparability of results, but also limiting the focus of parsing to a specific domain. TüBa-D/S is a treebank of transliterated spontaneous dialogues, which makes it an interesting training corpus for parsing since the problem of parsing spontaneous speech has not received much attention until now. Such a parser is an indispensable prerequisite for the successful design of dialogue systems.

1.2 Machine Learning

Machine learning (ML) is a term which is used in two different scientific disciplines: computer science and cognitive science. Both disciplines differ in their definition of the aims that are connected to the area of machine learning. The aim of ML research in cognitive science is to model human learning behavior by machines. This restricts the ML models used in this discipline to models that closely resemble the structure of the human brain. Machine learning in computer science, on the other hand, is based on a more general definition: here, the aim is problem solving in general, and the ML models are not restricted to specific architectures. We will concentrate on computer science approaches to machine learning since we do not want to restrict the parsing approaches here to models of human syntax learning. In this area, machine learning can be defined as follows:

> Learning denotes changes in the system that are adaptive in the sense that they enable the system to do the same tasks or tasks drawn from the same population more efficiently and more effectively the next time. (Simon, 1984, p. 28)

This definition consists of two main tenets. First, the change in knowledge, which is necessary to exclude improvement strategies such as using a faster computer or more memory to obtain better results. The second tenet concerns the improvement in efficiency, i.e. in results, and restricts ML approaches to goal-directed learning. Otherwise, the WWW could also be considered an ML system because it collects more knowledge every second.

The early stages of ML were focused on the development of individual algorithms for specific tasks (a thorough overview of many of these early algorithms can be found in (Pinker, 1979)). However, in due time, these attempts at finding algorithms resulted in a small collection of approaches that have become a standard inventory for the field of ML. This collection consists of approaches such as *neural networks* (Rumelhart et al., 1994), *memory-based learning* (Stanfill & Waltz, 1986), information theoretic approaches such as *maximum entropy learning* (cf. for example (Jelinek, 1997)) and *support vector machines* (Christianini & Shawe-Taylor, 2000), *genetic algorithms* (cf. for example (Mitchell, 1996)), and *conceptual clustering* (Everitt, 1981). Most of these algorithms perform classification, i.e., they assign one class out of a limited set of possible classes to the element to be classified.

Machine learning algorithms can be separated into two main groups: supervised and unsupervised learning. Supervised learning methods rely on the presence of training data which are already annotated according to the classification system to be learned. In part-of-speech (POS) tagging, for example, the set of POS tags constitutes the set of classes, and the classification task is defined as assigning a POS tag to each word. Consequently, the training data needs to consist of texts in which each word is annotated with its POS tag. Conversely, unsupervised methods work on unannotated data, which for tasks in NLP generally amounts to raw text. They perform learning either as hierarchical grouping of similar elements (conceptual clustering) or as selecting one hypothesis for structuring the search space by some more abstract principle such as *Minimum Description Length*.

NLP discovered machine learning as a useful method when it became clear that scaling up from toy systems to large-scale systems was not feasible by manually adding more knowledge. ML provided a methodology to acquire knowledge automatically. In this area, supervised learning methods are mostly used since the tasks generally were not restricted to solving a task such as driving a car, for example, in which the internal representation of different system states is irrelevant as long as certain rules are learned. In the linguistic domain, the task approached by machine learning methods can generally be defined as annotation or analysis of data, and the annotations or analyses are useful only if they are also linguistically meaningful.

This is ensured by giving the learning algorithm a set of annotated training data from which it can find the intended regularities (cf. the POS tagging example above).

In computer science, research in machine learning is centered around determining specific characteristics of different ML methods such as their behavior in the presence of noisy (i.e. incorrectly annotated) data or of irrelevant features. For this reason, tests are generally based on artificial data sets which can be tightly controlled with regard to the noise level, interdependence of features, etc. These results, however, are only of limited use for problems in NLP since natural language data are characterized by a mixture of noise, interdependent features, classes of varying cardinality, subregularities and exceptions which cannot be distinguished from noise (for a more detailed description see Section 2.3.1). For this reason, researchers who work on applying ML methods to problems in NLP need to focus on methods whose bias is suited to these data characteristics.

In this book, we will present approaches to parsing based on the machine learning paradigm of *memory-based learning*. Memory-based learning is a supervised learning method which does not abstract from the training data. Instead, the data are stored without modification in the instance base. For the classification of a new instance, the most similar instances from the instance base are selected by the application of a similarity metric, and the most frequent class of these instances is selected as the class for the new instance (for a more detailed description of the method see Section 2.1). Memory-based learning has a record of successful applications in NLP tasks, for example, for phoneme-grapheme conversion (Stanfill & Waltz, 1986; Daelemans, van den Bosch & Weijters, 1996), POS tagging (Cardie, 1993; Daelemans, Zavrel, Berck & Gillis, 1996; Zavrel & Daelemans, 1997*b*), and word sense disambiguation (Dagan et al., 1997; Escudero et al., 2000; Veenstra et al., 2000), to name only a few. This proves that the bias of memory-based learning is adequate for such tasks. It may be speculated that the main characteristic of memory-based learning, i.e. not generating any abstraction from the data, is advantageous in the presence of noise as well as subregularities. In the case of noisy instances, the effect of these instances is superseded by other, more numerous correctly annotated instances, while for subregularities, a very high similarity or even the identity of the instances will lead to the selection of the correct class from the subregular instance. An additional advantage of memory-based learning can be found in its capability of handling lexicalized data (cf. for example (Kübler, 2001), where an approach to base noun phrase (NP) chunking based on word form and POS tag features is described). This capability is due to the smoothing that is inherent in the similarity metric (cf. (Zavrel & Daelemans, 1997*a*)). Most probabilistic approaches, such as maximum entropy models, on the other hand, are incapable of handling such many-valued features successfully.

Memory-based learning is a propositional learning approach, i.e. it accepts instances consisting of a fixed number of feature value pairs. Therefore, a windowing approach is generally used for text annotation tasks. This means that an instance consists of the word to be classified plus a context of fixed size. This window moves to the right when the next word is classified. However, syntactic parsing is a very complex problem, in which a local context is often not sufficient, and so care needs to be taken to adapt the classifier to the characteristics of the task. There are approaches that tackle this problem with a cascaded architecture, in which each classifier in the cascade has a specialized task, and a careful selection of features. Other approaches concentrate on the modification of the original learning algorithm.

1.3 Outline

The remainder of this book is structured as follows. In Chapter 2, we will first introduce the basic concepts of the machine learning approach of *memory-based learning* (MBL) in its standard form and then present extensions to this model concerning the reduction of retrieval costs, storage reduction and adaptation to noisy data. Standard feature weighting metrics for MBL are introduced in Section 2.3.

In Chapter 3, we will give an overview of MBL applications for the tasks noun phrase chunking, partial parsing, grammatical relations assignment, and full parsing. The overview of the literature in this area clearly shows that memory-based learning has been successfully applied to such a complex task as parsing.

An overview of *Data-Oriented Parsing* (DOP) is given in Chapter 4. Apart from the work of Streiter (2001*a*,*b*), which is presented in Section 3.2, and the work on TüSBL in Chapter 5, this approach to parsing is the only one that uses tree fragments which go beyond rules for parsing. In DOP, tree fragments of varying size are extracted from the training corpus and are assigned probabilities. Parsing then uses these tree fragments as rules with internal structure. Since this approach leads to an exponential number of parses and each parse may be generated by exponentially many derivations, Monte Carlo disambiguation is used as a disambiguation heuristic (cf. Section 4.2.2). DOP performs well on small data sizes, with typical problems being speed and scaling up to larger treebanks (cf. Section 4.2.4).

Chapter 5 presents TüSBL, a novel approach to parsing in the memory-based framework. In Section 5.1, we introduce the treebank, TüBa-D/S, the treebank used for evaluating TüSBL. In Section 5.1.2, we give a short comparison of TüBa-D/S and the Penn treebank, which is the standard evaluation treebank for parsers for English. Section 5.2 describes the problems that arise if parsing is defined as a classification task by cascaded classifiers. In this section, we also explain how these problems can be avoided by approaching the problem of parsing as assigning a complete tree to the input sentence and how the standard memory-based approach needs to be modified to accommodate the specific requirements of this new approach. In Section 5.3, we describe how this memory-based parser is integrated into a hybrid architecture, which uses POS tagging and chunk parsing as preprocessing, in order to acquire a repository of information upon which the search for the most similar tree can be based. Section 5.5 gives a more detailed description of the task of parsing when defined as assigning a complete tree structure to an input sentence. It presents the types of information that are available to the parser and the search methods used for traversing the instance base. We then present an approach to feature weighting which differs from standard feature weighting metrics since the parser uses a flexible number of features. In Section 5.8 the backing-off module will be explained. Backing-off is necessary as the parser is not always able to find a similar sentence in the instance base. In such cases, TüSBL uses less reliable information such as the chunk sequence in order to find a similar sentence.

Chapter 6 presents the evaluation of TüSBL on the TüBa-D/S treebank. The evaluation is performed for the complete parser as well as for single components, and the results are compared to other parsers that have been evaluated on the same treebank. We show that, while TüSBL does not reach F-scores comparable to probabilistic parsers, its spanning analyses have a very high quality in terms of the assignment of grammatical functions. We also propose an evaluation measure, dependency-based evaluation, which, in our opinion, gives a clearer picture of the quality of partial parsers such as TüSBL.

In Chapter 7, we compare TüSBL to the three most similar approaches described in Chapters 3 and 4. Chapter 8 summarizes the results on memory-based parsing.

Chapter 2
Memory-Based Learning

Memory-based learning (MBL) is a machine learning technique for classification which is based on the k-nearest neighbor (k-nn) approach. It is also known as instance-based learning, exemplar-based learning, or case-based learning; all names stressing different aspects of the same method[1]. For the MBL approach, the task of classification is defined as finding the appropriate class for an example by learning from a set of examples. By generalizing from the examples in the training data, MBL can also classify unseen events. For each of the training examples the intended class is given, so the method clearly falls within the area of supervised learning. Memory-based learning is also related to case-based reasoning (Riesbeck & Schank, 1989; Kolodner, 1993; Baar & Lenz, 1996), an approach from the field of Artificial Intelligence which also learns from examples. But the answers that such case-based systems output go beyond mere classification and are generally more complex than those of pure classification systems. Therefore, equal importance is given to the further processing of information extracted from the training examples.

In the following section, we will first give an introduction to the basic concepts of memory-based learning and extensions to the basic approach which reduce retrieval costs, storage requirements, handle noise in the training data, and generalize over instances in the same area in the instance base and belonging to the same class. We will then look more closely at feature-weighting techniques and conclude with a summary.

2.1 The Memory-Based Learning Approach

Memory-based learning is part of the paradigm of *lazy learning*. Lazy learning can be described by the following characteristics: while other learning approaches abstract from the training data to learn rules or probabilities and then discard the actual data, lazy learners store the data without modification. This class of learners delays processing the data until a new instance is presented to the system and needs to be classified. Memory-based learning is based on the assumption that similar instances belong to the same class. So, the task can be defined as finding the most similar instance(s) in

[1] We have chosen the term "memory-based learning" because it is the one most widely used in NLP.

prev. word	**word**	next word	prev. POS	POS	next POS	class
NULL	das	geht	NULL	pds	vvfin	NP
das	geht	auf	pds	vvfin	appr	No-NP
geht	auf	die	vvfin	appr	art	No-NP
auf	die	Rechnung	appr	art	nn	NP
die	Rechnung	NULL	art	nn	NULL	NP

Table 2.1: *A toy world example for noun phrase recognition.*

the instance base and using the class which is the most frequent among the retrieved instances as the intended class of the new instance[2]. The instance base constitutes the collection of all instances extracted from the training data.

The data, i.e. the training and the test data, is presented to the memory-based learner as a set of instances. An instance consists of a set of features in the form of attribute-value pairs which contain information on the instance that is considered relevant for the classification task. Exactly one of the features contains the class attributed to the instance in question (this feature is necessarily missing in the test data). The number of features is generally fixed for a specific learning problem "although this restriction is not required by the paradigm itself ..." (Aha et al., 1991, p. 40). The set of n features defines the instance space, an n-dimensional search space.

Table 2.1 gives a toy world example of an instance base. The classification task here is defined as "Decide whether a word belongs to a noun phrase or not". Consequently, the classification is two-way, the two possible classes are "NP" and "Not-NP"[3]. The instance base consists of the instances for each word in the German sentence (2). The features considered relevant for the classification task were the word to be classified, the preceding and

[2] This assumption has a cognitive equivalent: Daelemans et al. base their work on the hypothesis "that performance in real-world tasks ... is based on reasoning on the basis of similarity of new situations to *stored representations of earlier experiences*, rather than on the application of *mental rules* abstracted from earlier experiences as in rules-based processing" (Daelemans, van den Bosch & Zavrel, 1999, p. 1, emphasis theirs). Since we do not aim to develop a cognitive model of syntax learning, we will not pursue the cognitive perspective further.

[3] This is a simplification of the problem of NP recognition. For an actual application, one would need a third class to mark the beginning of a noun phrase immediately following another noun phrase as in *Ich habe [ihm] [das Buch] gegeben.* (cf. Section 3.1 for a more complete description of this problem.).

prev. word	**word**	next word	prev. POS	POS	next POS	class
die	Termine	NULL	art	nn	NULL	???

Table 2.2: *A new instance.*

the following word, and their respective POS tags. The last column contains the information whether the word belongs to a noun phrase or not.

(2) das geht auf die Rechnung
that goes on the account
'that gets put on the account'

Now, if the new instance in Table 2.2 is presented to the MBL system for classification, it will be compared to all instances in the instance base, and the learner will (probably)[4] decide that the last instance is the most similar one and that the new instance also belongs to the class "NP".

A memory-based learner consists of two components: the learning component, which is memory-based, and the performance component, which is similarity-based. The learning component implements the *lazy learning* paradigm, storing the presented training instances without abstraction. This strategy contrasts with *eager learning* approaches for which the actual training data are processed and abstracted into rules or probabilities during the learning process, and the actual data are discarded for the classification task. One might argue that the processing of the actual language data into instances as well as the choice of which instances should be used for a specific classification task should be regarded as abstraction. This is undoubtedly true, but this processing is common to all learning approaches based on classification and therefore should not be regarded as abstraction inherent to the algorithm. The only abstraction inherent to memory-based learning is due to the similarity metric, which allows the classification of previously unseen instances.

Eager approaches are based on the assumption that their learning bias, i.e. the specific form of abstraction, is a valid representation of the problem to be learned. If this assumption is correct, they profit from high processing rates. If, on the other hand, the assumption turns out to be wrong, the actual training data is no longer available so the error cannot be rectified without repeating the training with a modified bias. Lazy learners, however,

[4] The decision depends on the specific similarity metric (cf. the next paragraph) used to measure the similarity of the features as well as on the weights assigned to the features.

"can respond to unanticipated queries in ways not available to eager learners ..." (Aha, 1998, p. 2) since they have access to the original data. Another advantage of keeping the data in the original form is that test instances that were already seen during the training phase can be classified with the certainty of being correct. If the classification is based on rules, the result needs to be inferred with the general likelihood of erroneous decisions even for instances that are part of the training data. In memory-based learners, however, an *exact match*, i.e. an identical instance in the instance base, will always be preferred.

The performance component uses the instance base to find the most similar instance(s) to a new instance. It compares the new instance to all instances and retrieves either the k most similar instances or the instances whose distance to the new instance belongs to the k closest ones. From these retrieved instances, the most frequent class is extracted and returned as the class of the new instance. If there is a tie among the most frequent classes in the set of retrieved instances, one of the classes is chosen randomly[5]. The best value for k for a specific problem needs to be decided empirically. However, there exist a few general rules: setting k to a small number means that only a small number of instances that were judged to be very similar to the test instance are considered in classification. This is useful in cases where a considerable number of subregularities need to be classified. A subregularity is likely to be represented by a small number of instances in the instance base. If, therefore, a large number of instances vote on the class, the majority will belong to a different class. The same is true if only a small instance base exists, then the instances are so sparse that the retrieval of a large number of neighbors will include instances of one or more neighboring classes. However, if the training data are likely to contain noise, i.e. wrong classifications, setting k to a higher number will increase the reliability of the classifier since, even in cases for which a noisy instance is the nearest neighbor, a number of correctly classified instances will be considered for classification. Typical tasks in NLP, though, are characterized by the presence of both types of data: subregularities as well as noise. In such cases, the classifier must be sensitive enough to recognize the former cases as such, but not too sensitive so as to confuse noisy instances with subregularities.

[5] There are also more sophisticated methods for solving ties; Daelemans et al. (2002), for example, increase the number of k and then make the choice based on the higher number of instances. If the tie still persists in the larger neighbor set, the class with the highest overall occurrence in the instance base is chosen.

The comparison of a new instance to instances in the instance base is executed by the use of a *similarity metric*. Since the memory-based approach does not use any abstraction from the training data, the success of the learner in classifying unseen instances crucially depends on the choice of the similarity metric. There are numerous possible metrics that can be used for distance metrics (cf. the literature on conceptual clustering, for example (Everitt, 1981)). For memory-based learning, however, only two very basic metrics are generally used: the *overlap metric* and the *Euclidean distance.* One of the main concerns in choosing a distance metric is the treatment of numeric features. If the set of features contains both numeric and symbolic features, it is especially important to normalize the higher distances between numeric feature values.

2.1.1 *Overlap Metric*

The *overlap metric* is the most basic metric that works especially well for features with symbolic values. The distance between instances X and Y is computed by comparing the n features and adding 1 to the distance if they are different and 0 otherwise. If the features are numeric, the distance between two features is calculated by the distance between the features divided by the distance of the maximally and minimally possible values for this feature. The equation for the distance of two instances, $distance(X, Y)$, is given in Equation 1, and the one for the feature distance, $\delta(x_i, y_i)$ in Equation 2. With this metric, the normalization of numeric features is based on the maximal distance of the values of a feature.

$$distance(X,Y) = \sum_{i=1}^{n} \delta(x_i, y_i) \tag{1}$$

$$\delta(x_i, y_i) = \begin{cases} \frac{|x_i - y_i|}{max_i - min_i} & \text{if the values are numeric, else} \\ 0 & \text{if } x_i = y_i \\ 1 & \text{if } x_i \neq y_i \end{cases} \tag{2}$$

2.1.2 *Euclidean Distance*

This metric is very similar to the overlap metric, the only difference being the form which the normalization of numeric features takes. Euclidean distance normalizes the feature distances by squaring them, as shown in Equation 4, before summing them and taking the square root, as in Equation 3. This form of normalization prefers instances with a number of small feature distances over instances with a few greater feature distances.

$$distance(X,Y) = \sqrt{\sum_{i=1}^{n} \delta(x_i, y_i)} \tag{3}$$

$$\delta(x_i, y_i) = \begin{cases} (x_i - y_i)^2 & \text{if the values are numeric, else} \\ 0 & \text{if } x_i = y_i \\ 1 & \text{if } x_i \neq y_i \end{cases} \tag{4}$$

In memory-based learning, there is a tendency to complement these basic distance metrics by feature weighting mechanisms rather than using more complex similarity metrics; an overview of the main feature weighting mechanisms will be given in Section 2.3. There exists a more elaborate metric that has been used for memory-based learning, the *value-difference metric* (Stanfill & Waltz, 1986). We will describe a modification of this metric by Cost & Salzberg (1993) in Section 2.3.2.

2.2 Extensions to the Basic Model

The basic memory-based learning approach, as presented in the previous section, suffers from the well known problems that affect all lazy learning approaches in their pure forms: higher storage requirements in comparison to eager approaches, resulting in higher retrieval costs if no indexing scheme is used, and intolerance of noise and irrelevant features. Therefore, several modifications to the basic algorithm have been suggested. They will be presented in the following paragraphs, but we will postpone the problem of irrelevant features until Section 2.3. The approach to reduce retrieval costs, on the one hand, is an improvement of the actual implementation and it does not, in general, affect the classification outcome. The methods for storage reduction, noise tolerance, and generalizing over instances, on the other hand, are heuristic in nature and can therefore have an effect on the selection of nearest neighbors and thus on accuracy.

2.2.1 *Reducing Retrieval Costs*

In their memory-based learning toolkit TiMBL, Daelemans et al. (2001) have implemented two indexing strategies in order to increase the retrieval of the most similar instances: they store the instances not as a list but in a tree-based memory, and they use inverted indices.

Instead of storing instances in an unordered list, TiMBL creates a decision tree (cf. (Mitchell, 1997; Quinlan, 1993)) in which each node represents

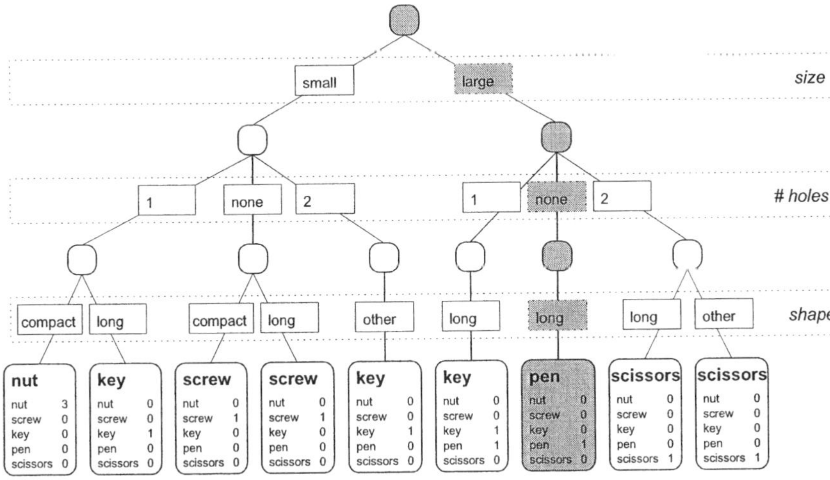

Fig. 2.1: *A section of the tree-structured instance base for object classification (Daelemans et al., 2001, p. 25).*

one feature, and the branches leaving this node represent the possible values for this feature. The main difference with regard to decision trees lies in the computation of how the features are ordered. While in standard top-down induction of decision trees, the daughter feature is computed individually for each node in the tree, TiMBL induces an *oblivious* decision tree, i.e. all nodes of the same depth from the root node represent the same feature (see Figure 2.1 for an example). An instance is thus represented by a path from the root node to one of the leaf nodes. The information of the class to which an instance belongs is stored in the leaf node of the instance. In traversing the tree, matching feature values are preferred so that this tree structure leads to very effective searches for exact matches. In all other cases, a depth-first search needs fewer comparisons of feature values as common path prefixes can be reused for calculating the new distance, and complete subtrees can be ignored if the distance of the features constituting their path prefix is greater than the distance of the current most similar instance. In order to obtain an efficient search strategy, an ordering of features must be found that produces a maximum number of common path prefixes. Daelemans et al. report that "an ordering which was found to produce small trees for many ... NLP data sets is Gain Ratio divided by the number of feature values ..." (Daelemans et al., 2001, p. 26). Therefore the features with the highest gain ratio, i.e. the features that give the most information about the class of the feature, are placed at the top of the decision tree. Gain ratio is a normalized variant of *information gain*, which gives a measure of how much information a feature contributes to the selection of the correct class, i.e. how great the reduction in entropy of the class is when this feature is known. A more detailed discussion of these concepts as feature weighting methods can be found in Section 2.3.

TiMBL also provides the means to create an inverted index of all feature values. In order to prevent the algorithm from comparing a test instance to instances that do not share even a single feature value, an index is created that stores for each feature value the instances that share this value. The index can only be used for instance bases without numeric values and combined with feature distance metrics that use global feature weights (cf. Section 2.3.2) since for all other cases it is possible that the nearest neighbor is an instance that does not share any feature values with the test instance.

Daelemans et al. add the following caveat: "Unfortunately, this also implies that the storage of both an instance base and an inverted index takes about twice the amount of memory. Therefore we have chosen to turn it off by default. However, especially for data with very large numbers of low frequent values it can be substantially faster to turn it on." (Daelemans et al., 2001, p. 26, footnote 4).

2.2.2 *Storage Reduction*

Aha et al. (1991) introduce the algorithm *IB2*, which is a modification of the standard, incremental memory-based learning algorithm *IB1*. *IB1* is an implementation of memory-based learning as described in Section 2.1 except that building the instance base is treated as an incremental learning process. Thus, the learning phase is an ongoing process which adds to the instance base all instances presented to the system for classification.

IB2 is an extension of the standard algorithm which allows a reduction of stored instances by an instance selection process. The reasoning behind the modification is that only informative instances, i.e. instances that contain new information about the class boundaries of the instance space, need to be stored. Since it is impossible to tell during the learning process which instance would be informative regarding possible future queries, Aha et al. (1991) employ a heuristic for selecting the instances to be stored: they argue that only instances that are misclassified during the incremental learning process need to be stored. *IB1* calculates the distance of each new instance from the training set from the instances in the instance base and then adds the new instance to the instance base. *IB2*, on the other hand, stores only those new instances that are classified incorrectly by the instances already in the instance base. Thus, instances for which there is already a good nearest neighbor in the instance base are discarded.

In a comparison of *IB1* and *IB2* for an artificial domain with a clear-cut linear boundary between the two classes, *IB2* performs only slightly worse, but the number of items stored is less than 10% if no noise is present in the training data. It is, however, intuitively clear that *IB2* has a tendency to store noisy data. Noisy instances constitute irregularities in the instance space. For this reason, they cannot be classified by the other instances in the instance base. As a consequence of a higher percentage of noisy instances in the instance base, the error rate of the classifier will increase since these instances are used more often in classification.

Daelemans, van den Bosch & Weijters (1996) have developed a compression technique, IGTree, that is based on top-down induction of decision trees (cf. (Mitchell, 1997; Quinlan, 1993)) as described in the section above. In order to reduce storage requirements, pruning is used. Pruning for IGTree consists of removing subtrees that lead to the same class. Thus, features that do not contribute any information to the selection of the most similar instance are discarded so that the number of comparisons made during classification is reduced. As a consequence of pruning, the decision tree no longer contains all features and feature values. This means that the search algorithm needs to be adapted so that instances for which no exact match exists can be classified correctly: the search for these instances does not reach a leaf in the tree as one of the features could not be found in the pruned tree. Therefore IGTree stores in each non-terminal node the most probable class given the feature values that have been used in the path from the root node.

Daelemans, van den Bosch & Weijters (1996) report results of a comparison between IGTree and the standard memory-based classifier that uses information gain as its weighting method, IB1-IG. The test problems were grapheme-phoneme conversion, hyphenation, and POS tagging. For the former two problems, they report slightly worse results for IGTree, 97.07% compared to 97.17% for grapheme-phoneme conversion, and 94.53% compared to 95.21% for hyphenation. IGTree obtains a compression rate of 95.1% for the first task and 91.1% for the second. For POS tagging, the results are inconclusive: Daelemans, van den Bosch & Weijters (1996) report a significantly better performance for IGTree: 95.1% compared to 94.7%. In a later publication, however, Daelemans, van den Bosch & Zavrel (1999) report a better performance of IB1-IG for a similar POS tagging task; in this case, however, a different set of features was used.

2.2.3 *Noise Tolerance*

Noisy data constitute a problem for any machine learning algorithm. However, the problem is multiplied when instance selection methods are applied as, for example, in *IB2* (cf. the previous section). This algorithm tends to store noisy instances since they seem to present new information about class boundaries in the instance space.

Since *IB2* is very sensitive to noisy training data (as described in Section 2.2.2) Aha et al. (1991) modified this algorithm to handle noise better. This approach can be applied not only with instance selection algorithms such as *IB2* but also for all other memory-based algorithms when noise constitutes a problem. The resulting algorithm *IB3* removes instances with a poor classification record during the incremental learning process from the instance base. To this end, the learner keeps for each instance a record of the number of correct and false classifications made for newly added instances. When a new instance is presented to the learner, it is compared to all instances in the instance base, but only instances with a good classification record qualify as nearest neighbors. Acceptability depends on the classification accuracy of an instance being significantly greater than its class's observed (relative) frequency. For classes with a high frequency, instances need features with a high classification accuracy in order to be accepted. For low-frequency classes though, features with a lower classification accuracy are sufficient. Thus, skewed feature distributions can be handled more easily. In a last step after considering a new instance, all instances with a poor classification record are removed from the instance base.

In a comparison of the three *IB*-algorithms in several standard applications, *IB3* outperformed the other two in domains with noisy data and in a domain with sparse data. Aha et al. also found that *IB3* performs significantly better than *IB1* and *IB2* when confronted with noisy data in a simple artificial domain. The new algorithm also reduces the percentage of stored instances, to 5.8% on a 10% noise level in the training data and to almost zero at high noise levels. "This occurred because few instances have good classification accuracies." (Aha et al., 1991, p. 58). Additionally, there is a reduction in the percentage of noisy instances accepted in the instances base.

2.2.4 *Nearest Hyperrectangle Approaches*

Memory-based learning is a version of k-nearest neighbors classifiers in that it retrieves exactly k most similar instances from the instance base to classify a new instance. The algorithm ignores the fact that the area in instance space from which the most similar instances are retrieved consists of either more or less than k instances of the same class.

Salzberg (1991) introduces a family of algorithms which generalize from instances to hyperrectangles, i.e. families of instances, which can then be used in classification instead of the instances. In this way, the complete family of instances is involved in classification.

During training, instances are incrementally clustered into the closest hyperrectangle if their classes coincide. The algorithm starts with a fixed number of randomly chosen seeds, which then form the initial hyperrectangles. These are trivial in that they cover exactly one instance. Then the algorithm loops over the remaining instances and tries to assign them to already existing hyperrectangles by calculating the distance between the instance and a hyperrectangle. If the closest one has the same class, the instance is included in the hyperrectangle, otherwise the class of the second closest hyperrectangle is compared to the instance's class. If both hyperrectangles belong to different classes to the instance, the instance forms a new hyperrectangle. Thus, instances are clustered into one family if they belong to one class and if they differ only in features which are irrelevant for class membership. The approach abstracts over the instances since it collapses different feature combinations so that combinations which cannot be witnessed in the training instances are also covered. This formulation of the algorithm often results in overlapping and nested hyperrectangles.

Each hyperrectangle H^j is defined by its lower left corner H^j_{ll} and its upper right corner H^j_{ur}. For this reason, the nearest hyperrectangle approach has an axis-parallel bias. The distance between an instance I and a hyperrectangle H^j is defined as follows:

$$distance(I, H^j) = w_{H^j} \times \sqrt{\sum_{i=1}^{n} w_i \delta_i(I, H^j)} \tag{5}$$

where n is the number of features, w_i the weight of feature i (cf. next section), w_{H^j} the weight of H^j calculated as the number of times H was compared to an instance divided by the number of times it had the same class as the instance. $\delta_i(I, H^j)$ is defined as follows:

$$\delta_i(I, H^j) = \begin{cases} I_i - H^j_{ur,i} & \text{if } I_i > H^j_{ur,i} \\ H^j_{ll,i} - I_i & \text{if } H^j_{ll,i} > I_i \\ 0 & \text{otherwise} \end{cases} \tag{6}$$

Wettschereck & Dietterich (1995) compared this approach to a standard k-nearest neighbors algorithm. They used three synthetic data sets and 8 data sets from the UC-Irvine repository (Murphy & Aha, 1994). Two of the three synthetic data sets are constructed so that they have axis-parallel decision boundaries, the third one having a diagonal decision boundary. Thus, the two sets are consistent with the bias of the nearest-hyperrectangular approach while the last one is not. The experiments of Wettschereck & Dietterich (1995) show that the k-nn learner is significantly better than the nearest hyperrectangular approach in all 8 UCI tasks. For the two synthetic tasks conforming to the bias of the latter approach, only specific settings improve its performance so that it significantly outperforms the k-nn approach.

Further experiments with several modifications of the nearest-hyperrectangle algorithm show that its inferior performance is mostly due to overlapping hyperrectangles, and to some extent, the suboptimal search algorithm. But even if both parameters are optimized and *information gain* (cf. the next section) is used for weighting, k-nn learning still outperforms the nearest-hyperrectangle approach.

Salzberg's algorithm (Salzberg, 1991) was reimplemented by van den Bosch (2002) in the system FAMBL2. The algorithm includes a more principled approach to the selection of the initial seeds: it uses *class-prediction strength* (CPS) (Salzberg, 1990) to order the instances based on their success in predicting the class of their surrounding nearest neighbors.

> Class-prediction strength of an instance i is typically defined …as the number of times the instance is a nearest neighbor of a training instance regardless of its class (N), minus the number of these nearest neighbors that are of a different class ($Ndif_i$), divided by N to express a portion between 0.0 and 1.0: $e_i = \frac{N_{\square}-Ndif_{\square}}{N}$. An instance with class-prediction strength $e = 1.0$ is a perfect predictor of its own class; an e near or at 0.0 indicates that the family [i.e. hyperrectangle] is a bad predictor. (van den Bosch, 2002, p. 214)

task	FAMBL2	IB1-IG	compression rate
GP	87.9%	88.1%	41.2%
POS	96.6%	96.6%	71.0%
NP	97.5%	97.5%	22.2%
PP	79.9%	80.8%	65.9%

Table 2.3: *A comparison of FAMBL to IB1-IG (van den Bosch, 2002, p. 218).*

FAMBL2 uses the instances with the highest CPS as seeds. In contrast to Salzberg (1991), van den Bosch restricts clustering to the closest hyperrectangle, thus restricting overlapping families to a minimum.

Van den Bosch (2002) compares FAMBL2 to IB1-IG (cf. Section 2.2.2) on different NLP tasks: English grapheme-phoneme conversion (GP), English POS tagging (POS), base-NP chunking (NP) and PP attachment (PP) among others. The results in Table 2.3 show that FAMBL2 does not improve generalization accuracy, but it does compress the instance base. Interestingly, however, a detailed error analysis shows that when FAMBL2 and IB1-IG disagree, then very often one of them predicted the correct class. This result might suggest that a combination of the two classifiers via weighted voting might improve results.

2.3 Feature Weighting Metrics

Standard memory-based algorithms are highly sensitive to the selection of features and to the definition of their distance function. In order to alleviate this problem, many algorithms use feature weighting to introduce a bias based on domain knowledge, so irrelevant or redundant features are given less weight in the computation of the distance. If weights are introduced, the overlap distance measure, for example, which is given in Equation 1, is modified so that the distance depends on a weight:

$$distance(X, Y) = \sum_{i=1}^{n} \delta(w(i), x_i, y_i) \tag{7}$$

where $w(i)$ defines the weight of feature i. k-nn methods define the weight as a constant function

$$w(i) = w_i \tag{8}$$

and define

$$\forall_{i \in F}\, w_i = s \tag{9}$$

where F is the feature space and s some scalar constant. Equation 9 restricts the weights to taking the same value for each feature.

In the remainder of this section, we will give an overview of the different methods used for feature weighting. As there are numerous feature weighting approaches, most of which have not been applied to problems in NLP, the following overview will necessarily refrain from describing the details of the individual methods. The interested reader is referred to the original publications for more information. The following overview is based on the reviews of Wettschereck et al. (1997) and Aha (1998). Both overviews compare feature weighting methods that differ in Equations 8 and 9.

Before starting to look into different feature weighting schemes, a short comment on the methods for empirical evaluation used in the following overview is necessary.

2.3.1 *Empirical Evaluation With Artificial Domains*

Most of the following feature weighting methods have been empirically evaluated on simulated, i.e. artificial, data, which is standard practice in the area of machine learning. Artificial data are constructed in a way that they model specific characteristics of the instance space. One data set, for example, might contain 10% noise, another irrelevant features. Since the data are artificial, these characteristics can be controlled to a very high degree. Friedman (1994) motivates this strategy by pointing out that experiments relying on simulated data provide more information:

> For several reasons, comparative studies on real data tend to be less informative than those based on simulated data. First, the true underlying structure in terms of the individual class density distributions is unknown for a real data set. When performance differences between methods are observed one cannot determine the underlying causes and make appropriate generalizations. Second, it is more difficult to reliably estimate such performance differences. A particular data set represents only one (random) sample drawn from the class probability distributions that characterize the system producing the data. This introduces a statistical uncertainty (variance) in the observed performance differences. Different training samples (of the same

> size) produced from the same system will generally give rise to different observed relative performances among the methods. In a simulation study one can average performances over a large number of randomly drawn training samples thereby reducing this source of uncertainty at will. (Friedman, 1994, p. 27)

This approach is certainly useful for scientifically motivated work in this area, i.e. for designing new feature weighting methods and for evaluating their strengths and weaknesses concerning specific types of problems. Friedman (1994) admits that evaluations based on real world data are necessary:

> The main advantage of real data is that it is produced without any knowledge of the particular classification procedures that will be used to test. Therefore, it cannot be customized to favor any particular procedure. Also, there is always the suspicion that artificially constructed examples will not correspond to situations that are likely to occur in practice. (Friedman, 1994, p. 27)

Again, Friedman takes the position of the scientist developing such methods. However, if these methods are used for applications with real data, comparisons based on evaluations in artificial domains are only of limited use for deciding which feature weighting method is best used for which real world problem. It is a well-known problem that in most cases, it is impossible to determine the exact characteristics of real world data sets, for example the level of noise. Therefore, as long as there is no classification of the real world problem in terms of characteristics of the instance space, the user of these feature weighting methods is forced to empirically evaluate each method for every specific problem that is to be learned by such a method.

The situation is especially difficult for problems in NLP. These problems are characterized, as far as it is possible to tell without further exploration of this topic, by classes of significantly varying sizes, by interdependent features, by noise, by subregularities or by exceptions which cannot be distinguished from noisy instances. To the best of our knowledge, there is no artificial data set that comes close to covering these characteristics. For this reason, the following overview on feature weighting methods only defines and structures the search space for choosing an appropriate feature weighting method for parsing problems: it cannot give clear-cut decision criteria.

dimension	possible values
bias	performance, preset
weight space	continuous, binary
representation	given, transformed
generality	global, local
knowledge	poor, intensive

Table 2.4: *Dimensions for categorizing feature weighting methods according to Wettschereck et al. (1997, p. 278).*

2.3.2 *Feature Weighting Dimensions*

Wettschereck et al. (1997) present an overview of feature weighting methods that use alternatives to Equation 9, i.e. they allow different weights for different features. The feature weighting methods reviewed are categorized according to the dimensions shown in Table 2.4.

Bias refers to the distinction whether the weight learning algorithm relies on feedback from the *performance* component, i.e. the classifier, or whether it determines a *preset* bias. Performance algorithms are also called *wrapper* models in machine learning, they attempt to take the learner's bias into consideration during the learning process. The search for optimal feature weight settings is influenced by how well these settings perform in actual classifications. Preset algorithms, also called *filter* models, rely only on the pre-existing model's bias. Here, the search for weight settings is directed by the aim of modeling the training data. The standard procedure is to minimize inter-class similarity while maximizing intra-class similarity. Thus, the distances of instances within one class reach a minimum, and the distance between different classes a maximum.

Performance algorithms can be further distinguished into methods that perform the search in the weight space *online* and those that pass through the training data more than once and perform *batch* optimization. Online optimizers pass through the data only once, and so these optimizers are dependent on the ordering of the data presented to the learner. Online optimizers are especially useful for applications with many irrelevant features because they generally give low weights to those features. "However, it is not clear to what extent they can recognize redundant or highly interacting features" (Wettschereck et al., 1997, p. 280). Batch optimizers, on the other hand, seem to depend to a high degree on design decisions as Wettschereck (1994) reports for the batch weighting approach k-nn$_{vsm}$.

Preset bias methods do not use feedback from the performance model, they use a pre existing model's bias instead. Wettschereck et al. describe methods that use *conditional probabilities, class projection*, and *mutual information*, respectively. We will concentrate on the latter two since they have been applied to problems in the area of NLP; furthermore, Wettschereck et al. report for the first method that "it tends to classify too many instances according to the majority class" (Wettschereck et al., 1997, p. 283). This behavior is especially unsuitable for problems in the area of NLP, which are characterized by a small number of majority classes, i.e. classes which cover the majority of word forms in the texts, and a multitude of classes containing only a few instances. A typical example for such a distribution of classes is POS tagging: here, a small number of classes covering open class words such as nouns, verbs, adjectives and adverbs describe more than 50% of the words in a corpus, depending on the language and the POS tagset[6]. Methods based on conditional probabilities show a tendency to select such majority classes simply because they occur in such large numbers. Classification errors would then occur for closed class words which are erroneously assigned open class labels. Such errors are very damaging for further syntactic analysis since closed class words particularly carry information about the structure of a sentence.

2.3.2.1 *Class Projection*

Stanfill & Waltz (1986) introduce the *value-difference metric* (VDM). This metric uses a complex similarity metric for symbolic features, which was later refined by Cost & Salzberg (1993) into then *Modified Value-Difference Metric* (MVDM).

The equation that MVDM uses to compute the distance of two instances X and Y is given in Equation 10 where n is the number of features:

$$distance(X,Y) = \sum_{i=1}^{n} w(X)\, w(Y) \delta(x_i, y_i)^r \qquad (10)$$

If r is set to 1, this equation yields an overlap metric, and if r is set to 2, it will result in the Euclidean Distance (cf. Section 2.1).

The feature distance $\delta(f_i, g_i)$ calculates the difference of the class probabilities given the feature values of the two instances:

[6] We found that in TüBa-D/S (Stegmann et al., 2000) 59.3% of the words belong to open classes, and 51.0% in TüBa-E (Kordoni, 2000).

$$\delta(f_i, g_i) = \sum_{c_j \in C} | p(c_j | f_i) - p(c_j | g_i) | \quad (11)$$

where C is the set of classes and c_j a member of this set. $p(c_j \mid v_i)$ is the observed relative frequency that instances in the instance base T with value v for feature i belong to class c_j. Equation 11 identifies two instances as similar if their feature values have similar class distributions.

Cost and Salzberg use a weighting scheme based on (Salzberg, 1990), which assigns weights to instances depending on their performance history. In contrast to the original version of Stanfill & Waltz (1986), MVDM can be combined with any weighting scheme.

Stanfill & Waltz (1986) have used their original similarity metric on a pronunciation task. However, they did not compare their method to other weighting approaches. Wettschereck et al. report that "surprisingly little evidence exists that feature-weighting variants of the VDM improve classification performance compared to unweighted variants. Daelemans & van den Bosch (1992) report that a method that assigns weights using information gain ... outperforms the VDM on a grapheme to phoneme conversion task and Aha (1991) reported that even the overlap function outperforms the VDM on some classification tasks" (Wettschereck et al., 1997, p. 283). MVDM, on the other hand, has been successfully applied, for example in word sense disambiguation.

2.3.2.2 *Mutual Information*

Mutual information (MI) (Shannon, 1948; Cover & Thomas, 1991) is a measure from information theory that describes the reduction in uncertainty of one feature value (i.e. the class) if the value of another feature is known[7]. MI is calculated as the difference of the entropy of feature A ($H(A)$) and the entropy of A given feature B ($H(A|B)$). Feature weighting is then calculated by the following equation:

$$w(i) = H(C) - H(C \mid X) = \sum_{v \in V_i} \sum_{c_j \in C} p(c_j, x_i = v) \log \frac{p(c_j, x_i = v)}{p(c_j)\, p(x_i = v)} \quad (12)$$

[7] This is the description for the application of mutual information in memory-based learning. More generally speaking, MI is the reduction in uncertainty of a random variable if the value of another random variable is known (cf. (Manning & Schütze, 1999, p. 66 ff.)) for an introduction).

where V_i is the set of values of feature i, $p(c_j)$ is the relative frequency of class c_j in the instance base, and $p(x_i = v)$ the relative frequency of value v in the instance base. For features that give no information about the class, Equation 12 returns zero, and for features that completely determine the class, it returns a value proportional to $\log(|C|)$.

Daelemans & van den Bosch (1992) use an extension of this feature weighting method in which the weight of a feature is determined by its *information gain* (Quinlan, 1986). Information gain gives a measure of how much a feature contributes to finding the correct class:

$$\begin{aligned} w(i) &= H(C) - \textstyle\sum_{v \in V_i} p(x_i = v) H(C \mid x_i = v) \\ &= \textstyle\sum_{c_j \in C} p(c_j, x_i = v) \\ &\quad - \textstyle\sum_{v \in V_i} \sum_{c_j \in C} -p(c_j \mid x_i = v) \log p(c_j \mid x_i = v) p(x_i = v) \end{aligned} \tag{13}$$

However, it shows a tendency to be sensitive to the number of values that are possible for one feature, therefore Daelemans et al. (2001) use the normalized version called *gain ratio* (Quinlan, 1993) for their memory-based learning toolkit TiMBL: gain ratio is information gain divided by *split info* $si(i)$:

$$w(i) = \frac{H(C) - \sum_{v \in V_i} p(x_i = v) H(C) \mid x_i = v)}{si(i)} \tag{14}$$

with $si(i)$ being the entropy of the feature values:

$$si(i) = -\sum_{v \in V_i} p(x_i = v) \log p(x_i = v) \tag{15}$$

Weighting based on gain ratio has been applied to NLP tasks:

Daelemans and van den Bosch report good results using this weighting method on a hyphenation task (Daelemans & van den Bosch, 1992) and for grapheme-phoneme conversion (van den Bosch & Daelemans, 1993). Daelemans et al. (1993) report the best results using gain ratio for stress assignment in a comparison of three algorithms.

The second dimension that Wettschereck et al. (1997) use after weighting bias is the weight space, i.e. the range of values the weights can take. The standard approach to feature weighting is the use of *continuous* weights. A special case, which has been applied to several lazy learning algorithms, is *feature selection*, which assigns only binary values. One method for implementing feature selection is the use of an induced decision tree. Cardie

(1993), for example, reports a significant improvement for lexical acquisition when using feature selection. Wettschereck et al. give a short summary of the findings concerning feature selection and continuous weighting:

> ...feature selection algorithms perform best when the features used to describe instances are either highly correlated with the class label or completely irrelevant. Feature weighting is more appropriate for tasks where features vary in their relevance, but such methods search larger spaces of weight assignments. (Wettschereck et al., 1997, p. 285)

They conclude that further research is needed to investigate this trade-off.

The third dimension that Wettschereck et al. investigate concerns the representation of features: instead of storing features in the form in which they are presented, the learner can *transform* them before weighting. By splitting up or recombining features, this method can avoid some of the problems of interacting or correlated features, which cause considerable problems for standard learning approaches. Another approach instead of transforming features relies on combining weights in the distance function. To our knowledge, no such method has been used for natural language problems. This might be due to the expectation that feature transformation methods generally expand the set of features. In a domain where sufficiently large sets of training data are difficult to obtain, this would be a major reason to avoid such practices. Another problem with feature transformation is that the resulting features often do not carry any discernible meaning, which "can constitute a significant shortfall of these methods if inspection of the (transformed) classifier is necessary (i.e., additional constraints on the transformation process are required to guarantee comprehensibility" (Wettschereck et al., 1997, p. 277)).

The fourth dimension, generality, concerns the distinction between *global* and *local* feature weighting methods. Global weights apply for all occurrences of a feature in the instance space, while local weights differ according to the specific location of the feature in the instance space. Local weight settings are one method for representing interacting features. If one feature is more relevant for classification under the condition that another feature has a specific value, this interaction can be modeled by higher weights for the first feature in such instances that also possess the second value. For example, for the prediction task whether to walk or to take the car, the feature "weather" will be much more important if it is known that the person is ill.

A variation of local weights can be found in VDM (Stanfill & Waltz, 1986), for example (see the paragraph on class projection above). There, the different feature values, rather than the features themselves, are assigned different weights, but they remain constant for every occurrence of the specific value in the instance space. Most algorithms, however, do not utilize this restriction. Another variant that has been investigated, for example by Aha & Goldstone (1990), is the combination of global and local weights.

2.3.2.3 *Generalized Context Model with Instance-Specific Weights*

Aha and Goldstone's algorithm is based on the Generalized Context Model (Nosofsky, 1986, 1987), and it computes the distance between an instance x from the instance base and the instance q to be classified by Equation 16.

$$distance(x, q) = s\sqrt{\sum_{i=1}^{n} w(i, x, q)\delta(x_i, q_i)^2} \tag{16}$$

s was set to 10 for all experiments. Aha and Goldstone use the Euclidean distance for $\delta(x_i, q_i)$, as defined in Equation 4. Weighting consists of adding the global weight of a feature to the context-sensitive local weight:

$$w(i, x, q) = w(i, x)\sqrt{1- \mid x_i - q_i \mid} + w(i)(1 - \sqrt{1- \mid x_i - q_i \mid}) \tag{17}$$

where $w(i)$ represents the global weight and $w(i, x)$ the local one. $\sqrt{1- \mid x_i - q_i \mid}$ is the factor that determines which weight is considered more important. Local weights are preferred when the difference in the values of the feature is small, and global weights are preferred when the difference is large. Thus, the metric depends on local weights when the instances are more similar and on the global weight when they are dissimilar. $w(i)$ is updated incrementally after a new training instance is presented "via a strategy akin to the delta rule (Rumelhart et al., 1986)" (Aha & Goldstone, 1992, p. 538), which is also used in connectionist approaches (cf. for example (Zell, 1994; Rumelhart et al., 1994; Mitchell, 1997)). $w(i, x)$ is updated by the same method except that only the weights of the specific instance are updated, not the weights of all instances.

Aha & Goldstone (1990) report that the locally weighted version of the algorithm shows significantly higher learning rates than the equivalent algorithm using global weights when the relevance of features depends on the values of other features. In further experiments, Aha & Goldstone (1992) also compare their locally weighted method, the equivalent globally weighted method, and one method without feature weighting to human performance on an artificial classification task, which is set up in such a way that humans cannot use background knowledge for the task. The experiments show that the locally weighted algorithm is cognitively more plausible than the other two in that it models human behavior more closely.

The fifth dimension in distinguishing feature weighting methods is based on whether they use domain-specific knowledge or not. In general, domain-specific knowledge is combined with automatic feature weighting algorithms. One possibility of introducing knowledge is to use *explanation-based learning* (Mitchell et al., 1986) in order to generate explanations of the class of an instance (cf. for example (Cain et al., 1991)).

Wettschereck et al. (1997) selected six algorithms that display different characteristics along the dimensions discussed above and tested them in comparison to the standard k-nn classifier on fourteen data sets varying in the number and types of features, as well as in the number of irrelevant features. They summarize their findings in the following four trends, for which they acknowledge that they might be restricted to the data sets that were used in the test.

T1: Preset bias methods can suffer substantially when the data are not carefully preprocessed[8].

T2: Performance bias methods attain higher accuracies than preset methods for tasks with interacting features.

T3: Performance bias methods have faster learning rates than preset bias methods.

T4: Feature weighting algorithms achieve higher generalization accuracies than feature selection algorithms for tasks where some features are useful but less important than others. (p. 23).

2.3.3 *Feature Weighting as Search*

While Wettschereck et al. (1997) use five unrelated dimensions to classify feature weighting methods, Aha (1998) uses the hierarchy of categories shown in Figure 2.2. Most of the distinctions in (Wettschereck et al., 1997), however, are represented in the hierarchy as well: the dimension

[8] Here, preprocessing refers to the method of discretizing continuous features.

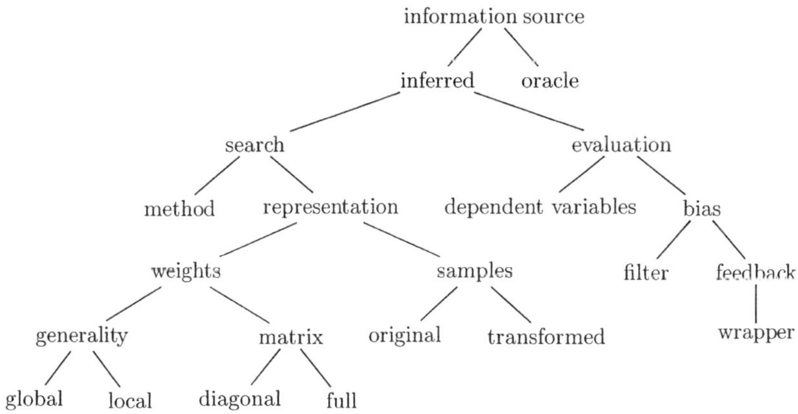

Fig. 2.2: *A framework for classifying feature weighting methods (Aha, 1998, p. 5).*

of *bias* is represented as such under the evaluation functions, *weight space* as *matrix*, *representation* changes to *samples*, and *generality* can be found in the *weights* subtree. The overview in (Aha, 1998) focuses on different search algorithms and evaluation functions which have not been covered by Wettschereck et al. (1997).

Search methods for choosing feature weights tend to be heuristic since the size of the weight space is exponential in relation to the number of features. One search strategy that can be used for filter and wrapper methods is *hill-climbing search*. Cardie (1993), for example, uses hill-climbing to induce a decision tree in which the redundant features are filtered out during pruning. Other possibilities which have been successfully used with wrapper methods are *beam search* or *conjugate gradient* combined with leave-one-out cross-validation error (cf. for example (Wettschereck, 1994)). Cardie & Howe (1997) use an induced decision tree for feature selection and continuous feature weighting. Features that do not appear in the decision tree are assigned the weight 0, while the weights for all others features are calculated according to their information gain on the training set given the feature values of the respective path through the decision tree:

$$w(f_{n_i}) = H(T) - H_{f_{n_1} \cdots f_{n_{l-i+1}}}(T) \tag{18}$$

where n_1 represents the root of the decision tree, and n_i the ith node in a path from the root to a leaf node n_l. f_{n_i} is the feature of node n_i, $H(T)$ the entropy of the entire training set, and $H_{f_{n_1} \cdots f_{n_{l-i+1}}}(T)$ the entropy in T when the features $n_1 \ldots n_{l-i+1}$ are known. Thus, the weight of the feature at node n_2, for example, "is the information gain associated with knowing the values of attributes of f_{n_1} through $f_{n_{l-1}}$" (Cardie & Howe, 1997, p. 60). This means that the lower a node is in the tree, i.e. the less important it is, the fewer the nodes are which are used for calculating the information gain. But for any node, the calculation will always use the nodes at the top of the tree, thus giving relatively high weights even to nodes at the lower end of the tree.

This approach is successful in learning skewed class distributions, which are common in NLP problems. Cardie and Howe explain the reasons for this success as follows:

> A possibly more intuitive approach would let the weight of f_{n_i} be the information gain associated with knowing the values of attributes f_{n_1} through f_{n_l}. This works less well than the method described here. We believe that this is because it biases retrieval toward cases that match features toward the top of the tree (which are probably important for majority class prediction) rather than features that appear lower in the tree (which may be useful for minority class prediction). (Cardie & Howe, 1997, p. 60, footnote 8)

The second main concern of Aha (1998) is evaluation functions. For classification tasks, evaluation functions are generally chosen for which *classification accuracy* is the dependent variable. However, Aha (1998) points out that other dependent variables exist, such as recall and precision for retrieval contexts or variables concerning memory requirements, speed, or cost, which can be used in evaluation. In cases where evaluation functions other than the performance function (i.e. classification accuracy) are used, the feature weighting algorithms might be influenced by bias mismatches between these functions. There is evidence that wrapper methods are better suited for classifiers than filter models when classification accuracy is the dependent variable (cf. for example (Wettschereck et al., 1997)). Wrapper methods, however, are generally linked with higher computational cost, so they can only be used where speed is of no concern.

2.4 Summary

In this chapter, we have given an introduction to the supervised learning algorithm of *memory-based learning*. Memory-based learning is based on the notion that training data are kept in the instance base without abstraction into rules or similar models. The classification of unseen instances is achieved by using a similarity function which retrieves the most similar instances from the instance base, the class of these instances then being used to classify the new instance. The extensions to the model discussed in Section 2.2 provide the means to reduce retrieval and storage costs (for example IGTree) and to increase robustness to noise.

Since memory-based learning is very sensitive to the presence of irrelevant or redundant features in the feature set, it is important to use feature weighting to counterbalance this sensitivity. There exists a large number of different feature weighting methods, which can be grouped along the following dimensions: performance-based or preset bias, continuous or binary weight space, given or transformed representation, global or local generality, and knowledge poor or intensive approaches. There exists no theory yet on the interdependence of problem characteristics and weighting methods. The different weighting methods have mainly been tested empirically on artificial domains, but even these evaluations have necessarily been restricted to comparisons of single methods on specific problems. For this reason, the choice of an appropriate weighting method for a specific problem is still based on hypotheses rather than on a well-defined theory.

Chapter 3
Memory-Based Approaches to Parsing

Many NLP problems which have been approached with memory-based learning techniques can easily be formulated as classification problems, which is a prerequisite for memory-based learning (cf. for example the work on phoneme-grapheme conversion (Stanfill & Waltz, 1986; Daelemans, van den Bosch & Weijters, 1996), POS tagging (Cardie, 1993; Daelemans, Zavrel, Berck & Gillis, 1996; Zavrel & Daelemans, 1997*b*), or word sense disambiguation (Dagan et al., 1997; Escudero et al., 2000; Veenstra et al., 2000), to name only a few). Natural language parsing, however, is not a task that can easily be defined in such terms since the set of grammatically well-formed trees in a language is, in principle, infinite[1]. Therefore, classification-based learning approaches to syntactic parsing go beyond ordinary classification tasks for which the set of classes is finite and of "manageable" cardinality. In syntactic parsing, a finite set of POS labels and phrasal syntactic categories can be combined recursively to produce a potentially infinite number of syntactic structures.

For this reason, there exists only a small number of memory-based approaches to the problem of syntactic parsing. These approaches exploit the fact that the potentially infinite set of candidate tree structures is in practice restricted by the finite length of the input sentence. The other source of infinite structures, i.e. recursive structures, are generally artificially limited to a preset number of recursions, which can then be analyzed sequentially. In order to define parsing as classification, most approaches split the task of annotation into sub-tasks that either deal with a segmentation problem, such as base noun phrase (NP) chunking, or with a labeling task, such as grammatical relations assignment. Complete syntactic annotation can thus be reached via a cascade of such classifiers for sub-problems. We are only aware of one approach to memory-based parsing that approaches the task of complete parsing in a single step.

There is related work on grammar induction by van Zaanen (2000*a*,*b*, 2003), which can also be subsumed under the paradigm of memory-based learning in that it uses past experience to make decisions. But since it concerns a different task, it will not be covered in detail here.

---

[1] But see for example the approach by (Black et al., 1992) for an alternative definition of the parsing problem.

3.1 Noun Phrase Chunking

Noun phrase (NP) chunking is generally the first step in a cascade of classifiers intended for partial parsing. The definition of noun chunks goes back to Abney (1991, 1996): noun chunks are defined as non-overlapping base noun phrases that include premodifiers but do not include postmodifiers. The sentence "A very clever traveling salesman sold his complete stock of washing machines the next day." would be analyzed as

> $[_{NP}$ A very clever traveling salesman $_{NP}]$ sold $[_{NP}$ his complete stock $_{NP}]$ of $[_{NP}$ washing machines $_{NP}]$ $[_{NP}$ the next day $_{NP}]$.

One method of annotating NP chunks with a classification approach is to define the problem as a tagging problem, as suggested by Ramshaw & Marcus (1995). They assign a tag to each word in a sentence to indicate whether the word is inside an NP chunk (tag *I*) or outside (tag *O*). The third tag (*B*) is reserved for marking the beginning of an NP chunk immediately following another NP chunk. The analysis of the sentence shown above receives the following annotation:

> A/*I* very/*I* clever/*I* traveling/*I* salesman/*I* sold/*O* his/*I* complete/*I* stock/*I* of/*O* washing/*I* machines/*I* the/*B* next/*I* day/*I* ./*O*

NP chunking based on the IOB representation served as part of the shared-task scenario for CoNLL-2000 (cf. (Tjong Kim Sang & Buchholz, 2000)). In general, the data set provided by Ramshaw and Marcus is used to provide a means for comparing different approaches to this task. Tjong Kim Sang & Veenstra (1999) devised a series of tests in order to find the best representation for NP chunking when using memory-based learning. They found that the standard IOB representation as defined by Ramshaw and Marcus achieves better classification results than other representations, which either mark only the end of a noun phrase, or consistently mark either the beginning or the end of noun phrases (and not only in the case of two adjacent noun phrases).

3.1.1 *The approach of Veenstra (1998)*

Veenstra (1998) used this IOB representation with Ramshaw and Marcus' data set for NP chunking in a memory-based learning approach. The instances consist of the focus word, a context of two words to the left of the focus word and one word to the right, as well as the corresponding POS tags of these words. Veenstra used TiMBL's IGTree classifier (Daelemans,

method	accuracy	precision	recall
IGTree – 1 level	96.8%	83.1%	97.0%
IGtree – 2 levels	97.2%	89.0%	94.3%
IB1-IG – 1 level	97.3%	89.4%	97.3%
IB1-IG – 2 levels	97.2%	87.4%	94.1%

Table 3.1: *Veenstra's results for NP chunking (Veenstra, 1998, p. 75).*

van den Bosch & Weijters, 1996) (cf. Section 2.2) and the memory-based POS tagger MBT (Daelemans, Zavrel, Berck & Gillis, 1996) to perform the chunking task. The results of this approach are shown in the first line in Table 3.1. It is worth noting that while accuracy and recall (i.e. the number of NPs that were found by the classifier) are high, the quality of the found NP chunks, i.e. precision, is quite low. In order to improve the precision score, Veenstra introduced a second classification phase in which the IOB tags from the first phase are used as additional context. The instances for this second phase contain the POS tags and the IOB tags of the focus word, the two words to the left, and one word to the right. The IOB tags are obtained by applying the first phase classifier in a tenfold cross validation to the training data and using the ten test sets thus annotated as training data for the second phase. The results (IGTree – 2 levels) in Table 3.1 show that this method gains a significant increase in precision; but, it also overcorrects, and recall decreases. The IOB tags therefore help to correct misclassifications of the first phase, but there is a tendency to "correct" in too many cases. Tests using the standard memory-based algorithm IB1-IG show that there is no significant improvement in comparison to the heuristic decision-tree variant IGTree.

3.1.2 *The approach of Tjong Kim Sang & Veenstra (1999)*

Tjong Kim Sang & Veenstra (1999) show that there exist methods to improve the results based on single classifiers as described above. Improvements can be achieved by combining two different classifiers for annotating the beginning and end of NP chunks. Tjong Kim Sang and Veenstra assume that this is due to "the fact that they are able to use two different context sizes for solving two different parts of the recognition problem" (Tjong Kim Sang & Veenstra, 1999, p. 176). Another method to improve results is based on a cascade of classifiers where subsequent classifiers have access to classifications of previous steps as already shown above by Veenstra (1998), but Tjong Kim Sang and Veenstra increase the number of levels. Using a sequence of classifiers designed for the same task is one way to integrate the classification of context words into the final classification of a word. This result implies that the correction of classification errors will provide enough information to correct other errors. Tjong Kim Sang and Veenstra report an increase in the F-score from 89.17 for a single classifier using standard IOB tag representation to 90.53 when using a cascade of four classifiers. Tjong Kim Sang (2000) and Tjong Kim Sang et al. (2000) extend the notion of classifier combination to include such different classifiers as theory refinement, decision tree learning, different versions of memory-based learning, maximum entropy learning, and an approach related to neural networks. They found that even a simple voting mechanism, majority voting, improves classification results significantly to an F-score of 93.86, the best result published at present.

3.2 Shallow Parsing and Grammatical Relation Assignment

Shallow parsing generally goes beyond noun phrase chunking in that it covers other types of chunks (i.e. prepositional chunks, verbal chunks, etc.) as well as basic grammatical relations such as subject-verb relations or verb-direct object relations.

3.2.1 *Memory-Based Sequence Learning*

Argamon et al. (1998, 1999) use *Memory-Based Sequence Learning* (MBSL) to learn noun chunks, verb-object relations and subject-verb relations. Memory-based sequence learning is based on the assumption that for learning tasks in the area of shallow parsing, the sequence of words is one of the most important types of information. However, exactly this type of information cannot be represented in a standard memory-based approach restricted to a fixed number of features. Argamon et al. show that syntactic patterns can be represented as sequences of POS tags instead of a predefined number of features. Contrary to a number of NP chunking approaches that assign IOB tags, Argamon et al. define the noun chunking task as bracketing. An input sentence to be bracketed is first split into all possible subsequences which serve as candidates for the target patterns (for example noun chunks). The instance base is then searched for corroborating evidence for each proposed pattern. Since it is unlikely that the complete sequence of POS tags

PP [DT ADJ NN]
PP [DT ADJ NN
...
PP [
[DT ADJ NN]
[DT ADJ NN
...
DT ADJ NN]
...
NN]

Table 3.2: *MBSL's list of tiles for the pattern "PP [DT ADJ NN] generated during training.*

will be found in the training data, MBSL rather relies on partial sequences that can be combined to cover the complete sentence. The instances, which are called *tiles*, consist of at least one bracket, a subsequence of the POS tags between the brackets and optionally a subsequence of the context. An overlapping of instances is desired since such an overlapping increases the probability that correct instances were chosen.

For each training pattern, all possible tiles are stored in the instance base. Thus, in NP chunking, the tiles given in Table 3.2 would be stored for the pattern "PP [DT ADJ NN]" (i.e.: preposition, determiner, adjective, noun)[2]. For each such tile, two counts are made: 1) the number of positive occurrences including the bracket, and 2) the total number of occurrences of the POS sequence, including occurrences where the bracket is in a different place or no bracket is included. For classification, only tiles are considered which exhibit a good classification accuracy, i.e. for which the ratio of positive count to total count is above a threshold θ.

During classification, each candidate, i.e. each subsequence of POS tags, receives a score that gives an indication of how much evidence there is in the instance base for this candidate. In order to calculate the score, MBSL searches for all *covers*, i.e. for all (potentially overlapping) sequences of tiles which cover the complete subsequence. By using tiles instead of the complete patterns, MBSL can also correctly analyze patterns which do not occur in the training pattern but for which tiles from different training patterns can be put together. The score for a candidate c is calculated by

[2] The sentences are annotated with the Penn treebank tagset, cf. (Santorini, 1990).

Equation 19. The highest-scoring candidate is approved, and all conflicting candidates (with lower scores) are removed from the candidate set.

$$score(c) = \alpha\, num(c) - \beta\, minsize(c) + \gamma\, maxcontent(c) + \delta\, maxoverlap(c) \quad (19)$$

In Equation 19, $num(c)$ is the number of covers, $minsize(c)$ the least number of tiles constituting a cover, $maxcontent(c)$ the maximal number of context POS tags in any cover, and $maxoverlap(c)$ the maximal number of overlapping tags in any cover. The weights, $\alpha \ldots \delta$ were selected to give a lexicographic ordering.

Argamon et al. tested their approach for the problems of NP chunking, verb-object relations, and subject-verb relations. For the first problem, they used the data set provided by Ramshaw & Marcus (1995); the tiles were extracted as described above. The other two problems were also defined as separate bracketing tasks, i.e. for subject-verb relations, the task was defined as finding the bracket that includes the subject and the verb of a clause. For these tasks, Argamon et al. extracted the necessary information from the Penn treebank (Marcus et al., 1993, 1994). For object-verb relations, the delimiters were set before the main verb and after the object head, and for subject-verb relations before the subject noun phrase and after the first verb. These heuristics lead to unintended patterns in the case of subjects that contain relative clauses. For these cases, the verb of the relative clause is erroneously selected as delimiter of the pattern. Argamon et al. argue that such a pattern "is not a properly grammatical [subject-verb relation], but it contains important information and may be regarded as grammatically meaningful in its own right" (Argamon et al., 1999, p. 84). This definition of subject-verb relations seems to result in a trivial task since the algorithm only needs to mark the first noun phrase element as the start of the intended pattern, and the last element of the following verbal phrase as the end. The only exceptions to this are wh-clauses with an auxiliary and topicalizations. The task, however, is non-trivial since the system has access only to a limited sequence of POS tags, which might not cover the complete subject-verb sequence.

The results of MBSL for the tasks described above are shown in Table 3.3. It is difficult to compare these results to other approaches since Argamon et al. used only POS tags in the instance base but no lexical information. In all likelihood, the latter would have improved the results, but this approach does not seem to be feasible for MBSL since the calculation of the different covers for candidates would be extremely time- and

task	context	threshold θ	recall	precision	F_1
NP chunking	3	0.6	91.6%	91.6%	91.6
verb-object	2	0.5	89.8%	77.1%	83.0
subject-verb	3	0.6	84.5%	88.6%	86.5

Table 3.3: *Argamon et al.'s results using MBSL for NP chunking, verb-object relations, and subject-verb relations (Argamon et al., 1999, p. 87).*

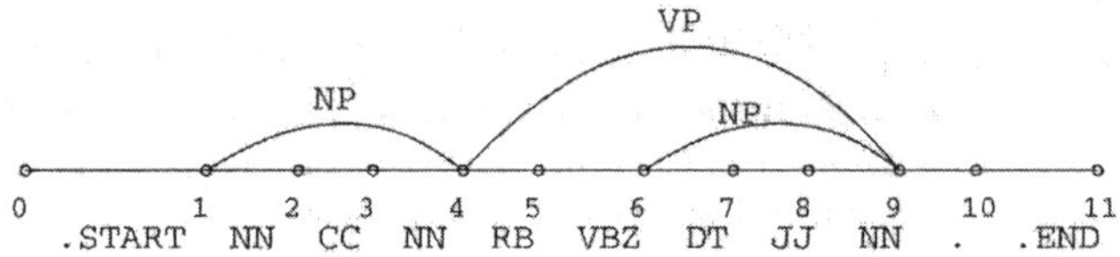

Fig. 3.1: *A sample sentence graph for the patterns NP and VP (Dagan & Krymolowski, 2003, p. 180).*

memory-consuming (p.c. Y. Krymolowski).

3.2.2 *Extended Memory-Based Sequence Learning*

Dagan and Krymolowski (Krymolowski & Dagan, 2000; Dagan & Krymolowski, 2003) extended the MBSL approach to include complex syntactic structures, to which they refer as "compositional evidence". Instead of restricting tiles to patterns of POS tags, they now allow tiles to include embedded structures. Thus, if VP chunks and NP chunks are to be learned with the same classifier, VP tiles may include the NP tag to represent an entire NP. Each sentence is represented by a *sentence graph* in which the nodes correspond to positions between words, and the edges describe either POS tags or target patterns. For the sentence shown in Figure 3.1, the set of tiles to describe the sentence not only includes tiles such as "[VP RB VBZ", "VBZ DT JJ NN VP]" or "NN VP] .", but also "[VP RB VBZ NP VP]" or "VBZ NP VP]"[3]. Candidates are again ranked according to their score as computed in Equation 19. But here, an additional score of the ratio of the

[3] In this example, "NP" is the label for a noun phrase suggested by the algorithm, all the other labels are POS tags from the Penn treebank POS tagset.

positive counts of all tiles to their overall count is added with the highest weight. The highest scoring candidate is approved, and all candidates that overlap with this candidate are eliminated. The results show that allowing one level of embedding increases recall from 45.4% to 82.6%, but decreases precision from 77.4% to 61.5%. The F-score increases from 57.2 to 70.5. By allowing embedded patterns in the tiles, Krymolowski and Dagan increase the span of the considered sequence, which obviously aids recognition of VPs since they generally contain more words than are allowed in a tile.

3.2.3 *The Approach of Buchholz (1998)*

Argamon et al. (1999) have approached chunking as well as assigning the most salient grammatical relations, i.e. for verb-object and subject-verb pairs. Buchholz (1998), on the other hand, concentrated on distinguishing complements from adjuncts. She argues that tests developed by linguists cannot be used for automatic approaches since, in general, they involve judgments about grammaticality or changes in meaning. Buchholz therefore investigated the types of information that can be automatically annotated in text to aid in distinguishing between complements and adjuncts. The tests reported in (Buchholz, 1998) were set up so that increasingly more information was given to the classifier. The data for the tests were extracted from the second version of the Penn treebank (Marcus et al., 1994), in which "[t]he difference between complements and adjuncts is not expressed by parse tree configuration ..., but can instead be derived from the combination of a constituent's syntactic category (NP, PP, etc.) and function tag (SBJ: subject, TMP: temporal, etc.)" (Buchholz, 1998, p. 43). In order to obtain a complete feature set, Buchholz extracted information about the head verb and all its complements and adjuncts for every VP. The verb additionally received a number characterizing its subcategorization behavior. The complements and adjuncts were represented by their category, their function tag, and a head feature, which contains different types of information for different categories, for example the preposition for a PP. In order to analyze sentences with different numbers of constituents, a windowing approach was used with the focus constituent and three context constituents on each side. Table 3.4 gives the instances for the sentence *The Mitsubishi family company VP[acquired NP[that property] PP-CLR[from the government] ADVP-TMP[some 100 years ago] SBAR-TMP[when it was ...]]*. The subcategorization number 628 in the example signifies that the verb is either intransitive or transitive with at most two PP complements.

feature	inst. 1	inst. 2	inst. 3	inst. 4
no.	628	628	628	628
verb	acquire	acquire	acquire	acquire
left cont.	-,-,-	-,-,-	-,-,-	np,-,-
	-,-,-	-,-,-	np,-,-	pp,-,from
	-,-,-	np,-,-	pp,-,from	advp,tmp,ago
focus	np,-,-	pp,-,from	advp,tmp,ago	sbar,tmp,when
right cont.	pp,-,from	advp,tmp,ago	sbar,tmp,when	-,-,-
	advp,tmp,ago	sbar,tmp,when	-,-,-	-,-,-
	sbar,tmp,when	-,-,-	-,-,-	-,-,-
category	C	C	A	A

Table 3.4: *The instances for the verb "acquired", each column representing one instance (Buchholz, 1998, p. 44).*

Buchholz then grouped the features into three categories: *syntactic features*, i.e. the first and third feature of each constituent, *function features*, i.e. the second feature, and the verb form and its subcategorization number. The first set of features can be extracted from a syntactic analysis. The second set is more difficult to acquire, and the third is generally learned from the results of the categorization into complements and adjuncts. Buchholz found that there are three good syntactic predictors: the head feature of the focus constituent, its syntactic category and the category of the preceding constituent. The classification accuracy when using these three features reaches 85.5% (baseline: 76.4%). If the category of the following constituent is added, the accuracy increases to 91.2%. The inclusion of all other syntactic features results in a further significant increase to 91.6% (which is equivalent to 93.3% precision and 95.9% recall). The best predictor of complement- vs. adjuncthood, however, is the functional category of the focus constituent. This feature alone reaches an accuracy of 92%.

3.2.4 *The Approach of Daelemans, Buchholz & Veenstra (1999)*

The tests of Buchholz (1998) show that the classification of constituents into complements and adjuncts is feasible even if only syntactic information is available. However, the experiments were conducted with "perfect" syntactic information, i.e. information extracted from the Penn treebank. In a more realistic setting, this type of information will be annotated automatically and thus will contain a certain percentage of errors. The question

task	accuracy	precision	recall	F_1
NP chunking	98.0%	93.7%	94.0%	93.8
VP chunking	99.2%	94.0%	95.5%	94.7
subject detection (IB1-IG)		76.2%	76.9%	76.5
object detection (IGTree)		77.2%	76.4%	76.8
subject + object (IGTree)	96.9%	79.5%	73.2%	76.2
subject + object (IB1-IG + IGTree)	97.4%	89.8%	68.6%	77.8

Table 3.5: *The results of Daelemans, Buchholz & Veenstra (1999, pp. 55-56) for partial parsing.*

arises whether such a classification will still be feasible under these more difficult conditions. This question was approached by Daelemans, Buchholz & Veenstra (1999). For their system MBSP, they used a sequence of two classifiers, the first annotating NP and VP chunks, the second subject-verb and verb-object relations. Chunking was defined as a tagging task corresponding to the work of Ramshaw & Marcus (1995) and others. Since two different chunk types are annotated simultaneously, however, the I and B tags are extended to describe the type of chunk as well: I_NP, B_NP, I_VP, and B_VP. Here, the O tag is used for all words that are neither part of an NP nor a VP. The instances consist of the focus word, two words to the left and one word to the right plus their corresponding POS tags. The results for both chunk types are shown in Table 3.5.

The task of the second classifier is to assign the labels "S" (for: *subject*), "O" (for: *object*), or "-" (for all other constituents) to pairs of words. Pairs consist of a verb and a word from the sentence. Since it is unnecessary to annotate for example noun modifiers with grammatical functions, for each chunk found in the previous step, only the head of the constituent is paired with a word to form an instance. Apart from the verb and the focus word/head, the instances contain a context of two words or heads of chunks to the left and one word or head to the right of the focus word; additionally, the distance of the focus from the verb, the number of other verbs between the verb and the focus, and the number of intervening commas are given. The results of this classifier are also given in Table 3.5. It is worth noting that by combining two different classifiers, precision increases by almost 10% (combined with a loss in recall of ca. 5%).

The task approached by Daelemans et al. is similar to the one by Argamon et al. (Argamon et al., 1998, 1999), it is, however, less restricted since

Argamon et al. only consider NP chunks directly preceding or following the verb phrase as possible subject or objects. For this reason, Daelemans et al. conducted a test based on the same restricted definition of subject and object. They reached comparable results: an F-score of 83.1 for subjects as compared to 86.5 by Argamon et al., and 86.5 as compared to 83.0 for objects. The approach by Daelemans et al. (MBL) shows several advantages: "[MBL's] efficiency, the ease with which information apart from POS tags can be added to the input (for example word information, morphological information, wordnet tags, chunk information for subject and object detection), and the fact that NP and VP chunking and different types of relation tagging can be achieved in one classification pass" (Daelemans, Buchholz & Veenstra, 1999, p. 57).

Buchholz et al. (1999) extended this approach to more complete annotations. They tested a cascade of classifiers which combines chunking levels with a final level of grammatical relation assignment. The first classifier in the cascade simultaneously annotates non-overlapping NP, VP, Prep, ADJDP, and ADVP chunks. A Prep chunk only contains the prepositional part of a PP, not the NP part. These two parts (and possibly more coordinated NPs) are combined into a PP chunk in the second classifier. The last chunking classifier assigns adverbial functions such as "locative" or "temporal" to all chunks. Chunking, again, was defined as a tagging task, with the IOB tags also carrying information about the type of chunk.

In the final level of the cascade, "several types of grammatical relations between pairs of words in the sentence" (Buchholz et al., 1999, p. 240) were annotated. Since only relations to a verb were of interest, the word pairs consisted of a verb and one of the remaining words in a sentence. Apart from the verb and the focus word, the instances contained a context of two words to the left and one word to the right of the focus word, and additionally some information about the clause structure: the distance of the focus from the verb, the number of other verbs between the verb and the focus, and the number of intervening commas. The results for different steps in the cascade of classifiers based on Penn treebank data are shown in Table 3.6. Grammatical relation assignment based on the words and POS tags only reaches an F-score of 49.1. When information is added from the chunking levels, the focus is represented by three additional features: the type of chunk in which the word is included, the prepositions if the chunk is a PP, and the adverbial function of the chunk. The context now represents complete chunks if possible, represented by the last word of the chunk. The distance between focus word and verb is now counted as the number of

type	precision	recall	F_1
NP chunks	92.5%	92.2%	92.3
VP chunks	91.9%	91.7%	91.8
ADJP chunks	68.4%	65.0%	66.7
ADVP chunks	78.0%	77.9%	77.9
Prep chunks	95.5%	96.7%	96.1
PP chunks	91.9%	92.2%	92.0
adverbial func.	78.0%	69.5%	73.5
gramm. rel. (words + POS)	60.7%	41.3%	49.1
gramm. rel. (+ all chunks)	74.8%	67.9%	71.2
gramm. rel. (+ treebank chunks)	86.3%	80.8%	83.5

Table 3.6: *Results of the cascade of chunking and grammatical relation assignment (Buchholz et al., 1999, pp. 241, 245).*

intervening chunks, and thus decreases as well.

The results of Buchholz et al. show that all types of information from the chunking levels aid in the classification of grammatical relations, but to different degrees for different relations. Adding NP chunks increases F_1 by 11.3% for subjects, 16.2% for objects, but only 3.9% for locatives and 3.7% for temporals. For the latter two relations, information about adverbial functions is more important, they increase by 6.3% and 15% respectively, while the gain for subjects and objects is less than 1%. If all types of chunking information are added, the classification reaches an F-score of 71.2. The upper limit for this classification task is shown on the last line of Table 3.6. This result can be reached if perfect chunking information is given to the second classification algorithm.

The results of Buchholz et al. for MBSP demonstrate that, on the one hand, even imperfect information from partial parsing steps can aid in classifying grammatical relations. It is, on the other hand, evident that the results vary significantly depending on the quality of previous annotation levels.

3.2.5 *Memory-Based Shallow Parsing Based on Words*

Van den Bosch & Buchholz (2002) explore the task of shallow parsing, i.e. of assigning grammatical functions to chunks with regard to whether such a system profits from the use of words as features. Many parsing systems

Penn treebank tree:

```
((S (ADV-TMP Once)
    (NP-SBJ-1 he)
    (VP was
        (VP held
            (NP *-1)
            (PP-TMP for
                    (three months))
            (PP without
                (S-NOM (NP-SBJ *-1)
                       (VP being
                           (VP charged)))))).))
```

partial parse:
[$_{ADVP}$ Once$^{ADVP-TMP}$] [$_{NP}$ he^{NP-SBJ}] [$_{VP}$ was held$^{VP/S}$] [$_{PP}$ for^{PP-TMP}] [$_{NP}$ three months^{NP}] [$_{PP}$ without^{PP}] [$_{VP}$ being charged$^{VP/S-NOM}$]

Fig. 3.2: *An example of the expected analysis for the experiments in (van den Bosch & Buchholz, 2002).*

use POS tags rather than words as their input in order to alleviate the problem of data sparseness. Van den Bosch & Buchholz (2002), however, argue that there are more resources available now. Additionally, the POS tags need to be provided by an external POS tagger. "This tagger can base its decision only on the information present in the sentence, i.e. on the words themselves. The question then arises whether we could use this information directly, and thus save the explicit tagging step" (van den Bosch & Buchholz, 2002, p. 343). For this reason, they designed an experiment which compares the influence of different types of input for a shallow parsing task. The shallow parsing task is defined as a combination of chunking and assigning grammatical functions to the head words of these chunks. Note that this is a simpler task than the work by Buchholz et al. (1999) presented in the previous section since it does not have to decide which verb is modified by a constituent.

The intended analysis of the system is the same as for the CoNLL-2000 shared-task scenario (Tjong Kim Sang, 2000). An example is shown in Figure 3.2. The nodes in the shallow structure consist of the syntactic category. The head word of each chunk is annotated with a function label which combines information from the constituent label of the parent and of ancestors with a different category (for example VP/S-NOM).

The task of the memory-based learner is to assign to each word a label which consists of the chunk label and the functional label. Chunk labels are based on the IOB representation format. The functional label for the head words of a chunk is its function (cf. Figure 3.2), for non-heads, it is "NOFUNC".

For the experiments, van den Bosch and Buchholz used the memory-based learner TRIBL (Daelemans et al., 1997), which first employs a decision tree until it reaches a predefined switch point. After the switch point is reached, the system uses a standard memory-based learner, TiMBL. For TRIBL, the switch point is set to 1 for experiments with only one type of information (words or POS tags) and to 2 for the experiment with both types of information present. The memory-based learner uses information gain to calculate feature weights, MVDM (cf. Section 2.2) for estimating differences between features, $k = 7$, and class voting based on the inverse distance of a neighbor to the test instance as weighting for the votes (Dudani, 1976).

Van den Bosch and Buchholz performed four experiments with different types of information: gold standard POS tags only, words only, attenuated words, and a combination of attenuated words and gold standard POS tags. In the experiments with attenuated words, all low frequency words are replaced by a label MORPH plus some characteristics of the word such as the final two letters, for example The word *developments* is transformed into *MORPH-ts*.

The experiments were conducted with different sizes of training data, using tenfold cross validation. The results (cf. Figure 3.3[4]) show that the word-based classification starts with a lower F-score than the POS-based one, but its learning curve is much steeper, such that it outperforms the POS-based classifier when more than 50 000 training sentences are available. With attenuated words, only 20 000 sentences are necessary to obtain better results. The best results, however, are reached by the combined classifier, which uses attenuated words as well as POS tags. Van den Bosch & Buchholz (2002) conclude that POS tags are a good replacement for words if only a smaller training set is available. Once enough data exists for training with words, the word information is more reliable, especially when low frequency words are attenuated. Attenuating words and adding POS tags to the feature set improves performance mostly with small training sets. Thus

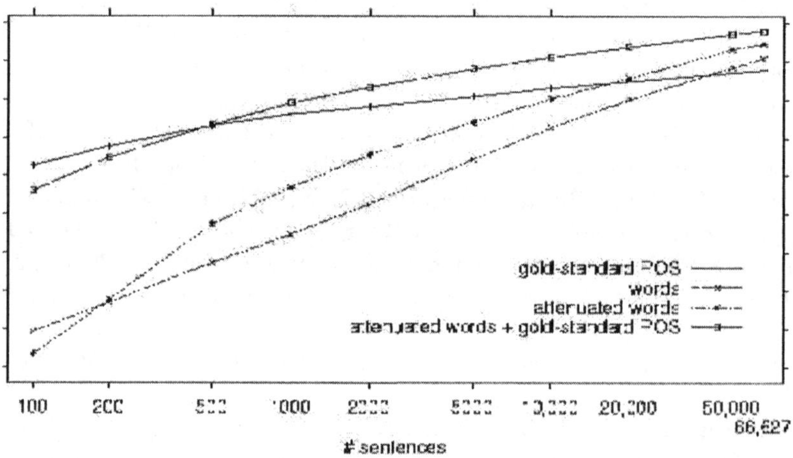

Fig. 3.3: *The results for different training sizes (van den Bosch & Buchholz, 2002, p. 437)*

input	precision	recall	F-score
gold standard POS	73.8%	73.9%	73.9
MBT POS	72.2%	72.4%	72.3
words	75.4%	75.4%	75.4
words + gold standard POS	76.5%	77.1%	76.8
words + MBT POS	75.8%	76.1%	75.9
att. words	77.3%	77.2%	77.3
att. words + gold standard POS	78.9%	79.1%	79.0
att. words + MBT POS	77.6%	77.7%	77.6

Table 3.7: *The results for the partial parsing task when comparing the use of gold standard and automatically assigned POS tags (van den Bosch & Buchholz, 2002, p. 338).*

if enough training data is available, POS tagging becomes unnecessary.

The next question which van den Bosch & Buchholz (2002) investigated was the effect of automatically assigned POS tags. For these experiments, they used MBT, a memory-based tagger (Daelemans, Zavrel, Berck & Gillis, 1996) trained on the Penn treebank. MBT reached an accuracy of 96.7%. The results for the partial parsing task using the maximal amount of training data are shown in Table 3.7. For the experiments with combined information, it becomes clear that automatically assigned POS tags result in a small increase in performance, however, the increase is nowhere as pronounced as it is for gold standard POS tags.

3.2.6 *The Approach of Buchholz (2002)*

Buchholz (2002) extended the work of Buchholz et al. (1999) by a thorough investigation of optimal parameter settings and features used for the classification of grammatical relations. The task remained the same, i.e. finding grammatical relations between verb chunks and non-verb chunks for the Penn treebank data. The task of the system is therefore to decide for each pair of verb chunk and non-verb chunk whether they share a grammatical relation, and if so, which relation. Since training and testing very soon reach prohibitively large time requirements, it is impossible to test all possible combinations of system parameters and possible features. Therefore, Buchholz first optimized system parameters on the basis of the features used in (Buchholz et al., 1999), and then tested different feature combinations with the system parameters fixed to the optimal values found in the first set of experiments. Here, we will only present the changes that resulted in an improved performance of the system.

The initial feature set included the following features:

- the distance, i.e. the number of chunks or words not grouped into a chunk, between the verb chunk and the focus chunk (i.e. the chunk for which the system needs to decide whether it has a grammatical relation to the verb chunk) – negative numbers indicate that the focus chunk is to the left of the verb chunk
- the number of verb chunks intervening between the verb chunk and the focus chunk
- the head word of the verb chunk
- information about the focus chunk: the (semantic) head word, its POS tag, the chunk type, and the syntactic head if the chunk is a prepositional chunk
- information about the element (chunk or word) immediately preceding the focus chunk
- information about the element immediately following the focus chunk

In the first step, the search space was restricted. Originally, each non-verb chunk was classified in relation to every verb chunk present in the sentence. The modification restricted the eligible verb chunks to the two closest verb chunks to the right (i.e. with possibly one intervening verb chunk). This modification makes it impossible to analyze very complex sentences completely correctly, but such cases constitute only 3.5% of the instances. Processing time, however, is reduced from 2 hours 30 minutes to slightly more than one hour.

Buchholz reached optimal results by using the following parameter settings: IB1-IG with gain ratio as weighting scheme, modified value difference metric (MVDM) as similarity metric (cf. Section 2.3), and k=9. Since the value for k is rather high, it proved useful to prefer instances that were closer to the new instance in class voting. Here, the best method proved to be *exponential decay* (cf. (Daelemans et al., 2002)) with a decay factor of $\alpha = 30$. The results of the system with the default settings are shown in the first line in Table 3.8, the results for the optimal parameter settings in the second line.

It needs to be noted that both the results for the default settings and the parameter optimization, as well as the results for feature selection, are based on optimal input data. The grammatical relations finder as described by Buchholz needs POS tagged and chunked data as its input. In a realistic setting, these annotations are obtained by applying a POS tagger and a

	recall	precision	F_1	time (h:m)
default	71.79%	77.20%	74.40	1:06
parameter optimization	75.39%	85.41%	80.09	4:48
feature reduction	75.79%	85.11%	80.18	3:27
feature splitting	75.94%	85.16%	80.29	2:46
adding more information	79.24%	86.87%	82.88	5:58
deleting infrequent feature values	80.01%	86.45%	83.10	3:14
tagger + chunker (train. + test.)	66.47%	79.96%	72.59	4:24
tagger + chunker (only testing)	67.90%	75.24%	71.38	4:01

Table 3.8: *Results of parameter optimization and feature selection for grammatical relation assignment (Buchholz, 2002).*

chunk parser. As a consequence, the input for the grammatical relations finder will not always be correct. In order to abstract from errors in POS tagging and chunking, Buchholz extracted POS tags and chunk structures directly from the treebank. Thus, only a very small amount of errors are introduced which result from cases where the treebank annotation does not give enough information for determining chunk boundaries. These do not necessarily coincide with the phrase boundaries of the treebank annotation.

The first step in feature selection was the search for redundant or harmful features of the initial feature set. Buchholz (2002) first tested for each feature separately whether the results decreased if this feature was ignored. She found that many features, such as the POS tag or the chunk type of the preceding element, or all four features describing the following element, are redundant if only a single feature of those is pruned. However, if a combination of these features was pruned, the results in most cases decreased significantly. The only combination of ignored features that did not harm performance was the combination of two features of the left context element and three features of the right context. This reduction was applied to the feature set, and reduces memory requirements from 107 MB to 77 MB and time requirements from 4 hours 48 minutes to 3 hours 27 minutes, while the differences in precision and recall are not significant (cf. line 3 in Table 3.8).

The next step concerned the splitting of features. If features contain a combination of different types of information, it is often useful to separate these into different features. Thus, their weights can be increased or decreased individually. Buchholz found that splitting the distance feature into absolute distance and direction resulted in increased speed (cf. line 4 of Table 3.8).

The next logical step is increasing the feature set in order to include more information. The tests showed that the combination of the following new features is beneficial for the task: the word immediately preceding the verb chunk, the head word of the element preceding the immediate left context element of the focus chunk, numeric information about the occurrence of elements such as commas, SBAR chunks, etc., and the POS tag of the head of a verb chunk. Adding these features resulted in an increase of the F-score to 82.88 (cf. line 5 in Table 3.8).

The last improvement concerning features results from the removal of infrequent feature values. If all feature values that occur with a frequency of 5 or less in the training corpus are replaced by the value "HAPAX", results improve significantly (cf. line 6 of Table 3.8).

All the results reported above were obtained when POS and chunk information were extracted directly from the treebank. However, Buchholz (2002) also examined the influence of imperfect input data on classification results. She integrated her grammatical relations finder (GLF) into the cascaded parsing system MBSP, in which GLF processes the output of the previous modules, the POS tagger MBT (Daelemans, Zavrel, Berck & Gillis, 1996) and the chunk parser presented by Veenstra & van den Bosch (2000). She found that using MBSP in training and testing resulted in a smaller loss in performance than training on perfect data and testing on imperfect data from the POS tagger and chunk parser (cf. lines 7 and 8 of Table 3.8).

The work of Buchholz (2002) is an in-depth analysis of the factors that influence the classification of grammatical relations between verb chunks and other chunks. She showed that by a careful selection of system parameters and features, a considerable gain in performance can be reached. It is interesting to see that results are promising although no linguistic information is used beyond the information which can be extracted from POS tagging and chunk parsing, two methods that give limited but fairly robust information about syntactic constituency. This information is rather different from the more complex information that linguists use, for example in tests for distinguishing complements and adjuncts.

3.3 Memory-Based Full Parsing

In the previous section, we described several approaches to partial parsing. Partial parsing is generally restricted to analyzing either completely non-recursive structures (chunk parsing) or to an approximation of recursive structures, which imposes an artificial upper limit on the depth of recursive structures. We are aware of only one approach to memory-based parsing without these restrictions: OCTOPUS (Streiter, 2001*a*,*b*). OCTOPUS was designed to parse the CKIP Chinese treebank (Chen et al., 1999) by finding the most similar sentences in the instance base via a fuzzy match and then adapting the tree structure to the input sentence. The instance base for OCTOPUS contains not only the complete trees for the sentences in the training data, but also all the subtrees and modifications of tree structures in which words or phrases were removed randomly. This strategy of also storing tree fragments is reminiscent of DOP (Bod, 1998) (cf. Chapter 4).

Since OCTOPUS retrieves a complete tree in a single step of the analysis, it cannot use the standard memory-based similarity metrics. Instead, the parser identifies "sets of keywords which are distinctive for a small number of structures" (Streiter, 2001*b*, p. 4)[5] during the training phase and indexes the sentences accordingly. During parsing, the same step is repeated for the input sentences. The keywords that are extracted from the input sentence are then used to retrieve the k nearest neighbors in the instance base. For the identification of keywords, first a word count is performed for the complete training corpus. Then the least frequent (in the training corpus) words are removed from a sentence until the sequence of the remaining (high frequency) words can be found with a certain frequency in the training corpus. These words are then considered keywords. Thus, the search for the most similar sentences is based on co-occurrence frequencies of combinations of single words rather than on linguistic criteria such as heads of phrases or chunks. This is due to the characteristics of Chinese, which has a high number of non-local dependencies (p.c. O. Streiter). These keywords are not used as a bag of words but rather as a sequence which must be matched completely in order to retrieve a sentence from the instance base. Ideally, this would give the parser information about the major syntactic constructions of a sentence. It is, however, unclear in how many cases these sequences of keywords actually correspond to linguistically relevant constructions.

Once the parser has retrieved the k most similar sentences, it aligns these sentences with the input sentence. During sentence alignment, words can be deleted either from the input sentence or from the instance base sentence. This step can regarded as a refinement of the search for the single nearest neighbor since "with this limited set of retrieved examples a more precise

[5] The page numbers given in the following section are based on the electronic version of the papers available at http://dev.eurac.edu:8080/autoren/mitarbeiter/ostreiter

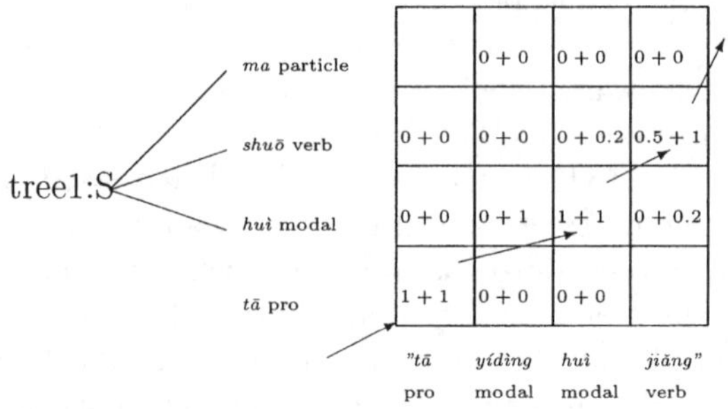

Fig. 3.4: *An alignment of the input sentence and a sentence from the instance base (Streiter, 2001*a*, p. 3).*

evaluation is possible" (Streiter, 2001*b*, p. 6). Figure 3.4[6] gives an example for such an alignment of an input sentence and a sentence from the instance base.

In (Streiter, 2001*b*), each alignment is assigned a score based on the number of identical words. But the score does not only register the number of matched words; each word is also assigned a weight during the training phase. The weights are intended to describe the importance of each word for the tree structure. They are assigned by a simple procedure: Streiter assumes that each sentence has a total weight of 1, which is assigned to the root node. Then this weight is equally distributed over all immediate daughter nodes, and the process is repeated recursively until the leaf nodes are reached. A binary tree thus distributes the weights equally to all daughter nodes so that the weights indicate the distance of a word from the root node. In a flat tree, however, weights represent a combination of the distance from the root and the number of sister nodes of each node dominating the word in question. It is unclear whether the fact that "unimportant" words are characterized by a large distance from the root or by being grouped into a flat constituent is reflected in the annotation scheme of the Chinese treebank used as gold standard[7].

After the alignment, the sentence with the highest score in the alignment

[6] Reprinted with permission from PACLIC.

[7] Streiter (p.c.) motivates the use of such a weighting scheme by the need to parse the major constituents of a sentence correctly. The internal structure of these major constituents can then be corrected by reparsing these parts of the sentences.

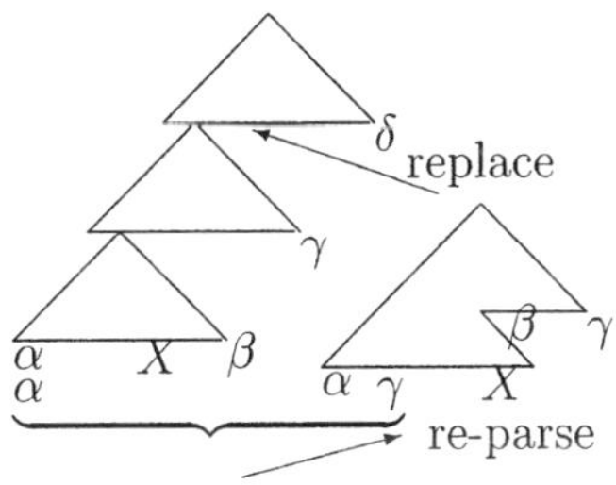

Fig. 3.5: *Reparsing the sequence from word α to word γ (Streiter, 2001*a*, p. 3).*

is chosen, its tree structure is retrieved, the words are replaced by the words of the input sentence, and unmatched words in the tree structure are deleted. After this step, the tree needs to be adapted to the input sentence. This adaptation is performed in 3 steps:

1. Insertion of deleted words from the input sentence. All words of the input sentence that could not be matched are inserted into the tree structure. They are generally inserted at the deepest level.
2. Derivational Adaptation: This type of adaptation is triggered by mismatches between words and the POS tags they received during alignment. In such cases, the largest possible subtree spanning these words is chosen and reparsed. Reparsing here means that the complete parsing procedure is repeated for the subtree. This is possible because during training all subtrees of the training sentences were extracted and stored with the complete trees. The original subtree is then replaced by the subtree from the reparsing step. A schematic example of this process is shown in Figure 3.5.
3. Structural Adaptation: This type of adaptation is triggered by a mismatch of a single word and its assigned POS tag. In such cases, the most probable POS tag for the word and its semantic relation are extracted from the training data and inserted into the tree structure.

Since this approach as described above is not satisfying with regard to coverage, especially for long sentences, Streiter (2001*a*) introduced an extension of the parsing algorithm based on the notion of chunks. He argues that if a sequence of words (i.e. a chunk) can be found in the instance base, the corresponding tree structure from the instance base can be accepted as the correct analysis for this chunk. The chunk is then replaced in the input sentence by the head of the rightmost head of the chunk, and parsing continues with the reduced sentence. However, it remains unclear how chunks are selected during the training phase and whether they correspond to the linguistic notion of chunks (cf. (Abney, 1991)).

Streiter's evaluation of his approach shows that OCTOPUS reached an F-score of 63.0 (and with a slightly modified algorithm, 70.0 (Streiter, 2002)) when trained on 20 000 sentences. In comparison, if no chunk collection is used in the parser, the F-score decreased to 61.7.

Streiter's approach to memory-based parsing shows that parsing as classification is possible even if one does not subscribe to the notion of cascaded classifiers. If parsing is viewed as finding the most similar sentence in the set of training examples and using the tree structure of this sentence as the basis for analyzing the input sentence, then the performance of the parser depends to a high degree on the design of the adaptation module. Streiter here relies mostly on reparsing sentence fragments for which mismatches between the input sentence and the retrieved structure have been detected.

3.4 Summary

In this chapter, we gave an overview of memory-based parsing approaches to noun phrase chunking, shallow parsing, grammatical relation assignment, and full parsing. All of these approaches, with the exception of Streiter's parser (Streiter, 2001*a*,*b*), are based on classification. They define parsing as assigning labels marking the beginning and end of constituents or grammatical functions to words or to previously analyzed constituents. For most approaches, this strategy results in an architecture in which highly specialized classifiers are cascaded so that results from earlier classifiers can be used as input for later ones. The classifiers themselves use a sliding window approach, thus relying on local context, sometimes combined with sentence global features. Streiter's approach is more holistic in that it attempts to assign the most similar tree structure to a complete input sentence. If the structure does not fit the sentence, parts of the sentence are reparsed, which often simplifies the problem.

The systems presented in this chapter prove that parsing can be reliably performed with memory-based learning methods. They show that words can be used successfully as features, and that POS tags become unnecessary when enough training data are available.

Chapter 4
Data-Oriented Parsing

Standard stochastic parsing approaches are based on the assumption that the linguistic information necessary for parsing can be abstracted into rules. This assumption presupposes that the decision of how to group constituents can be based for the most part on information that can be taken from a very local context in the tree, i.e. the type of constituents to be grouped and possibly the lexical heads of these constituents. Recent experiments, however, have shown (for example (Collins, 1999; Charniak, 2001)) that this is not necessarily true. Thus, stochastic parsers have been developed which use a more extensive set of parameters in the stochastic model to make these decisions: the parameters include information about, for example, neighboring nodes, grandparent nodes, or a subset of non-head words. These extensions of the locality assumption, though, need to be restricted to a small set since the estimation of a larger set of parameters requires larger training sets.

Data-Oriented Parsing (DOP) (Bod & Scha, 1996; Bod, 1998) is the first approach that relies on larger structures which go beyond mere context-free rewrite rules instead of using more parameters. DOP is based on the assumption that human syntactic analysis is related to "representations of concrete past language experiences rather than [to] abstract linguistic rules" (Bod & Scha, 1996, p. 2)[1]. Similar to other supervised stochastic parsing algorithms, DOP assumes a corpus of utterances annotated with labeled phrase structure trees or similar annotations (utterance-analyses). Instead of inducing a model of rules and a probability distribution, DOP uses these syntactic annotations as representations of formerly experienced utterances, equivalent to those representations Bod and Scha postulate in human sentence processing. From these representations, fragments are extracted which are then used to process new input utterances. Since it is not clear which definition of these fragments would result in the most suitable representation, DOP takes an extreme view on this issue and defines fragments to be subtrees of the original trees.

The basic DOP framework can be applied to corpora annotated within

[1] The cognitive aspect of syntactic processing is used as motivation for using past experiences, but the actual parsing system is explicitly described as "a language-technological approach" (Bod & Scha, 1996, p. 3). We will therefore concentrate on the language-technological perspective.

different linguistic frameworks as well as corpora with different definitions of fragments. In order to specify a particular DOP model, the following four parameters need to be set:

1. a formal definition of a well-formed *representation for utterance-analyses*
2. a definition of the *fragments* of the utterance-analyses that may be used as units in constructing an analysis of a new utterance
3. a set of *composition operations* by which such fragments may be combined
4. a *probability model* that indicates how the probability of a new utterance-analysis is computed on the basis of the probabilities of the fragments that combine to cover the complete utterance (Bod, 1998, p. 6).

DOP is in many respects very similar to memory-based learning; they both have a number of common properties (cf. also (De Pauw, 2002, pp. 37-38)):

- *Memory:* Both approaches emphasize the role which memory plays in processing. Both approaches are based on the psycholinguistic argument that humans retrieve previously seen examples from memory when they process sentences.
- *Aquisition:* Both approaches rely on a trivial learning phase: they store items or fragments without abstracting over them. Thus, the same items can be retrieved without modification or construction efforts.
- *Similarity:* Both approaches define the instances or tree fragments to be retrieved in terms of similarity to the input.
- *Low-Frequency Events:* Both approaches store low-frequency events, which enables them to treat irregularities and subregularities properly without having to resort to using a more high-frequency analysis for them.

In the following section, we discuss the most simple instantiation of DOP based on the phrase structure trees of the Penn treebank (Marcus et al., 1993), DOP1. Next, we describe the algorithm that allows DOP to find the most probable parse for a sentence and present empirical evaluations of this approach. To date, DOP has been evaluated on different treebanks for English, the only exception is the work by Hearne & Way (2004), who apply DOP to Chinese. Section 4.4 discusses the treatment of unknown words in DOP3. Section 4.5 describes a PCFG version of DOP, and Section

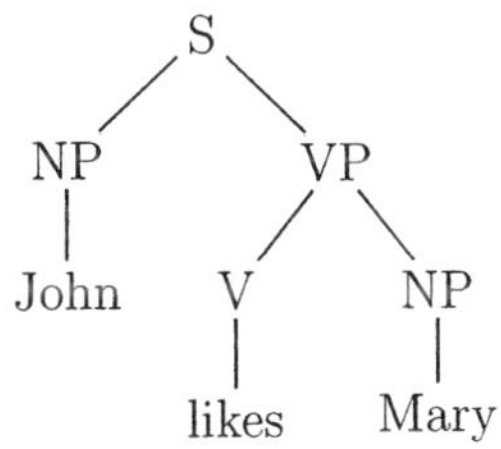

Fig. 4.1: *A possible phrase structure tree for "John likes Mary" (Bod, 1998, p. 13).*

4.6 a memory-based interpretation of DOP. We conclude this chapter with a summary.

4.1 A DOP Model for Phrase Structure Representations: DOP1

Representation. DOP1 (Bod, 1992) is intended to model phrase structure trees in which the labels are atomic categories for syntactic constituents. In these trees, there is no representation for functional or semantic information[2]. Thus the sentence *John likes Mary* may be assigned the tree given in Figure 4.1.

Tree Fragments. DOP1 extracts fragment subtrees which need to conform to the following requirements:

A subtree of a tree T is a subgraph t of T such that

1. t consists of more than one node,
2. t is connected,
3. each node in t has the same daughter nodes as the corresponding node in T, the only exceptions being the leaf nodes.

The first condition ensures that a derivation for a sentence is a process with a finite number of steps. The third condition ensures that either all or none of the daughters are removed; it does not allow structural generalizations such as changing the number of objects of a verb. Figure 4.2 gives examples of valid fragments of the tree in Figure 4.1.

[2] There are applications of DOP to higher-level grammar formalisms such as LFG (Bod & Kaplan, 1998, 2003) and HGSP (Neumann, 2003) but these go beyond the scope of the present book.

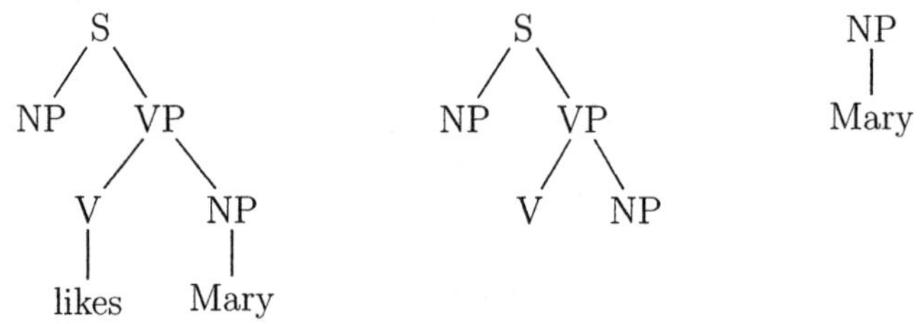

Fig. 4.2: *Examples of valid fragments for the tree in Fig. 4.1 (Bod, 1998, p. 13).*

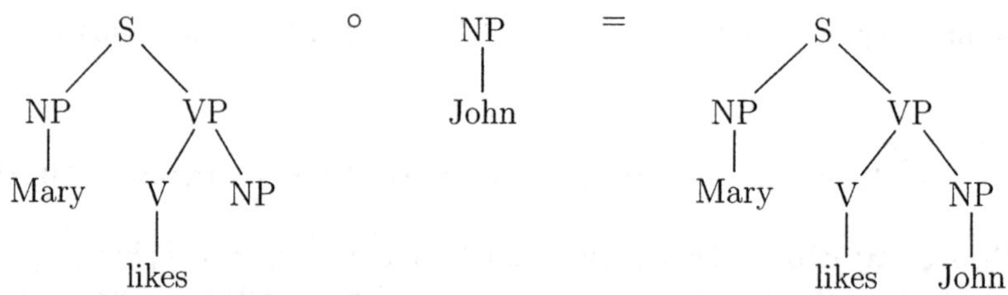

Fig. 4.3: *One possible derivation for "Mary likes John" (Bod, 1998, p. 15).*

Composition. In DOP1, only one composition operator is defined: a node-substitution which substitutes the leftmost non-terminal leaf of a tree by the root node of a second tree. Thus, the composition operator $\circ$ is a partial function on pairs of labeled trees. The composition of tree t and tree u, $t \circ u$ is defined if the label of the leaf to be substituted is identical to the root node label of the second tree. Restricting the operation to the *leftmost* non-terminal leaf makes the composition unique.

Given a (left-associative) sequence of compositions, $t \circ u \circ v$ yielding a tree T, the sequence of compositions is called a *derivation* if the resulting T contains no non-terminals as leaves. Figure 4.3 gives an example of a derivation of two subtrees for the sentence *Mary likes John.*

Given a bag of subtrees B, the set of trees without non-terminal leaves that can be generated by iterative composition of fragments in B gives the *tree language* of B, and the set of strings yielded by these trees is the *string language* of B. Given a corpus C, the tree language induced by C consists of the tree language of the bag of fragments of C, and the string language induced by C is the string language of the bag of fragments of C.

Probability Calculation. In DOP, the tree fragments extracted from a corpus take the place of a grammar of rules in traditional approaches. This grammar can be defined as a *stochastic* grammar if the process of syntactic analysis is redefined as a stochastic process that uses the frequency distribution of fragments.

The probability of a derivation is the joint probability of selecting the subtrees used in the derivation, i.e. the product of the probabilities of the subtrees:

$$P(t_1 \circ \ldots \circ t_n) = \prod_{i=1}^{n} P(t_i) \tag{20}$$

The probability of a subtree t is the relative frequency of t, i.e. the frequency of t divided by the frequency of all subtrees with the same root node label:

$$P(t) = \frac{freq(t)}{\sum_{t':root(t')=root(t)} freq(t')} \tag{21}$$

where $root(t)$ is the root node label of fragment t. The probability of a parse tree is the sum of all its derivations. The probability of a sentence is the sum of the probabilities of all its parses.

This calculation of probabilities is based on two assumptions: 1. that all fragments are stochastically independent and 2. that the collection of fragments is complete, i.e. that it contains all the fragments expected to occur in the future. Bod and Scha stress that "both assumptions are wrong. The occurrence-probabilities of the subtrees are certainly correlated to some extent, because many distinct overlapping subtrees are derived from one and the same corpus tree" (Bod & Scha, 1996, p. 9). They assume that this assumption "may nevertheless be relatively harmless as long as *all* (arbitrarily large) subtrees are taken into account" (Bod & Scha, 1996, p. 9). The second assumption is more difficult to justify since it assumes that all words as well as all possible subtrees are known. Therefore, the model is extended to treat both unknown words and words which are ambiguous in their word class. The treatment of such words, based on Good-Turing smoothing (cf. (Katz, 1987; Manning & Schütze, 1999) for an introduction to this smoothing method), is described in Section 4.4. This solution, however does not provide any solution for sentences, which can only be parsed if previously unseen tree structures can be accessed.

Another problem with the probability model is described by Johnson (2002), who proves that the model is biased and inconsistent. And while

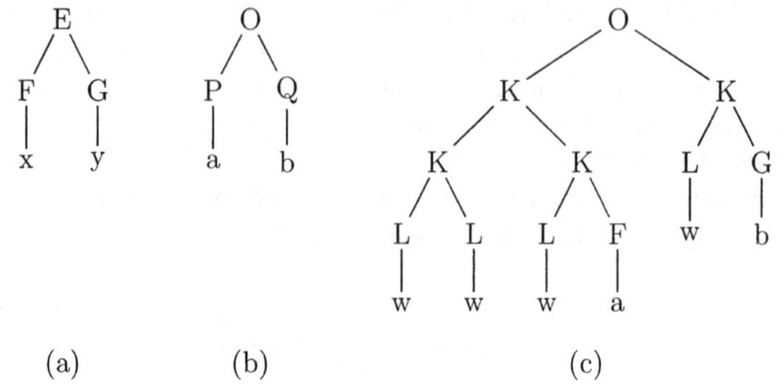

Fig. 4.4: *A sample treebank with one large tree (Bonnema & Scha, 2003, p. 28).*

"[b]ias is not necessarily a defect in an estimator, . . . , inconsistency is usually viewed as a fatal flaw of a estimator" (Johnson, 2002, p. 76). Additionally, Bonnema & Scha (2003) show that an unproportionally large portion of the probability mass goes to large subtrees. This can be shown when using the sample treebank shown in Figure 4.4 to parse the sentence *ab*. Intuitively, the correct analysis should be tree (b), but since there are 134 different subtrees with root O, each of these subtrees is assigned the probability $\frac{1}{134}$. The tree in Figure 4.5, however, is chosen because there are only 4 subtrees with root E. Bonnema and Scha's solution to this problem is based on the fact that there is no evidence as to which subtrees were used in the construction of the trees in the corpus. Thus all possible derivations for a corpus tree are regarded as equally probable. The probability of a subtree is then defined as the expected relative frequency of the application of that subtree in the process of constructing the trees in the corpus. For a more detailed description of the probability model, the reader is referred to (Bonnema & Scha, 2003).

4.2 Parsing DOP1

Parsing in DOP1 can be separated into two steps: the actual parsing step, in which the parse forest is generated, and disambiguation, in which the most probable parse from the parse forest needs to be found.

Fig. 4.5: *The most likely parse for sentence ab based on the treebank shown in Figure 4.4.*

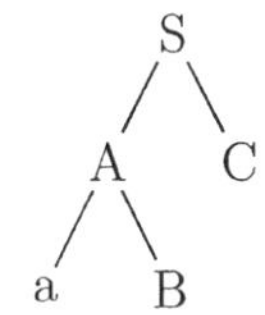

Fig. 4.6: *A sample fragment (Bod, 1998, p. 44).*

4.2.1 *Parsing*

For the generation of the parse forest of an input sentence, DOP1 does not have any requirements that deviate from those of standard context-free grammars. For this reason, any context-free parsing algorithm that uses a chart to store intermediate parsing results can be used for DOP. Examples for such algorithms can be found in (Jelinek et al., 1990; Naumann & Langer, 1994) for example.

Chart parsing can be applied to DOP1 since it is possible to view tree fragments as context-free rewrite rules: $root(t) \rightarrow yield(t)$ where $root(t)$ is the root node label, and $yield(t)$ the sequence of words covered by subtree t. The fragment shown in Figure 4.6, for example, is represented as $S \rightarrow aBC$. Since the rule does not store the internal structure between the root and the leaves, this information needs to be stored separately in order to be retrieved when the most probable parse is constructed. Contrary to standard context-free parsing, identical derivations can be achieved by composing different fragments. Unfortunately, parsing algorithms for DOP cannot collapse derivations that lead to identical trees. In such cases, the internal structure of the rewrite rules would have to be composed and the resulting structures compared to other derivations. There is no known efficient algorithm for this problem. For a string *abcd* and the bag of fragments shown in Figure 4.7, four different derivations leading to two different

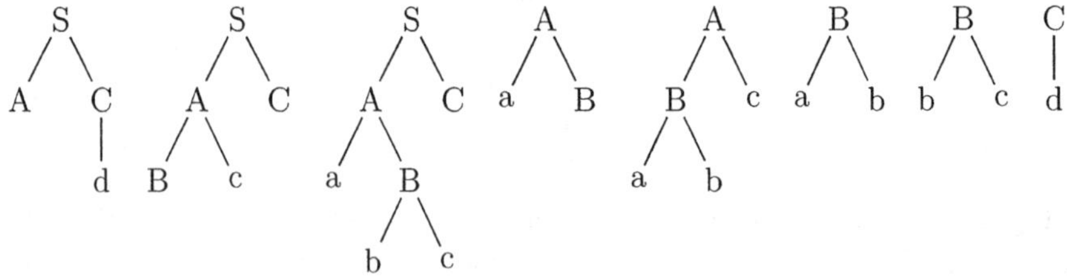

Fig. 4.7: *Tree fragments for parsing the string "abcd" (Bod, 1998, p. 41).*

trees can be found. Figure 4.8 shows the resulting derivation forest: arcs represent entries in the chart; the arc from 0 to 2, for example, represents the chart entry spanning the words 'a' and 'b'. The arcs are labeled by linked fragments that constitute the partial derivations of the string. The derivation forest shows that each derivation is generated twice, and that different tree fragments are used for these identical derivations. Since these fragments will be assigned different probabilities (which are not represented in the figure since they are only used for disambiguation), the forest needs to be unpacked in order to find the most probable parse.

4.2.2 *Monte Carlo Disambiguation*

The parsing step based on chart parsing can be achieved in polynomial time. Disambiguation for DOP parsing, however, cannot be achieved in the same time constraints since sentences may be assigned exponentially many parses and these parses can be generated by exponentially many derivations. Sima'an (2003) proves that finding the most likely parse in disambiguation with a DOP grammar is NP-hard. For this reason, it is not efficient to unpack the parse forest exhaustively. Therefore, DOP uses an estimation technique to approximate the selection of the derivation that leads to the most probable parse heuristically.

For standard stochastic context-free grammars, the most probable derivation can be found in cubic time by Viterbi optimization (Viterbi, 1967; Manning & Schütze, 1999). Viterbi optimization is a bottom-up, best-first search strategy which eliminates subtrees with lower probabilities when encountering several subtrees spanning the same sequence of input words and having the same root node label. This method guarantees finding the best derivation, since from these subtrees with identical root and identical yield, only the most probable one will be used in the most probable derivation.

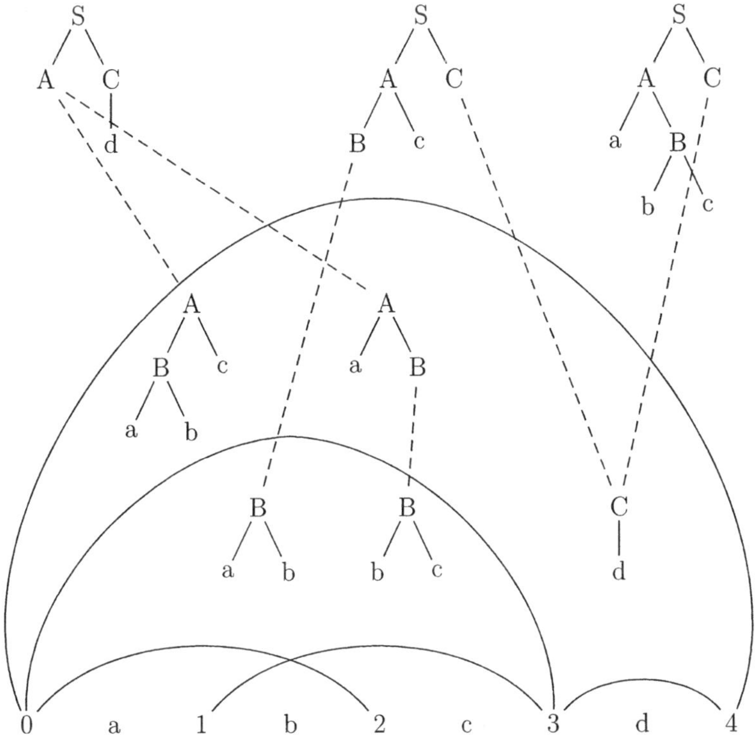

Fig. 4.8: *Derivation forest for the string abcd and the bag of fragments shown in Figure 4.7 (Bod, 1998, p. 42).*

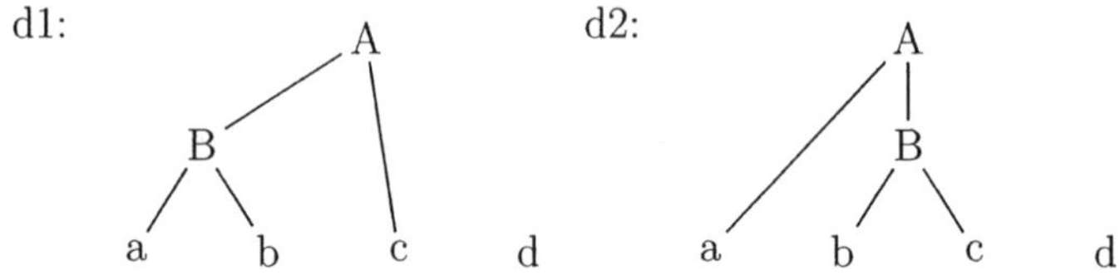

Fig. 4.9: *Two derivations d1 and d2 for the substring "abc" (Bod, 1998, p. 44).*

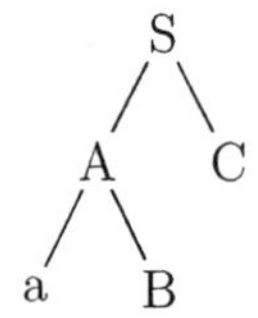

Fig. 4.10: *An additional fragment (Bod, 1998, p. 44).*

And since for stochastic context-free grammars, the most probable parse is generated by exactly one derivation, the most probable derivation found by Viterbi optimization is also the most probable parse for the input sentence.

For DOP, however, Viterbi optimization does not guarantee finding the most probable parse for two reasons: first, different derivations may lead to the same parse tree. A parse in DOP is the sum of all derivations generating the same structure. Therefore, finding the most probable derivation is not equivalent to finding the most probable parse. Second, the elimination of less probable subtrees is not possible for DOP parsing. This can be shown by the following example: if there exist two subtrees for the string *abc* as shown in Figure 4.9, where *d1* has a higher probability than *d2*, *d1* will be used for the most probable **derivation**, comparable to stochastic context-free parsing, but *d2* may still be part of the most probable **parse tree**. If, for example, an additional fragment, *d3*, as shown in Figure 4.10, is available, this fragment may be developed into a parse tree that can also be generated using *d2* but not by using *d1*. Additionally, the sum of the two derivations using *d2* and *d3* may be greater than the derivation based on *d1*.

For this reason, DOP needs to use *Monte Carlo Parsing*[3], a random-first search strategy. The parsing strategy is based on the Law of Large Numbers

[3] For an overview of Monte Carlo algorithms, cf. (Motwani & Ragavan, 1995).

(Feller, 1968), which states in this case that the most frequently generated parse converges to the most probable parse if the number of random samples is sufficiently large. By iteratively generating a high number of randomly chosen derivations, the most probable parse can be approximated as the parse which results with the highest frequency from these derivations. The selection of a random derivation from the parse forest can be achieved by a bottom-up algorithm similar to Viterbi optimization. However, instead of selecting the most probable subtree out of different subtrees identical in root node label and yield, a subtree is randomly chosen, based on the probability distribution of these subtrees. Therefore, a subtree s_i that is $p(i)$ times as probable as a subtree s_j, is $p(i)$ times as likely to be chosen as the other subtree. All the other subtrees are deleted from the chart. When the root node of the tree is reached, the remaining subtrees constitute the randomly chosen derivation. "[T]he time complexity of generating a random derivation of an input sentence is equal to the time complexity of finding the most probable derivation, i.e. linear in grammar size G and cubic in sentence length n: $O(Gn^3)$" (Bod, 1998, p. 46). The number N of derivations selected from the parse forest depends on the standard derivations σ: $N \geq \frac{1}{(4\sigma^2)}$. So, in order to obtain a standard error $\sigma \leq 0.05$, N needs to be greater than 100.

4.2.3 *Empirical Evaluation of DOP1 on ATIS*

DOP1 was empirically evaluated on the *Air Travel Information System* (ATIS) corpus in order to decide how different aspects, such as selecting the most probable parse versus the most probable derivation, or the impact of fragment size, influence parsing accuracy. ATIS is part of the Penn treebank corpus (Marcus et al., 1993), containing 750 sentences annotated with syntactic phrase structures according to the Penn treebank annotation guidelines (Santorini, 1990, 1991). For the tests, annotation errors were corrected, and "all epsilon productions and all analyses with so-called 'pseudo-attachments' " (Bod, 1998, p. 51) were removed. Thus, the tests were performed using a corpus that contained no noise, which is far from a normal test situation since this procedure is not feasible for larger corpora. Then, the ATIS corpus was split into a 90% training set (675 sentences) and a 10% test set (75 sentences). The splitting process was randomized, but the test set was chosen in such a way that only sentences which solely contained "known" words, i.e. words that appeared in at least one sentence in the training set were selected. The selection of this particular, highly-specialized subcorpus, its very limited size, and the restriction of the test set to known words make a comparison to other stochastic parsers very difficult if not impossible. The restriction to known words is dropped in later work by Bod described in the following section, but the limited size is necessary to make a testing regime possible. Bod (1998, p. 53) reports that "the calculation of only one random derivation takes already about 6 seconds ... and a full run on the 75 test set sentences, using 100 sampled derivations per sentence, takes more than 18 hours". Therefore, the evaluations described in the remainder of this section can only be used for internal evaluation of different factors.

The baseline for testing the influence of different factors on parsing accuracy was obtained by using all fragments, without any restriction, for training and employing this information to parse the 75 test sentences. The tests of factors such as using the most probable derivation instead of the most probable parse or lexicalization either restrict the number of parses or the number of fragments. The parse accuracy, i.e. the percentage of correctly parsed sentences, reached by the baseline approach was 85%. This figure, like all of the following results, is obviously rounded, although Bod does not explicitly state this or explain the method used.

The results of these tests can be summarized as follows:

- The first factor to be tested was the impact of using the most probable derivation (which can be calculated efficiently by Viterbi optimization) versus the most probable parse tree. When using the most probable derivation, parse accuracy drops to 69%, a good indication of the importance of using overlapping fragments in different derivations.
- The second factor was the impact of the maximal fragment size. Large fragments are capable of capturing more lexical and syntactic dependencies. On the other hand, the larger the fragments are, the less frequently they will occur in the training set. Restricting the fragments to a specific maximal depth will therefore give an indication of how important these dependencies within the fragments are. The experiments with a maximal fragment depth between 1 and 6, as well as unbounded depth, show that parse accuracy increases the greater the allowed depth is. Even from depth 6 to unbounded, there is still an improvement from 84% to 85% - it should be noted though, that this improvement is in the order of 1 out of 75 sentences and thus might be due to chance[4].

[4] With such a small test set, a test for significance might help to clarify the picture.

- The third factor was the impact of lexicalization on parse accuracy. Lexicalization here means that the presence of terminal leaves, i.e. lexical entries, is required. The presence of more than one word in a tree fragment represents collocational information, which might provide important information in the parsing process. If, however, there is too much lexicalization, the fragments tend to be too specific to be selected. For this reason, Bod tested how the restriction of terminal leaf nodes to a maximum influences parse accuracy. The experiments were carried out with a maximal tree depth of 6. When using only trees with at most one terminal leaf node, the parser reaches an accuracy of 57%. Parsing accuracy increases to 87% with a maximum of 8 terminal nodes in a fragment, while maximal fragment sizes between 3 and 6 remains constant at 83%, which constitutes a difference of three out of 75 sentences.
- The fourth factor was the removal of low frequency fragments. In standard probabilistic approaches, this is generally used to reduce noisy data in training. The results for DOP1, however, show that even the removal of fragments that occur only once in training data leads to a decrease of parsing accuracy from 85% to 77%.
- The fifth factor concerned the impact of the presence of non-head words in the fragments. The experiments show that parsing accuracy decreases to 74% if fragments are removed that contain only non-head terminal nodes. If only those fragments are removed that contain one non-head terminal, the accuracy decreases to 80%. Bod attributes the importance of non-head words in the fragment to dependencies that are not explicitly annotated, as in the sentence *Show the nearest airport to Dallas* where the adjective *nearest* determines the attachment of the prepositional phrase *to Dallas*.

The results presented above are good in comparison to other parsers, but one needs to bear in mind that the corpus size is very limited, and the restriction to known words in the test set is very likely to prefer sentences that are similar or identical to other sentences in the training set. This assumption may be corroborated by a test performed with a very basic model for treating unknown words (cf. (Bod, 1998, p. 71)). For this test, the test sentences were chosen completely randomly, i.e. they might contain unknown words. The result for the set of sentences that do not contain unknown words is significantly lower (73%) than the result reported in this section (79%) for the same depth of fragments.

A closer look at these results reveals that there is only one method of defining fragments that gives a higher accuracy than the baseline, which allows the use of all fragments: the restriction of fragments to maximally 8 terminals increases accuracy from 85% to 87%. But even in this instance, there is the issue of whether the difference is statistically significant. The fact that unrestricted fragments lead to better results than most of the restricted fragment sampling methods raises the question whether this behavior is due to *data sparseness*. Data sparseness is proven to be a problem for stochastic approaches using rewrite rules, which are generally trained on the one million word corpus of the Penn treebank. Since larger tree fragments occur in texts with an even lower frequency, it might be expected that more training data are needed to build a reliable probabilistic model. Unfortunately, the prohibitive processing costs of DOP parsing make it very difficult, if not impossible, to train the system on larger, state-of-the-art corpora.

4.2.4 *Evaluating DOP1 on the Penn Treebank*

A major point of criticism concerning the evaluation presented in the previous section is that the corpus used was very limited in size. Such small corpus sizes do not allow reliable statements about the quality of the method. Bod (2000*a*) therefore uses the Penn treebank to evaluate DOP1 on a broader basis. He concedes, however, that

> [w]hile [Monte Carlo parsing] has been successfully applied to parsing the ATIS section in the Penn treebank ..., it is extremely time consuming. This is mainly because the number of random derivations that should be sampled to reliably estimate the most probable parse increases exponentially with the sentence length (see (Goodman, 1998; Scha et al., 1999)). It is therefore questionable whether Bod's sampling technique can be scaled to larger domains such as the WSJ portion in the Penn treebank" (Bod, 2000*a*, p. 5).

For this reason, Bod used a Viterbi *n*-best search to find the 1 000 most probable derivations and to estimate the most probable parse on this basis since Monte Carlo parsing "turned out to be prohibitive for WSJ sentences" (Bod, 2000*a*, p. 6). For parsing, Bod uses the standard CKY parser, but in order to avoid a prohibitively high number of subderivations, he used a pruning technique (cf. (Collins, 1999, pp. 263 – 264)) which calculates the score of an item, based on its prior probability, and removes all items that score less than 10^{-5} times that of the best item.

parser	lab. precision	lab. recall	lab. precision	lab. recall
	≤ 40 words		≤ 100 words	
Collins	88.7%	88.5%	88.3%	88.1%
Bod	89.5%	89.3 %	88.6%	88.3%
Charniak	90.1%	90.1%	89.5%	89.6%

Table 4.1: *Bod's baseline for the Penn treebank as compared to other state-of-the-art stochastic parsers (Bod, 2000*a*, p. 8).*

The evaluation was conducted with the sections 2 through 21, which contain approximately 40 000 sentences, as training data and section 23 as the test set. Section 23 contains 2 416 sentences with less than 100 words each. Bod removed semantic tags, co-reference information, and quotation marks from all trees. Due to memory limitations, possible subtrees of a depth greater than one had to be restricted to a subset of 400 000 randomly chosen subtrees for each depth. The sampling procedure consisted of randomly selecting a node in a random tree and randomly expanding this node until the required depth is reached. All subtrees of depth one were used, and subtrees of a depth greater than 14 were ignored. This procedure resulted in a set of 5 217 529 fragments. For unknown words, the POS tag was guessed by the method described in (Weischedel et al., 1993), which uses statistics on word-endings, hyphenation, and capitalization.

Contrary to the evaluation in the previous section, Bod used the standard PARSEVAL measures (Black et al., 1991) of labeled precision and labeled recall to evaluate his parsing approach. The results for the baseline set of fragments described above as compared to the parsers of Collins (1999) and Charniak (2000) are shown in Table 4.1. For the tests to determine whether certain factors influence parsing accuracy, subsets from this baseline set were selected that conform to the restrictions. The results found for the Penn treebank reflect the tendencies for the ATIS corpus presented in the section above:

- Reducing the depth of fragments leads to a loss in precision and recall; if only fragments of size 1 (i.e. only context-free rules) are chosen, precision decreases to 76.0%, and recall to 71.8%. Both figures increase steadily, and for a maximal fragment depth of 12, precision increases to 89.1%, and recall to 88.8%.
- If the number of terminal leaves (i.e. words) is restricted in the fragments, results may even improve over the unrestricted sampling

method. Both precision and recall increase from 84.4% and 84.0% respectively for at most one word in a fragment to 90.8% and 90.5% respectively if at most 12 words are allowed. If even more than 12 words are present in the fragments, both precision and recall decrease to a minimum of 89.5% and 89.3% respectively for an unrestricted number of terminals.

- The exclusion of unlexicalized fragments, i.e. fragments that do not contain terminal leaves, with a depth greater than 6 increases precision to 90.8% and recall 90.6%; if unlexicalized trees of smaller depths are also removed, both figures decrease to a minimum of 79.9% precision and 77.7% recall for a selection which does not contain any lexicalized trees.
- If fragments containing a maximal number of non-head words are removed from the bag of fragments, precision and recall decrease slightly. The difference in both measures between using all non-head fragments and none at all, however, is in the order of 1%. Thus the effect is considerably less pronounced than for the ATIS corpus where parsing accuracy decreased from 85% to 74%.

The fact that lexicalization reaches an optimum if maximally 6 words are used indicates that there is a trade-off between the positive influence of having access to information on lexical dependencies between words and the problem of data sparseness. And the fact that several sampling methods improve precision and recall corroborates our hypothesis that the use of all fragments can be used as a balance for data sparseness. It is expected that the effects would be even more pronounced if more training data were available.

4.3 Non-Probabilistic DOP

Bod (2000*b*) presents a non-probabilistic version of DOP which finds the best parse by calculating the shortest derivation. For standard, rule-based stochastic parsers, finding the shortest derivation is equivalent to finding the parse tree with the least number of nodes. Since the probability of a parse tree is the product of the probabilities of all rules used in a derivation, derivations with fewer rules tend to receive higher probabilities. In general, this behavior is considered harmful and is avoided, for example, by normalizing the derivation. Since DOP employs tree fragments of arbitrary size, the shortest derivation, i.e. the derivation using the least number of fragments, corresponds to the derivation using the largest possible fragments from the

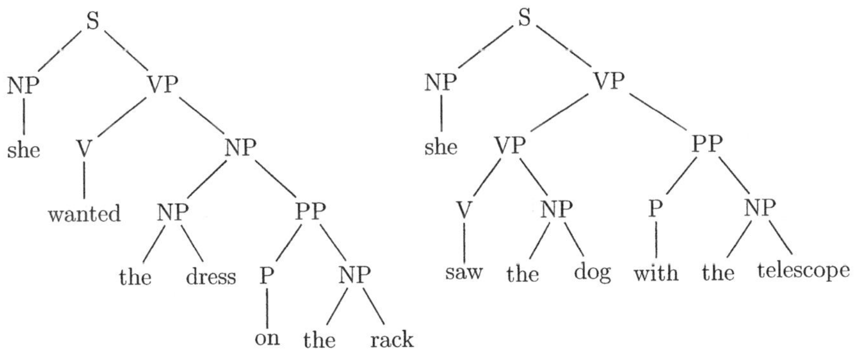

Fig. 4.11: *A sample corpus (Bod, 2000b, p. 2)*[5].

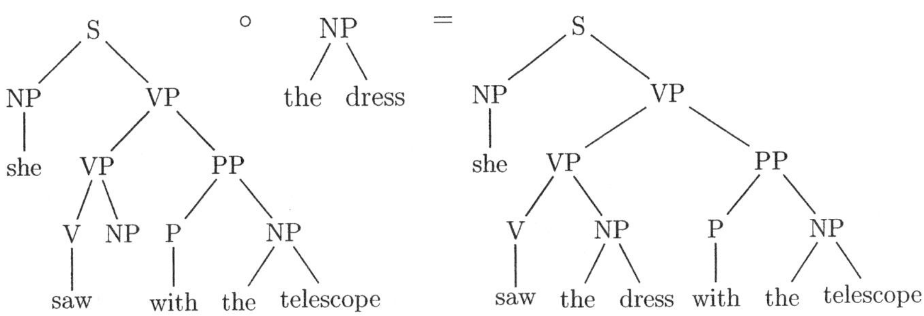

Fig. 4.12: *An example for a non-probabilistic parse (Bod, 2000b, p. 2).*

corpus. For the corpus shown in Figure 4.11, *She saw the dress with the telescope* is composed of the two subtrees shown in Figure 4.12. If there exists more than one shortest derivation, Bod uses a heuristic that ranks all fragments by their frequency and chooses the derivation that receives the smallest sum of ranks (i.e. that uses the most frequent fragments).

The shortest derivation in DOP can be computed by converting the fragments into rewrite rules (cf. Section 4.2.1) and giving all such rules equal probabilities. The shortest derivation coincides with the most probable derivation, that is, the derivation using the least number of such fragment rewrite rules. Thus it can be computed by Viterbi optimization.

[5] The page numbers for this article are based on the electronic version available from http://staff.science.uva.nl/~rens/.

max. frag. depth	ATIS			WSJ			
	Monte Carlo	Viterbi	non-prob.	Viterbi		non-prob.	
	parse accuracy			LP	LR	LP	LR
1	46.7%	46.7%	24.8%				
≤ 2	67.5%	67.5%	40.3%				
≤ 3	78.1%	78.2%	57.1%				
≤ 4	83.6%	83.0%	81.5%	84.7%	84.1%	81.6%	80.1%
≤ 5	83.9%	83.4%	83.6%				
≤ 6	84.1%	84.0%	85.6%	86.2%	86.0%	85.0%	84.7%
≤ 8				87.9%	87.1%	87.2%	87.0%
≤ 10				88.6%	88.0%	86.8%	86.5%
≤ 12				89.1%	88.8%	87.1%	86.9%
≤ 14				89.5%	89.3%	87.2%	86.9%

Table 4.2: *A comparison of probabilistic and non-probabilistic DOP parsing (Bod, 2000*b*, pp. 4 – 5).*

The non-probabilistic version of DOP has been tested on the ATIS section of the Penn treebank and on the WSJ (we will omit the evaluation on the OVIS corpus (Bonnema et al., 1997) since the results are similar to the results for ATIS). For ATIS, 10% of the sentences were chosen as test data, the selection being random but performed in such a way that no unknown words were included in the test set. For WSJ, sections 1-21 were used as training data, and section 23 as the test set. Here, the same sampling and smoothing methods as well as the treatment of unknown words were used as described in Section 4.2.4: only fragments with a maximal depth of 14 were used, and for each depth, a random sample of 400 000 fragments was extracted, which were then smoothed by the Good-Turing estimator (Good, 1953; Manning & Schütze, 1999) (cf. Section 4.4 for a description of the estimator). For unknown words, the POS category was guessed based on word-endings, hyphenation, and capitalization.

The results of this evaluation as compared to the probabilistic model are shown in Table 4.2. The evaluation for the ATIS corpus is based on *parse accuracy*, the percentage of exact matches, the evaluation of the WSJ corpus on the PARSEVAL measures *labeled precision* (LR) and *labeled recall* (LR). For both corpora, the non-probabilistic model performs considerably worse for small maximal fragment depths. If the maximal depth increases, the performance of the non-probabilistic model approaches the results of the probabilistic model. For ATIS, the former model even outperforms the latter one by 1.5% but here again one needs to keep in mind that the test set contains 75 sentences, so this difference probably corresponds to one sentence. For the WSJ, the non-probabilistic model gives very similar results to the probabilistic model when fragment depth is restricted to a maximum of 8. However, if larger trees are used, both precision and recall decrease for the non-probabilistic model. The good results of the non-probabilistic model for the ATIS corpus again indicate that using larger fragments balances the problem of data sparseness, at least to some degree. For the WSJ, for which more training data are available and therefore more reliable probabilities can be extracted, this advantage of using larger fragments is less pronounced.

4.4 The Treatment of Unknown Words: DOP3

DOP1, as presented in Section 4.1, can only find analyses for sentences for which every word is known, i.e., there exists at least one fragment which can cover this word. Sentences with an unknown word would not receive an analysis since only spanning analyses are taken into account.

Another problem posed by DOP1 is caused by words that are ambiguous concerning their POS tag. These words can be found very frequently in English since there exists a systematic ambiguity between nouns and verbs. If a word occurs, for example, only as a noun in the training corpus, DOP1 cannot suggest an analysis as a verb.

Therefore, in order to treat unknown words and words with word classes not encountered in the training corpus, an extension of the basic model is necessary: DOP3[6]. Bod (1998) bases this extension on the idea that the required tree fragment can be retrieved if the system is allowed to replace terminals in the fragment with the unknown word or the word with the unknown category. Such a replacement of the word *flight* with the unknown word *aircraft* is shown in Figure 4.13.

While it is not a problem to decide whether a word is unknown, the decision whether the word class of a word is unknown is not trivial. For this reason, Bod allows any word in a fragment to be replaced. The algorithms will prefer parses with as few word replacements as possible: the new fragments receive only minimal probabilities.

[6] DOP2 is a much simpler version for treating unknown words. It assigns all lexical categories to unknown words and then selects the most probable parse. However, the experimental result only reached 63% for a maximal depth of 3.

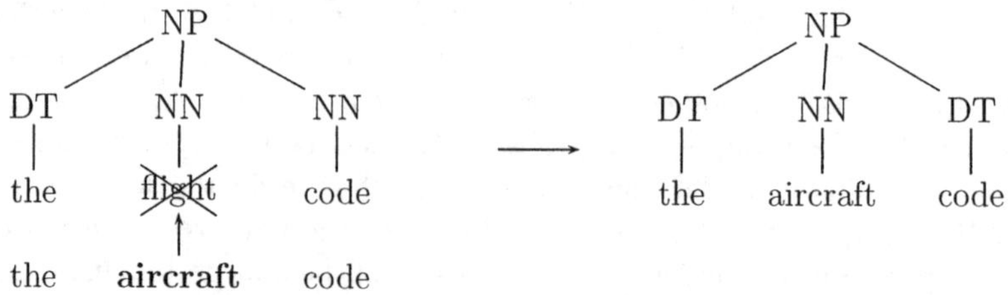

Fig. 4.13: *Replacing a word in a tree fragment with an unknown word (Bod, 1998, p. 82).*

Since a new lexicalization of a fragment also changes the fragment's probability, a method needs to be found that assigns suitable probabilities to these new fragments not covered by the corpus. For this problem, the *Good-Turing* estimator (Good, 1953; Manning & Schütze, 1999) presents a solution, since this method does not assume a specific distribution.

The Good-Turing estimator estimates the *adjusted* frequency r^* of an event by adding one to its *observed* frequency r depending on which probability the new frequency class is assigned:

$$r^* = (r+1)\frac{n_{r+1}}{n_r} \qquad (22)$$

where n_x is the number of events that occur x times. The expected probability of a new event t is then estimated by the following equation:

$$P(t) = \frac{r^*}{N} \qquad (23)$$

where N is the total number of observed events.

A new fragment, therefore, receives the adjusted frequency of the number of fragments occurring exactly once, divided by the number of fragments not occurring in the corpus. Because the bags of fragments with specific root node labels constitute different distributions in DOP the Good-Turing estimator is applied to each subclass of fragments separately, i.e. for fragments with S as root, with NP, VP, etc. In order to calculate the adjusted frequency of new fragments, however, the number of fragments not occurring in the corpus is needed. This figure is calculated as the difference between the number of all possible fragments with the same root as the new fragment and the number of observed fragments with this root. The number of all possible fragments "may be computed by Good's approximation formula for the sample/population proportion $(1 - n_1)/N$; but a direct application of this formula would lead to severe underestimation of the number of possible ... subtrees, since our method allows *any* subtree-terminal to mismatch with *any* word of an input sentence" (Bod, 1998, p. 86). Therefore, Bod uses this approximator to estimate the total number of words (and not the total number of fragments), and then calculates the number of ways in which these words can be inserted into the fragments.

For the empirical evaluation of DOP3 including the treatment of unknown words, Bod concludes that "treating all unknown words as possible unknown-category words [i.e. words with an unknown word class] would certainly lead to an impractically large number of subtrees in the derivation forest" (Bod, 1998, p. 90). So, he restricts the replacements to unknown words and for nouns and verbs. For the test, the same division of training and test data was used, i.e. 90% training data and 10% test data, but now the test sentences may contain unknown words. The splitting resulted in 26 sentences out of 75 containing 33 unknown words. The parse accuracy for these 26 sentences reaches 62%, (i.e. 16 sentences), and Bod attributes the failure to parse the remaining 10 sentences containing unknown words to the unavailability of morphological information, which (in our opinion) suggests that using a separate POS tagger might improve results. The accuracy for the remaining 49 sentences containing possibly ambiguous words is 86% (i.e. 42 sentences). The latter figure is 1% higher than the baseline model calculated for known words only (which might also be ambiguous). It is therefore unclear whether DOP3 results in an improved treatment of such words which are ambiguous regarding their word class.

4.5 Reducing DOP to a PCFG

Goodman (1996*a*, 2003) describes an approach to parsing which reduces DOP to PCFG-style parsing. Goodman's approach is very similar to the original DOP in that it results in the same distribution over parse trees, but it does not suffer from DOP's problems of an exponentially growing grammar and an inefficient search for the most probable parse tree. Goodman's modifications concern two different parts of the DOP model: Firstly, he suggests an alternative to extracting the set of subtrees from the training corpus. Instead of a bag of fragments, he uses an indexed version of PCFG rules and thus reduces the size of the resulting grammar. The second modification concerns the search criterion: instead of maximizing the most probable parse criterion, Goodman (2003) suggests maximizing the number of constituents which are expected to be correct. This criterion is more similar to the commonly used evaluation criteria *precision* and *recall* than the original most probable parse criterion.

Both modifications can be used separately, i.e. the PCFG version can also be used with Monte Carlo Parsing techniques, and the new maximization criterion can be used with the original subtree representation of the treebank, but it is expected that only the combined use will optimally exploit their strengths.

4.5.1 *The PCFG Representation of Subtrees*

Goodman (2003) points out that the representation of a corpus in classic DOP is extremely expensive in terms of memory. If all possible subtrees are stored in memory, the size of the grammar increases exponentially in relation to the size of each training tree. Even if 95% of the subtrees are discarded, the resulting grammar is still too large for efficient handling. Goodman suggests a reduction of the trees of the training corpus in a way which results in at most eight PCFG rules for each node in the training data. Since this reduction is much smaller than the original DOP reduction, it is not necessary to discard fragments from the training corpus.

The role of DOP's subtrees is to provide a larger context than the standard PCFG rules, which are known to be unable to handle long-distance relationships. Thus, the context of a node is explicitly represented in the subtree. Goodman's reduction is based on the idea that the context can be represented implicitly by an index. Consequently, each node in the training corpus is assigned a unique number, its address. This address is different for each node in the corpus, representing the unique context in which it is found. Figure 4.14 shows an example of a tree with such addresses. For each non-terminal node A in the training corpus, a new node A_k is created, its non-terminal is A_k. Non-terminals with an index are called *interior*, while the original non-terminals, without an index, are called *exterior*. Let a_k be the number of all possible (non-trivial) subtrees headed by node $A@k$, and a the number of possible (non-trivial) subtrees headed by nodes with the non-terminal A, i.e. $\sum_j a_j$. Thus, for the example in Figure 4.14, $np_2 = np_4 = 1$, $vp_3 = 2$, and $s_1 = 6$.

If PCFG rules were extracted from indexed trees by using non-terminals plus their addresses, the resulting grammar would not be able to generalize. The rule $S_1 \rightarrow NP_2\, VP_3$ extracted from the tree in Figure 4.14 can only result in the exact same tree because differently structured NPs, for example,

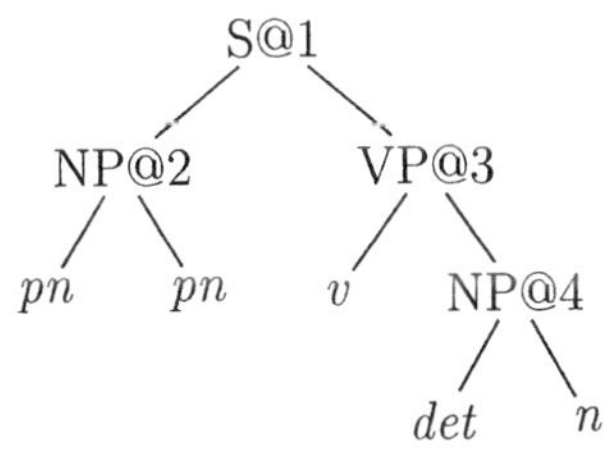

Fig. 4.14: *A tree with addresses at the nodes (Goodman, 2003, p. 130).*

possess different addresses. For this reason, Goodman (2003) extracts eight rules for each local tree,

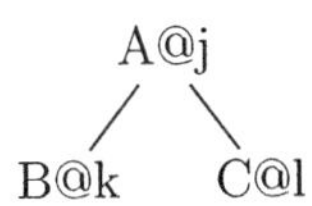

each rule having a different distribution of interior and exterior non-terminals (the probabilities are given in parentheses)[7]:

$$\begin{array}{llll} A_j \rightarrow B\,C & (1/a_j) & A \rightarrow B\,C & (1/a) \\ A_j \rightarrow B_k\,C & (b_k/a_j) & A \rightarrow B_k\,C & (b_k/a) \\ A_j \rightarrow B\,C_l & (c_l/a_j) & A \rightarrow B\,C_l & (c_l/a) \\ A_j \rightarrow B_k\,C_l & (b_k c_l/a_j) & A \rightarrow B_k\,C_l & (b_k c_l/a) \end{array}$$

The probability distribution over these rules assigns higher probabilities to, and so prefers, those rules with indices.

Now a DOP subtree can be represented as a subderivation which has exterior non-terminals as root and leaves, while all other nodes are represented by interior non-terminals. Figure 4.15 gives an example of a subtree and its subderivation. Such subderivations are considered homomorphic to the original DOP subtrees. Goodman (2003) proves that a homomorphic subderivation headed by A has probability a and that a homomorphic subderivation headed by A_j has probability a_j.

A PCFG derivation is considered homomorphic to a DOP derivation if for every subtree there is a corresponding homomorphic subderivation. Figure 4.16 shows an example of homomorphic derivations involving two

[7] This approach as presented requires binary trees. It can be extended to more unbalanced trees, but then the number of necessary rules increases with the number of daughters in a local tree.

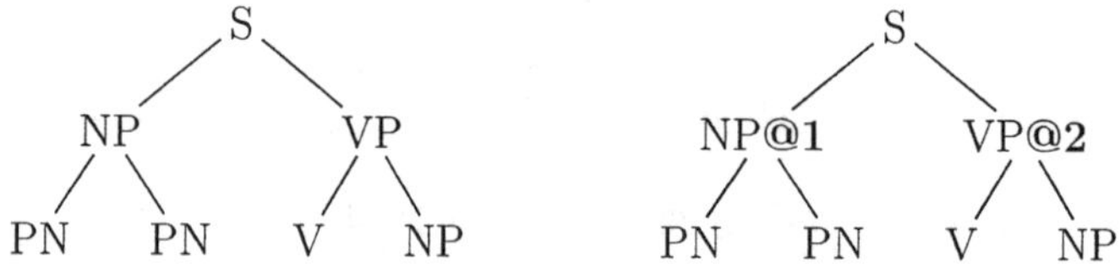

Fig. 4.15: *A DOP subtree (left) and its representation as a PCFG subderivation (right) (Goodman, 2003, p. 130). Internal nodes are highlighted.*

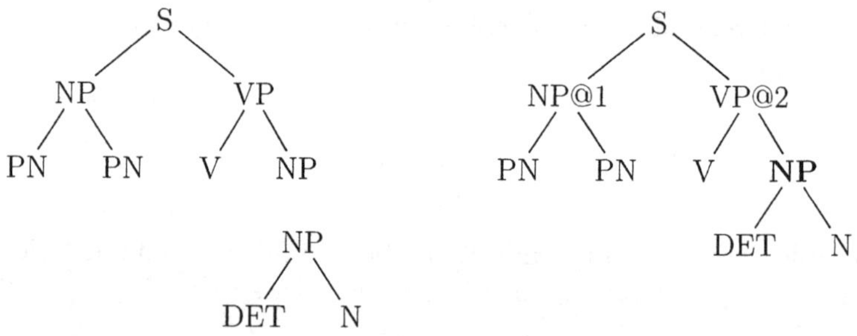

Fig. 4.16: *A DOP derivation (left) and a homomorphic PCFG derivation (right) (Goodman, 2003, p. 132). The corresponding node in the PCFG derivation to the substitution site in the DOP derivation is marked in bold.*

subtrees on the one hand and four PCFG rules on the other. The substitution site in the DOP derivation, i.e. the NP node in the VP, can be recognized as such in the PCFG derivation since it uses an exterior nonterminal although it is neither root nor a leaf in the tree. Goodman (2003) proves that this results in trees homomorphic to DOP trees (identical when ignoring the addresses) with equal probabilities.

Goodman (2003) shows that there are also equivalent PCFG representations for DOP models which restrict the maximal depth of subtrees and for the non-probabilistic DOP version presented in Section 4.3.

4.5.2 *Maximum Constituent Parsing*

Goodman (1998) shows that the choice of optimization metric is closely linked to the choice of evaluation metric. Goodman (1996*b*, 2003) suggests

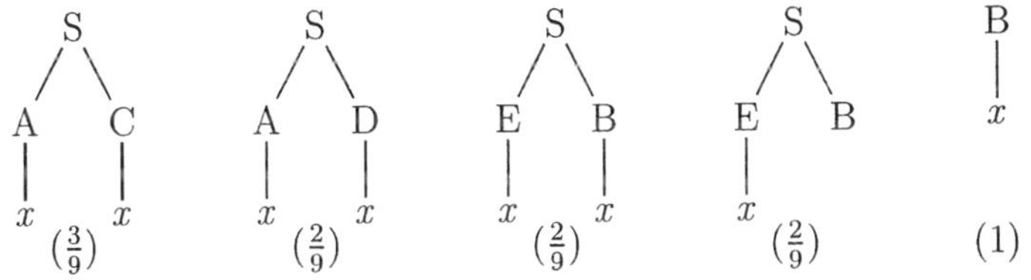

Fig. 4.17: *A small corpus of subtrees (Goodman, 2003, p. 128).*

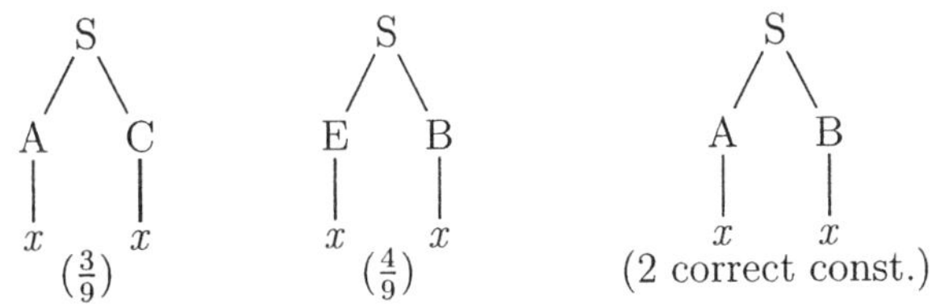

Fig. 4.18: *The best parses according to the most probable derivation(left), the most probable parse (middle), and the maximum constituents parse (right) (Goodman, 2003, p. 137).*

a new optimization metric for parsers: maximizing the expected number of correct constituents in a parse. He shows that this criterion can be maximized in $O(n^3)$ time, which is more efficient than the most probable parse, which can only be approximated by Monte Carlo sampling (cf. Section 4.2.2). Since it is closely related to the measures of precision and recall, it can be expected to perform well.

Figure 4.18 gives an example of the different parses according to the three criteria *most probable derivation*, *most probable parse*, and *maximum constituents* for the grammar shown in Figure 4.17. For the maximum constituents parse, the expectation for the different nodes must be calculated. The probability that S is correct is 1, and the probability for constituent A is $\frac{3}{9} + \frac{2}{9} = \frac{5}{9}$, for constituent B it is $\frac{4}{9}$. The number of constituents expected to be correct is the sum of these probabilities, i.e. 2. Note that this tree cannot be derived from the grammar since there is no tree containing $S \rightarrow A\,B$. This characteristic of maximum constituent parsing may lead to unwanted analyses, but Goodman (2003, p. 137) reports that "[i]n practice, however, the trees produced do tend to be both grammatical, and to score well on the exact match criterion".

The algorithm, which is only sketched here and which can be found in more detail in (Goodman, 1996*b*), is based on the *Inside-Outside* algorithm (Baker, 1979) (cf. (Manning & Schütze, 1999) for a short introduction). But while the original Inside-Outside algorithm is intended for training PCFGs, Goodman's modification allows its use for parsing. The intuition behind the parsing algorithm is that the probability for a possible constituent X (starting with word s and ending with word t) to be in the parse can be computed via the inside-outside probabilities. The parser then searches bottom-up for the most likely constituents.

The probability that constituent X is in the parse is defined as follows:

$$P(X \stackrel{*}{\Rightarrow} w_s \ldots w_t \mid S \stackrel{*}{\Rightarrow} w_1 \ldots w_n) \tag{24}$$

This probability is stored in $g(s,t,X)$. It can be computed using the inside ($i(s,t,X)$) and outside ($o(s,t,X)$) probabilities:

$$g(s,t,X) = \frac{o(s,t,X) \times i(s,t,X)}{i(1,n,S)} \tag{25}$$

Every constituent with a non-zero probability must be licensed by a complete parse because it can be derived from the root node via the outside probabilities and from the leaves via the inside probabilities.

In a second step, the parser proceeds bottom-up and finds for each span the most likely constituent Y by looking at its inside-outside probability and the probabilities of the best split. Since Goodman assumes binary trees, the split must consist of exactly two nodes, which together span Y completely and uninterruptedly. The search for the best split is not restricted by the requirement that both participants in the split must be licensed by a rule, thus allowing new structures as shown in Figure 4.18.

Goodman (2003, p. 141) evaluated his approach using the suggested reduction to indexed PCFG rules and the maximum constituent parse. He used the ATIS corpus, in a minimally edited version and in the cleaned up version, which was also used by Bod (1998) in a ten-fold cross-validation setup. The results are shown in Table 4.3. They show that Goodman's approach of a PCFG-version of DOP is a valid alternative to the full scale DOP system although the numbers reported by Bod (1998, p. 54) are not reached. Goodman (1996*a*) attributes this difference to Bod's cleaning of the data.

	minimally edited		cleaned up	
criteria	mean	std. dev	mean	std. dev.
crossing brackets accuracy	90.15%	2.65%	97.16%	0.93%
zero crossing brackets	66.11%	5.56%	86.13%	3.99%

Table 4.3: *Goodman's results for ATIS (Goodman, 2003, p. 140).*

4.6 Memory-Based DOP

Goodman's (Goodman, 2003) indexing method described in the previous section derives an indexed version of a PCFG grammar which uses the complete tree as the context in which a rule is applicable. De Pauw (2000, 2002, 2003) uses a similar indexing strategy to obtain an indexed PCFG grammar. His strategy, however, restricts the context to the subtree dominated by the rule in question. De Pauw argues that this indexing allows a memory-based look-up, in which, in contrast to DOP, "a sentence can be analyzed by looking for the most similar sentence in memory and by consequently extrapolating its tree-structure" (De Pauw, 2002, p. 38). In practice, this means that the largest subtrees found in memory are used for parsing.

De Pauw's indexing algorithm proceeds bottom-up: if a node is found that dominates only terminals or already indexed non-terminals, this node is assigned an index. The index can be either retrieved from memory if the current rule has already been observed (including the indices of the daughter non-terminals), or a new index can be created if a new rule is observed. Thus, the tree shown in Figure 4.19 is indexed as shown in Figure 4.20. The tree is based on an ATIS style annotation, as De Pauw retains the syntactic flags such as the subject marker -SBJ, while semantic flags are removed from the data. In the tree in Figure 4.20, the two PP nodes receive the same index because both of them have the same daughters, *to* and *NP@2*. The tree contains four different NPs, of which only the two dominating the proper nouns receive a common index.

The example clearly shows the difference to Goodman's (Goodman, 2003) approach: here, nodes with the same subtree receive the same index, while Goodman's indexing scheme would have assigned different indices to, for example, the PP nodes Thus, Goodman's indexing strategy also considers the context outside the subtree. Additionally, De Pauw does not require the trees to be binary.

From the indexed tree, De Pauw derives a PCFG grammar which trans-

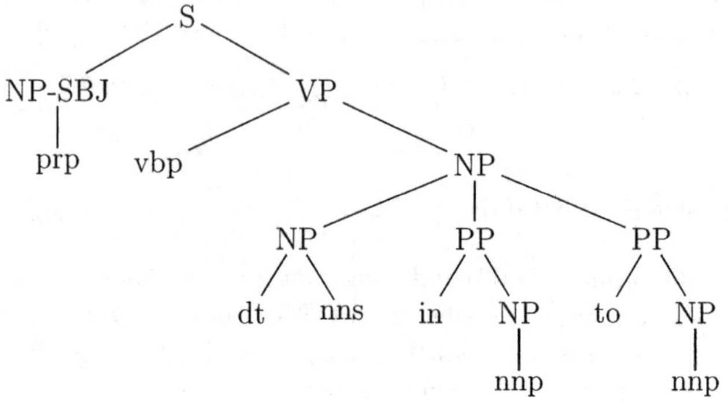

Fig. 4.19: *An ATIS-style tree for the sentence "I want a flight from Rome to Buffalo" (De Pauw, 2003, p. 156).*

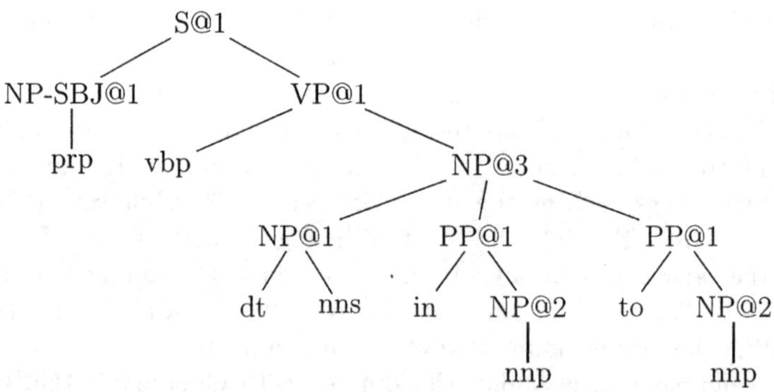

Fig. 4.20: *The indexed version of the tree in Figure 4.19 (De Pauw, 2003, p. 157).*

NP@3	→	NP@1 PP@1 PP@1
NP@3	→	NP@1 PP@1 PP
NP@3	→	NP@1 PP PP@1
NP@3	→	NP@1 PP PP
NP@3	→	NP PP@1 PP@1
NP@3	→	NP PP@1 PP
NP@3	→	NP PP PP@1
NP@3	→	NP PP PP
NP	→	NP@1 PP@1 PP@1
NP	→	NP@1 PP@1 PP
NP	→	NP@1 PP PP@1
NP	→	NP@1 PP PP
NP	→	NP PP@1 PP@1
NP	→	NP PP@1 PP
NP	→	NP PP PP@1
NP	→	NP PP PP

Table 4.4: *The rules which are extracted for node NP@3 from the tree in Figure 4.20.*

lates each non-terminal node into a number of rules which cover all possible combinations of indexed and non-indexed nodes. The node NP@3 in Figure 4.20, for example, is translated into the rules shown in Table 4.4. The higher number of rules resulting from one node in De Pauw's indexing method should be counterbalanced to some degree by a reduction in the number of rules caused by the use of a common index for identical subtrees. However, since neither Goodman nor De Pauw give the number of rules, this intuition cannot be corroborated.

Similar to DOP1, De Pauw uses a two-step parsing architecture (PMPG). First of all a CYK parser (Chappelier & Rajman, 1998) is used to generate a parse forest. The disambiguation phase is similar to the indexing phase during training as explained above, the only difference is that no new indices are created. If no rule is found in the grammar, the node is left without an index. For the probability calculation, the subtrees of the highest indexed nodes are pruned. Based on the remaining tree, the probability of the parse is calculated using the PCFG manner, ignoring the indices. The tree shown on the right remains after pruning the parsed and indexed tree on the left in Figure 4.21. The probability of this parse tree is calculated as

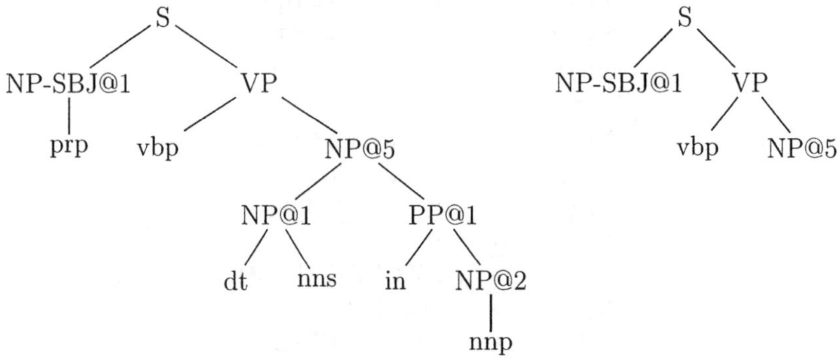

Fig. 4.21: *A parsed tree (left) and the indexed tree (right) for the sentence "I want a flight from Paris", based on De Pauw's indexing strategy (De Pauw, 2002, p. 159).*

treebank	parser	exact match	F_1
ATIS	PCFG	60.03%	84.54
	PMPG	68.34%	85.37
	PCFG + PMPG	74.05%	90.52
WSJ	PCFG	8.49%	62.27
	PMPG	12.29%	63.55
	PCFG + PMPG	14.94%	78.01

Table 4.5: *The results of De Pauw (2003, p. 154).*

$P(t) = P(S \rightarrow NP - SBJ\,VP) \times P(VP \rightarrow vbp\,NP@4)$. This calculation effectively assigns the probability 1 to all subtrees retrieved from memory. The reason for this approach remains unclear, and an alternative may be to use the DOP1 probability of the subtree instead.

De Pauw (2003, p. 154) evaluates his approach (PMPG) on data from ATIS and from the Wall Street Journal (WSJ) section of the Penn treebank. PMPG is compared to a standard PCFG and to a combined model in which the PCFG selects the n most probable parses from the parse forest and the memory-based indexing approach selects the most probable sentence from this selection. The results are given in Table 4.5. De Pauw's error analysis for PMPG (De Pauw, 2002, p. 67) shows that the model's tendency of selecting the largest possible subtree may not always be fortuitous. This tendency can be counteracted by the combined model.

4.7 Summary

In this chapter, we have given an introduction to *Data-Oriented Parsing* (DOP). Similar to other stochastic approaches, DOP extracts information necessary for parsing from a syntactically annotated corpus. It is, however, the first approach that does not abstract this information into pure context-free rules, instead it uses larger fragments extracted from the corpus. Here, the corpus serves as a repository of "past experiences", which guide parsing.

The use of these "past experiences" is to some degree similar to memory-based learning (cf. Chapter 2), which refrains from any abstraction of the data. DOP, though, uses a less strict regime, since it allows the splitting of syntactic trees into fragments of flexible size, thus allowing a certain degree of generalization. Instead of using a similarity metric, as in memory-based learning, to retrieve the most suitable tree for a new sentence, DOP uses standard probability models.

One of the main insights that the work on DOP gives is that the use of larger fragments instead of local rules has a beneficial influence on parsing accuracy. Restricting the sampling of tree fragments to a maximal number of terminal nodes (i.e. words) improves accuracy even more. This indicates that DOP is one method of incorporating lexical information without the (or with less of a) problem of having to estimate a huge number of parameters for a very limited amount of training data.

This increase on parsing accuracy, however, is traded for a considerable increase in processing load: for DOP, it is not sufficient to calculate the most probable derivation, instead the most probable parse based on a possibly exponential number of derivations needs to be computed. One possible solution to this problem may lie in using the shortest derivation instead. Results for small amounts of training data especially suggest that this method could outperform the original DOP model.

Another solution to the problem of efficiency can be found in transforming the DOP model into a PCFG. The transformation uses indices, which act in place of the actual context of a rule. By using a PCFG-based version taking the complete context into consideration (Goodman, 1996*a*, 2003), homomorphic trees are generated in parsing. If the restriction of indexing a node based on its daughters is combined with a probability model which assigned probability 1 to subtrees found in memory (De Pauw, 2002, 2003), a preference for larger subtrees is instilled in the model.

Chapter 5
TüSBL: A Memory-Based Parser

Memory-based learning (MBL), as well as all other symbolic machine learning methods, needs to be adjusted to every new learning task to which it is applied. The choice of features and the setting of parameters is unique to each task. More specifically, when applying memory-based learning to a new problem, one needs to make a number of important decisions:

1. The problem to be solved needs to be defined as a *classification task* and the set of classes must be chosen.
2. The *similarity metric* needs to be chosen.
3. The *weighting scheme* needs to be chosen. This choice is not independent from the previous choice – on the contrary, these two choices are mutually dependent.
4. The *feature set* needs to be determined. This choice involves a decision on which types of information are important for the classification task.

For some problems, such as for POS tagging, the solution to the first problem is evident: the set of classes is the set of POS tags, and the task can be described as assigning a class, i.e. a POS tag, to each word in a sentence. For other tasks, such as for syntactic parsing, there exist no such evident solutions. It is not clear what exactly should be classified: each word, or the sentences as a whole? The same holds for the decision concerning the feature set; for POS tagging, it is well known that the vast majority of decisions can be made when only a very local context of 2-3 words is available, combined with previous classifications for the context to the left. In syntactic parsing, however, the situation is less clear. Here, the intended annotation is generally a tree structure, which implies that not only neighboring words but also previous decisions on different levels need to be considered. Additionally, most researchers in NLP agree that the degree of long-distance relations is much higher in syntactic parsing than in POS tagging, so that a wider context should be taken into consideration for parsing. As to decisions concerning the choice of the similarity metric and the weighting scheme, there is only a limited amount of empirical research giving very preliminary assumptions on which similarity metric or weighting scheme will be useful for which type of classification task.

This chapter describes the memory-based parsing approach TüSBL (Kübler, 2002, 2003). But first, a short introduction to the training data and the annotation scheme, which are different from the Penn treebank in many respects, will be given.

As explained in Section 1.1, parsing algorithms depend on the expressive power of the grammar that will be used. In contrast, TüSBL does not use rules of any form, thus it cannot be related directly to a particular class of grammars in the Chomsky hierarchy. Instead, there are restrictions that hold for the annotations in the instance base: these annotations must consist of tree structures that do not contain crossing branches or empty categories. The annotations used in the treebank on which TüSBL is trained and evaluated, however, go beyond pure tree structures, in the sense that some nodes may not be connected to the surrounding (connected) nodes. This type of structure arises if the sentence contains parenthetical clauses, which occur frequently in speech data. Another case of non-canonical tree structures are structures which consist of more than one tree without a common root node, or *embedded trees*. These types of annotations arise in the case of elliptical expressions or false starts, both of which are very typical in speech data.

The presence of these non-canonical tree structures in the treebank annotations also influences the design of the parsing algorithm. For this reason, we will describe the treebank, TüBa-D/S, in Section 5.1.1[1]. TüBa-D/S is a treebank of German based on transliterations of dialogues. It should be noted that the parser can, in principle, be used with any treebank whose annotations adhere to the same restrictions as the corpus presented here. Since the data set is based on spontaneous speech, it confronts the parser with characteristic problems that are in many instances different from the challenges typical for written texts.

We will describe and motivate TüSBL's solution concerning the choice of the classification task in Section 5.2: the whole syntactic tree is used as a class. This decision necessitates a certain amount of reformulation of the remaining questions. First, in order to approach such a complex task, the system needs a detailed annotation of the sentences to be parsed that goes beyond mere morpho-syntactic annotation. For this reason, we have introduced a finite-state chunk parser as a "preprocessing stage". We will introduce the hybrid architecture into which the learning component is incorporated in Section 5.3 and describe the preprocessing steps and their output structures. Section 5.4 gives an overview of the complete system. In Section 5.5, we will have a closer look at what this preprocessing implies

[1] This will also help to familiarize the reader with the annotation scheme used for all examples in the following chapters.

for the learning task and what type of information is available after the chunk parsing step. This will also give an answer to the decision concerning the feature set, since the need for all available information leads to using all words in the sentence instead of only a window of specific length. We will then show a sample parse in Section 5.6. As a consequence of using all words as features, it is impossible to use the weighting schemes described in the literature. We have therefore decided to use a simple overlap metric combined with a feature weighting metric based on the cost of modifying the tree structure if parts of the sentences are left out. This method will be described in Section 5.7. The feature weighting method described in Section 5.7 optimally requires a high amount of syntactically annotated training data; the available treebanks, on the other hand, are very restricted in size for complex learning tasks. In order to offset the drawback of the chosen weighting scheme in combination with a small instance base, we describe in Section 5.8 a backing-off strategy, which, to some extent, replaces feature weighting. We will conclude with a summary in Section 5.9.

5.1 Parsing, Training Corpora, And Related Issues

Parsing spontaneous speech is an area in NLP which has not received very much attention until recently. This problem needs to be addressed in order for the design of dialogue systems based on deep processing (as opposed to completely statistical approaches) to be successful. Since most of the work on data-oriented parsing concentrates on using the Penn treebank as training data, few approaches based on speech data have been reported (cf. for example (Ruland, 2001; Kiefer et al., 2000)). Another, more practical, reason for using TüBa-D/S was that at the time when the work on TüSBL started, there was no other treebank for German of comparable size available. The only existing treebank for German was the NEGRA treebank (Skut et al., 1998), whose publicly available version contained 10 000 sentences. Another approach might have been to combine these two treebanks, but then we would have had to cope with differences in text types as well as in annotation schemes, both of which are non-trivial problems, as experience has shown.

Section 5.1.2 gives a comparison of TüBa-D/S to the Penn treebank, and in Section 5.1.3, we will have a closer look at specific features of TüBa-D/S that necessitate modifications in the parsing algorithm.

5.1.1 *The TüBa-D/S Treebank*

The treebank used for evaluating TüSBL is the TüBa-D/S treebank (Stegmann et al., 2000; Hinrichs, Bartels, Kawata, Kordoni & Telljohann, 2000*a*,*b*). This treebank was developed in the context of VERBMOBIL, a long-term Machine Translation project funded by the German Ministry for Education, Science, Research, and Technology (BMBF). VERBMOBIL had as its goal the speaker-independent translation of spontaneous speech in the domains of business appointments, travel scheduling, and hotel reservations. As a consequence, the TüBa-D/S treebank contains transliterations of spontaneous dialogues in the above mentioned domains. Thus, the data provide special challenges for the annotators as well as for parsers that are trained on such data: To begin with, the natural segmentation of spontaneous speech is a *dialogue turn*, i.e. a single, generally uninterrupted contribution of one participant to the dialogue. It is far from clear how such dialogue turns can be segmented into sentences, the primary units in syntactic annotation. For TüBa-D/S, the decisions on sentence boundaries were made by the human transliterators based on intonational features. These sentences may be very short, such as sentence (3) or (4), or they may consist of more than one sentence in the linguistic sense, such as in sentence (5)[2].

(3) ja
yes

(4) hallo Herr Schuster
hello Mr. Schuster

(5) ja da gibt es zwei Hotels mit Sauna Hotel Nöhre in Hannover
well there gives it two hotels with sauna hotel Nöhre in Hanover
oder Prinzenhof das ist gar nicht so lustig oder Prinzenhof-Hotel
or Prinzenhof that is at all not so funny or Prinzenhof hotel
das eine ist wesentlich teurer das Prinzenhof-Hotel
the one is considerably more expensive the Prinzenhof hotel
'well there are two hotels there with a sauna hotel Nöhre in Hanover or Prinzenhof that is not so funny at all or Prinzenhof hotel the one is considerably more expensive the Prinzenhof hotel'

[2] Whenever possible, the examples in this and the following chapters are taken from the TüBa-D/S treebank. The translations are, if available, the official translations from the VERBMOBIL project, which were also provided by Tübingen.

Additionally, the transliterated data exhibit all the characteristics of spontaneous speech, including hesitations, false starts, interruptions, repetitions, and fragmentary utterances. The utterance in (6) is typical in many respects: it contains several discourse markers such as "ja", a fragmentary utterance "das ist schon", and the repeated adverb "dann".

(6) ja ja das ist schon nee dann dann mache ich das lieber im
yes well that is already no then then do I that rather in the
April
April
'yes well that is already no then then I would rather do that in April'

TüBa-D/S consists of more than 38 000 annotated sentences. In order to give a more realistic picture of the size of the treebank in terms of the definition of a sentence in a speech corpus, we counted the number of separate trees that were annotated: approximately 67 000 trees. From this number, we can conclude that the treebank contains approximately 67 000 sentences (in the linguistic sense) and fragmentary utterances.

For the TüBa-D/S treebank, a theory-neutral and surface-oriented annotation scheme has been adopted that is based on the notion of *topological fields* – in the sense of Herling (1821), Erdmann (1886), Drach (1937), Reis (1980), and Höhle (1986) – and enriched by a level of function-argument structure. The linguistic annotations pertain to the levels of morpho-syntax (POS tagging), syntactic phrase structure, and function-argument structure. The structuring into topological fields favors bracketings that do not rely on crossing branches and traces to describe discontinuous constituents in non-configurational languages such as German.

Figure 5.1[3] gives an example of this annotation scheme. The tree structure contains different types of syntactic information in the following way: as the primary clustering principle, the theory of topological fields (following Höhle (1986)) is adopted, which captures the fundamental word order regularities of German sentence structure. In verb-second sentences, such as in sentence (7), the finite verb of the main clause "könnte" constitutes the *left sentence bracket* (LK) and the verb complex of the main clause "sein" the *right sentence bracket* (VC). This sentence bracket divides the sentence into the following topological order of fields: *initial field* (VF), LK, *middle field* (MF), VC, *final field* (NF).

[3] This tree, as well as all other complete trees in the remainder of the document, follow the data format for trees defined by the NEGRA project of the Sonderforschungsbereich 378 at the University of the Saarland, Saarbrücken. They were printed by the NEGRA annotation tool *Annotate* (Brants & Skut, 1998; Plaehn, 1998).

(7) das könnte auch noch bei den Spesen drin sein wenn wir jetzt
that could also still with the expenses in be if we now
das billigere Hotel nehmen
the cheaper hotel take
'that could also still be included in the expenses if we take the cheaper hotel now'

Below the level of topological fields, i.e. strictly within the bounds of the topological fields, a phrase level of *function-argument structure* is established. The function-argument structure has its own descriptive inventory based on a minimal set of assumptions concerning constituenthood, phrase attachment, and grammatical functions that must be captured by any syntactic theory. In the present annotation scheme, nodes are labeled with syntactic categories on four different levels of annotation (sentence level, field level, phrase level, and lexical level), edges denote grammatical functions on the phrase level (i.e. immediately below the topological fields) as well as head/non-head distinctions within phrases. On the level of POS tagging, the Stuttgart-Tübingen tagset (STTS)(Schiller et al., 1995; Thielen & Schiller, 1994) , a tagset for German based on distributional regularities of German, was used. The tagset contains 54 different POS tags, the complete list of which is given in Appendix A.

The constituents below the topological fields are assigned grammatical functions. They describe two different types of information; in general, the edge labels describe the grammatical function of complements and modifiers, which depend on the head of the sentence. The same inventory is used to describe long-distance relations among these complements or modifiers as well as between conjuncts of split-up coordinations. In the example in Figure 5.1, the first constituent is marked as a subject (ON), the finite verb constitutes the head of the sentence (HD), the middle field consists of three modifiers (MOD and V-MOD) and the predicate (PRED), and the verb complex contains the verbal object (OV). The final field contains a subordinate clause, which also constitutes a modifier of the matrix clause. The subordinate clause, in turn, consists of a complementizer field (C) containing the subordinating conjunction, the middle field containing the subject (ON), a modifier, and the direct object (OA), and the verb complex containing the finite verb of the subordinate clause.

As mentioned above, the annotation scheme does not support crossing branches and traces to describe discontinuous constituents. Instead, long-distance relations are marked by specific labels. Figure 5.2 shows an example for such a long-distance relation: In sentence (8), the extraposed

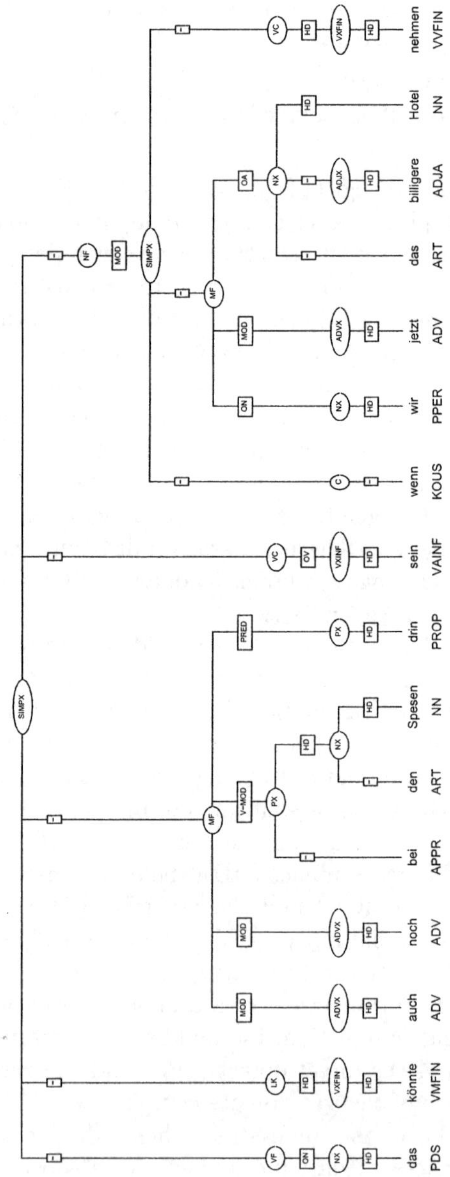

Fig. 5.1: *A sample tree structure of the TüBa-D/S treebank.*

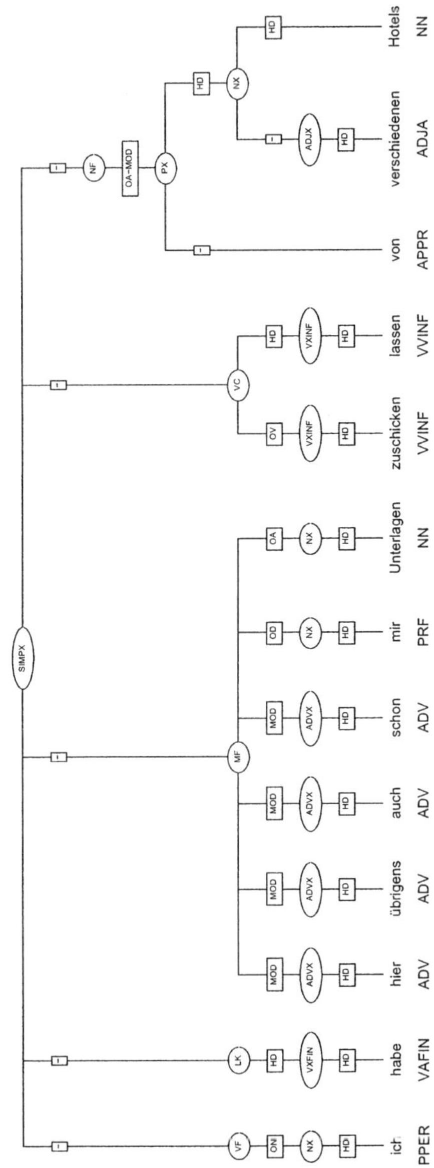

Fig. 5.2: *An example of a long-distance relation in TüBa-D/S.*

prepositional phrase (PX) "von verschiedenen Hotels" in the final field modifies the direct object "Unterlagen". This long-distance relation is marked by the functional label of the extraposed prepositional phrase, OA-MOD.

(8) ich habe hier übrigens auch schon mir Unterlagen zuschicken
I have here by the way also already to me brochures sent
lassen von verschiedenen Hotels
let of different hotels
'by the way here I have also had brochures sent to me about different hotels already'

Within the phrase level, two specific edge labels denote whether a constituent has the function of a head (HD) or a non-head (-). On any annotation level, there is at most one head. The head of a sentence structure (for example SIMPX) is always the finite verb, which can be found in the left sentence bracket (LK). If there is no LK, the head is represented by the finite verb in the verb complex (VC). In coordinations, each conjunct depends on the head of the whole construction. Therefore, conjuncts are denoted with the non-head edge label. An example of a complex coordination is shown in Figure 5.3. In sentence (9), the first and the second noun phrase are coordinated on the phrase level. The third noun phrase is extraposed, and the functional label OAK marks it as the rightmost conjunct in a split-up coordination of the direct object OA.

(9) das Hotel hat sogar ein Schwimmbad und ein Solarium
the hotel has even a swimming pool and a tanning booth
dabei und einen Fitnessraum
with it and a fitness room
'the hotel even has a swimming pool and a tanning booth and a fitness room'

As mentioned above, TüBa-D/S consists of transliterated spontaneous speech data. For this reason, the annotation scheme needs to define standards for the annotation of fragmentary utterances and repetitions. The general decision was that a simplex tree (SIMPX) ends when a syntactically well-formed sentence ends according to the *longest-match principle*. Only constituents that cannot be assigned a proper grammatical function are not attached. The remaining fragments, as well as repetitions and corrections, receive as much structural annotation as possible. The utterance in (6) is assigned the structure shown in Figure 5.4. Here, the fragmentary utterance "das ist schon" is projected to sentence level while the repetition "dann" can only be projected to phrase level.

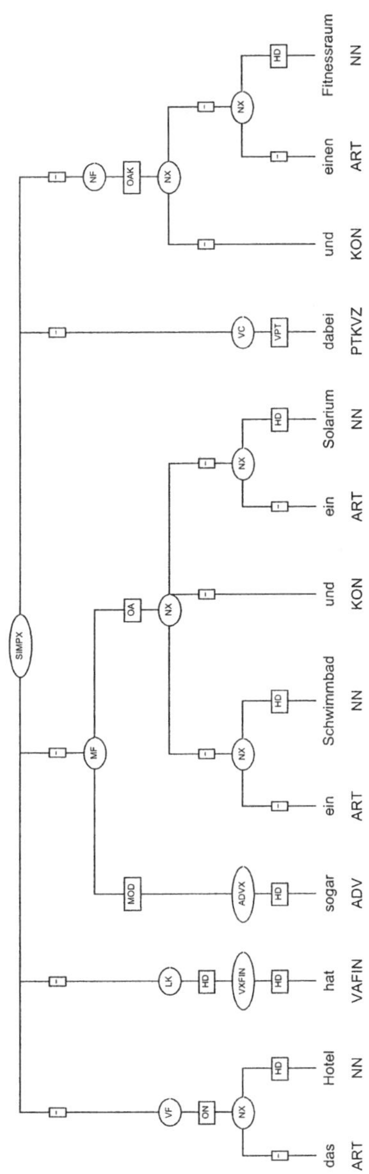

Fig. 5.3: *An example of a complex coordination in TüBa-D/S.*

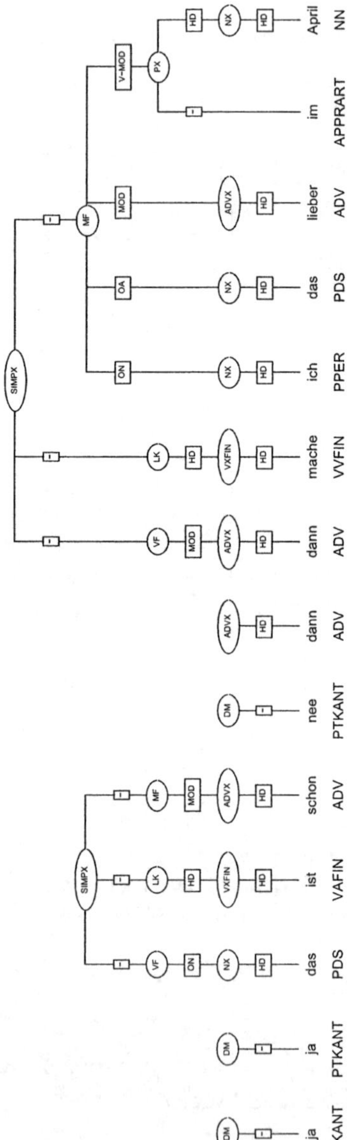

Fig. 5.4: *The annotation of spontaneous speech in TüBa-D/S.*

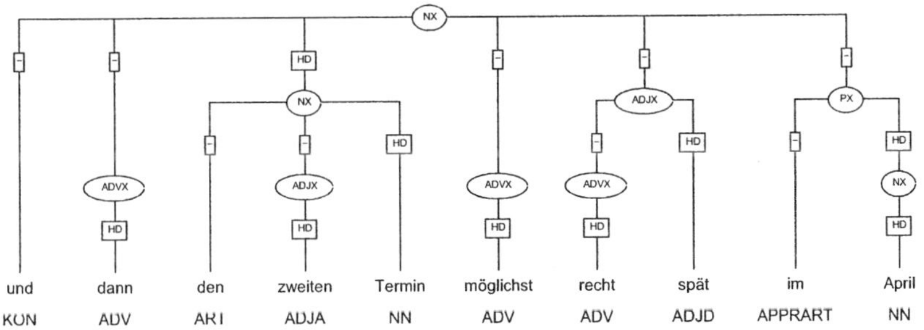

Fig. 5.5: *The annotation of a sentence fragment.*

Another peculiarity of spontaneous speech is the high frequency of isolated phrases and fragmentary sentences which lack a verb. Such utterances are analyzed according to the *longest-match principle* as complex phrases, i.e. the analysis includes as many parts of the utterance as possible. This treatment of fragmentary sentences results in phrase structures which are not allowed in complete SIMPX trees. An extreme example for such a fragmentary sentence, sentence (10), analyzed as a complex noun phrase (NX) is shown in Figure 5.5. If this fragment were part of a complete sentence, all the constituents that are immediately dominated by the root node would be directly attached to one of the fields.

(10) und dann den zweiten Termin möglichst recht spät im April
and then the second date preferably quite late in the April
'and then the second date if possible quite late in April"

This description of the annotation scheme can only give a very brief overview. A more detailed description can be found in (Stegmann et al., 2000). In order to make the examples readable, however, the complete set of syntactic categories and grammatical functions with short descriptions is listed in Appendix B.

5.1.2 *A Short Comparison of TüBa-D/S and Penn Treebank*

Parsing algorithms which use a training component are often trained and evaluated on the *Wall Street Journal* (WSJ) portion of the Penn treebank (Marcus et al., 1993, 1994), a syntactically annotated corpus in the domain of financial news.

There are a great number of similarities between the Penn treebank and TüBa-D/S. Both treebanks model a narrowly defined domain. In the case of the Penn treebank, it is mostly financial news, and in the case of TüBa-D/S, the domain is restricted to business appointments, travel scheduling, and hotel reservations. Both treebanks are annotated syntactically according to annotation schemes that prefer flat representations. Both annotation schemes are restricted to pure tree structures in their syntactic bracketing, and both extend the purely constituent-based annotation by grammatical functions.

The individual characteristics of the two treebanks are often consequences of the different text types: while the Penn treebank models written language in a domain with its own technical sublanguage, TüBa-D/S models spontaneous speech, which presents different challenges for the design of a parser, as described in the section above.

In the remainder of the section, we will have a look at differences in linguistic decisions of the two treebanks. The most important of these differences adhere to the analysis of noun phrases and to the use of grammatical functions.

5.1.2.1 *Noun Phrases*

In the field of NLP, noun phrases receive a high amount of attention. This is partly due to the fact that they can be efficiently and reliably annotated, and that they carry a high amount of information which can be used in tasks such as information retrieval, information extraction, question answering, and word sense disambiguation. For this reason, the annotation and recognition of noun phrases is of high importance for a parser.

In the Penn treebank, noun phrases receive a flat annotation, in most cases without internal structure. Premodifiers are included in one bracket with the head of the noun phrase. An example for such a flat noun phrase is shown in Figure 5.6. Here, the complete noun phrase "not a single congressional hearing" is bracketed without internal groupings.

In TüBa-D/S, in contrast, adjectival and adverbial phrases are projected to the phrasal level before they are grouped in the noun phrase. Sentence (11) gives an example of a premodified noun phrase containing the adverbial phrase "so", sentence (12) gives an example of a noun phrase containing a complex adjectival phrase. The respective syntactic analyses of these sentences are shown in Figure 5.7 and Figure 5.8.

(11) also so eine Stadtrundfahrt wäre sicher mal nett
so such a trip around town would be certainly once nice
'so such a trip around town would certainly be nice'

```
...
(S
  (NP-SBJ-2
    (NP (RB not) (DT a) (JJ single) (JJ congressional) (NN hearing))
    (PP (-NONE- *ICH*-3) ))
  (VP (VBZ has)
    (VP (VBN been)
      (VP (VBN held)
        (NP (-NONE- *-2) )
        (PP-3 (IN on)
          (NP
            (NP (DT any) )
            (PP (IN of)
              (NP (PRP them) ))))))))
(. .) ))
```

Fig. 5.6: *A sample sentence for a flat NP from the Penn treebank.*

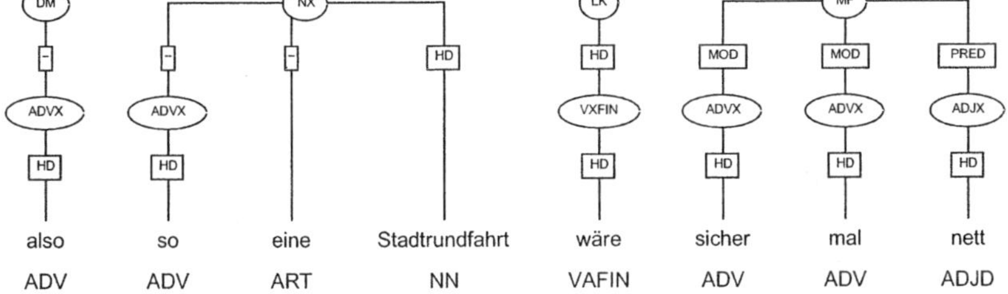

Fig. 5.7: *A comparable sentence from TüBa-D/S to the sentence in Figure 5.6.*

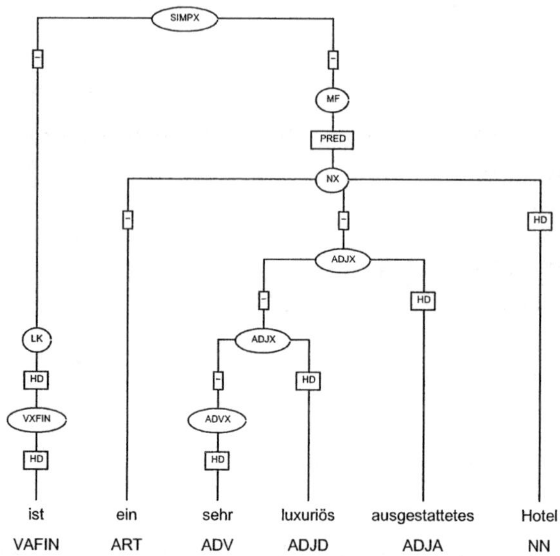

Fig. 5.8: *An example for a complex premodified noun phrase.*

(12) ist ein sehr luxuriös ausgestattetes Hotel
is a very luxuriously equipped hotel
'it is a very luxuriously equipped hotel'

In the Penn treebank, adverbial postmodifiers of a noun phrase are also attached in a flat structure. An example for such a flat annotation of a noun phrase containing a postmodifier is shown in Figure 5.9.

In TüBa-D/S, on the other hand, all postmodifiers are attached high, i.e. the noun phrase is first projected before the postmodifier is attached. A corresponding example for an adverbial postmodifier is shown in Figure 5.10 for sentence (13). Here, the noun phrase "eine Weile" is first grouped on the noun phrase level before the postmodifying adverb "hin" is attached.

(13) ist ja doch noch eine Weile hin
is certainly still well a time off
'it is certainly still well a time off'

The presence of internal structure within the noun phrases in TüBa-D/S is necessary, since German noun phrases may contain recursive structures, for example in the case of complex adjectives such as in (14) or in the case

```
( (S
    (S
      (NP-SBJ (NNP HUD) )
      (VP (VBZ has)
        (NP
          (NP (DT no) (NN paper) (NN work) (RB whatsoever) )
          (PP (IN on)
            (NP
              (NP (CD 30) )
              (PP (IN of)
                (NP (DT the) (NNS projects) )))))))
    (, ,)
... ))
```

Fig. 5.9: *A postmodified NP from the Penn Treebank.*

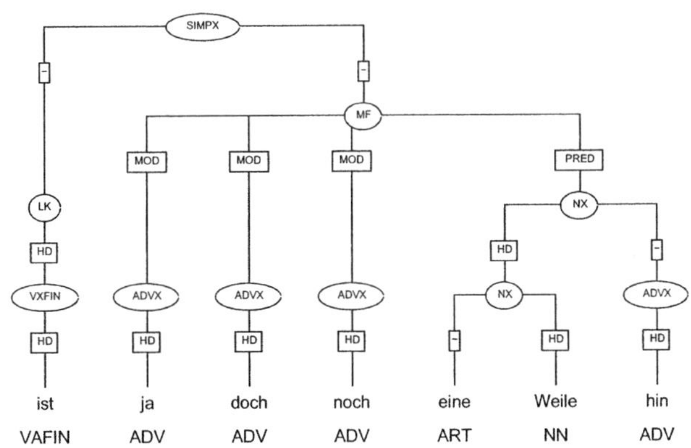

Fig. 5.10: *A comparable sentence from TüBa-D/S to the sentence in Figure 5.9.*

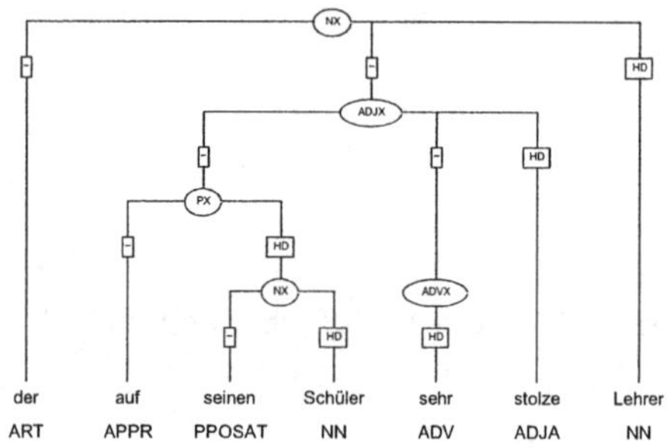

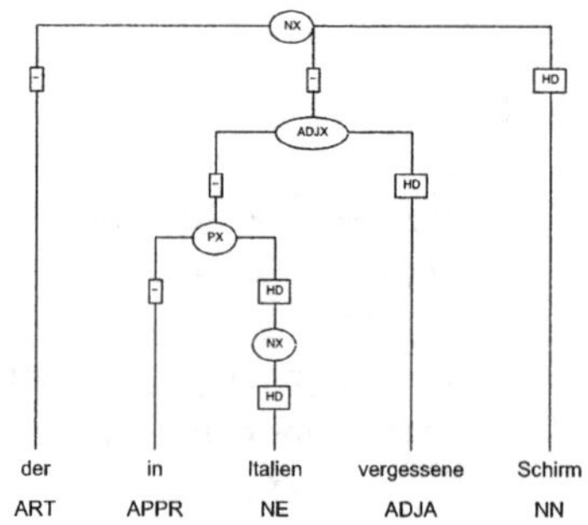

Fig. 5.11: *Two examples of complex noun phrases.*

of attributive participles such as in (15). These two phrases would receive the annotations shown in Figure 5.11.

(14) der auf seinen Schüler sehr stolze Lehrer
the on his student very proud teacher
'the teacher who is very proud of his student'

(15) der in Italien vergessene Schirm
the in Italy forgotten umbrella
'the umbrella forgotten in Italy'

5.1.2.2 *Grammatical Functions*

Grammatical functions are considered important by most grammar formalisms since they constitute an interface between syntax and semantics; LFG, for example, regards grammatical functions as linguistic primitives (cf. for example (Kaplan & Bresnan, 1982)). Grammatical functions are especially important in the description of non-configurational languages such as German. While in configurational languages grammatical functions are generally expressed by the position of a constituent in the syntactic structure and can thus be retrieved from the syntactic structure alone, this is not possible for languages such as German. Here, it it necessary to have an inventory of labels to describe relations of constituents that are not adjacent.

Grammatical functions, however, are not only relevant for linguistic theory, they are also very important for a large number of applications in NLP, such as machine translation. If the German sentence in (16) is to be translated into English, the translation system needs to determine the subject, the direct (accusative) object, and the indirect (dative) object of the main clause.

(16) deswegen hat mir meine Sekretärin auch schon alles
therefore has to me my secretary also already everything
hergerichtet was man irgendwie braucht
prepared what one somehow needs
'that is why my secretary has already prepared everything what one needs somehow'

Both the phrases "meine Sekretärin" and "alles" are ambiguous between nominative and accusative, and the sequential ordering of noun phrases in German is subject only to preference. As a consequence, the respective information cannot be extracted by either morphological processing or by pure detection of syntactic structure. Rather, the assignment of grammatical functions can only succeed when the parser has access to information on similar examples or on probabilities that model such preferences. Marcus et al. (1994) report that they started annotating grammatical functions in the second phase of the Penn treebank project after many requests from treebank users for this type of information.

There exist several different treebanks whose annotation also includes grammatical functions: Apart from the Penn treebank, there is also the SUSANNE treebank (Sampson, 1993) for English and the NEGRA treebank (Skut et al., 1998) and TüBa-D/S for German. Both the Penn treebank and the SUSANNE treebank include the grammatical functions in the category labels of syntactic constituents, while NEGRA and TüBa-D/S represent them as edge labels. NEGRA and TüBa-D/S, however, differ in the representation of long-distance relations. As explained in Section 5.1.1, TüBa-D/S represents such relations via a specific label set. NEGRA, on the other hand, allows crossing branches in the annotation scheme. However, if crossing branches are allowed in the annotation scheme, the resulting structures are no longer context-free, which results in a higher complexity of the parsing task. Such an annotation scheme can be described by discontinuous trees (Bunt, 1996), for which the order of daughter nodes of one mother node is underspecified. Plaehn (1999) describes a parsing algorithm that extends an Earley-style parser in order to process discontinuous trees. The modification, however, resulted in a significant loss in efficiency (cf. (Plaehn, 1999, p. 80)).

Both the Penn treebank and the TüBa-D/S treebank use annotation schemes that are based on pure tree structures. They mark long-distance

```
((SINV ‘‘
      (S-TPC-2 (NP-SBJ-1 We)
               (VP like
                   (S (NP-SBJ *-1)
                      (VP to
                          (VP make
                              (NP (NP our own judgments)
                                  ’’
                                  (PP about
                                      (NP Mr. Morishita)))))))
      ,
      (VP says
          (SBAR 0
                (S *T*-2)))
      (NP-SBJ (NP Christopher Davidge)
              ,
              (NP (NP Christies ’)
                  group managing director))
      .))
```

Fig. 5.12: *The direct object in Penn treebank style is not explicitly marked.*

relations by traces or by labeling conventions (cf. below). For the annotation of grammatical functions, the Penn treebank follows a strategy that assigns functional labels only if the information is not recoverable from the constituent structure of the sentence. Thus, direct objects are only marked by their position in the sentence; the direct object is defined as the noun phrase on the verb phrase level which is not followed by another noun phrase (cf. (Bies et al., 1995, p. 12)). An example for such an annotation is shown in Figure 5.12.

In TüBa-D/S, in comparison, all constituents are explicitly marked with their grammatical function. An example for a similar structure in TüBa-D/S is shown in Figure 5.13 for sentence (17), in which the noun phrase "wir" is marked as the subject (ON), and "den Termin" as direct object (OA). It is also evident that while the Penn treebank only assigns grammatical functions to constituents, TüBa-D/S also describes head/non-head dependencies within phrases.

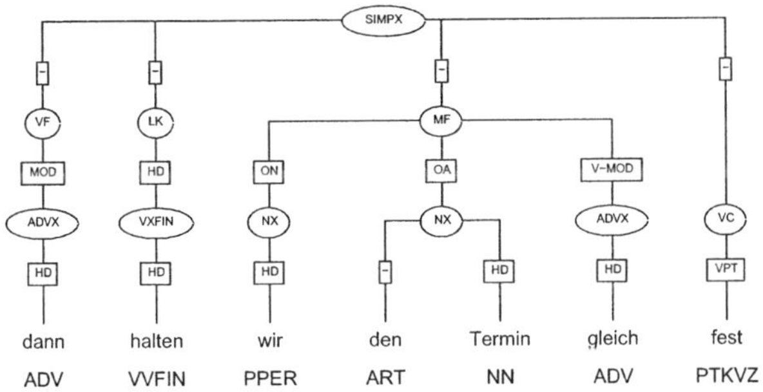

Fig. 5.13: *A comparable sentence from TüBa-D/S to the sentence in Figure 5.12.*

(17) dann halten wir den Termin gleich fest
then hold we that date right away on
'then let us hold on to that date right away'

Within the sets of functional labels, both treebanks allow a distinction of complements and adjuncts. But while in TüBa-D/S this information is directly recoverable from the label set (ON, OA, OD for subject, direct, and indirect object, and OPP and FOPP for (optional) complements and MOD for adjuncts), the Penn treebank annotation scheme marks both complements and adjuncts according to grammatical roles. A subset of these roles are defined as complements. This subset includes, apart from arguments and clauses, the following roles: benefactive (-BNF), closely related (-CLR), dative (-DTV), predicate (-PRD), and locative of put clause (-PUT) (cf. (Bies et al., 1995, p. 13)).

Long-distance relations are marked in the Penn treebank by a specific label. In the sentence in Figure 5.14, the prepositional phrase is considered a postmodifier of the subject noun phrase. This is expressed by the empty PP marked by -NONE- and the label *ICH* which marks the position at which the extraposed modifier should be attached. The number serves as a unique identifier.

In TüBa-D/S, such long-distance relations are more common. Since no empty categories such as the PP -NONE- in Figure 5.14 are allowed in the annotation scheme, such relations are marked in the functional labeling. Figure 5.15 gives an example for the sentence in (18). Here, the relative clause "wann Sie mich dann abholen" modifies the direct object "einen Termin", which is marked by the label OA-MOD.

```
( (S
    (NP-SBJ
      (NP (NNS Prices) )
      (PP (-NONE- *ICH*-1) ))
    (VP (VBD fell)
      (ADVP (RB marginally) )
      (PP-1 (IN for)
        (NP (NN fuel)
          (CC and)
          (NN electricity) )))
    (. .) ))
```

Fig. 5.14: *A sentence from the Penn treebank containing a long-distance relation.*

(18) dann könnten wir einen Termin vereinbaren wann Sie mich dann
then can we a time arrange when you me then
abholen
pick up
'then we can arrange a time when you pick me up then'

The Penn treebank also uses the notion of empty categories for describing traces. In Figure 5.16, the subject of the verb phrase "to boost" is marked as empty, -NONE-, and the trace * connects this empty subject to the subject of the matrix clause, "The project".

In the TüBa-D/S annotation scheme, such information remains underspecified. In the utterance in (19), the annotation in Figure 5.17 does not explicitly mark whether the complement "für Fliegen" modifies the main verb of the matrix clause or the infinite phrase "zu haben". In a majority of the cases, however, this underspecified representation does not lead to ambiguities.

(19) von mir aus gerne ich bin immer für Fliegen zu haben
from me out willingly I am always for flying to have
'as far as I am concerned by all means yes I can always go for flying'

5.1.3 *Going Beyond Pure Tree Structures*

The tree structures in TüBa-D/S, as described in the above section, can be described by a standard context-free grammar. There are different possibil-

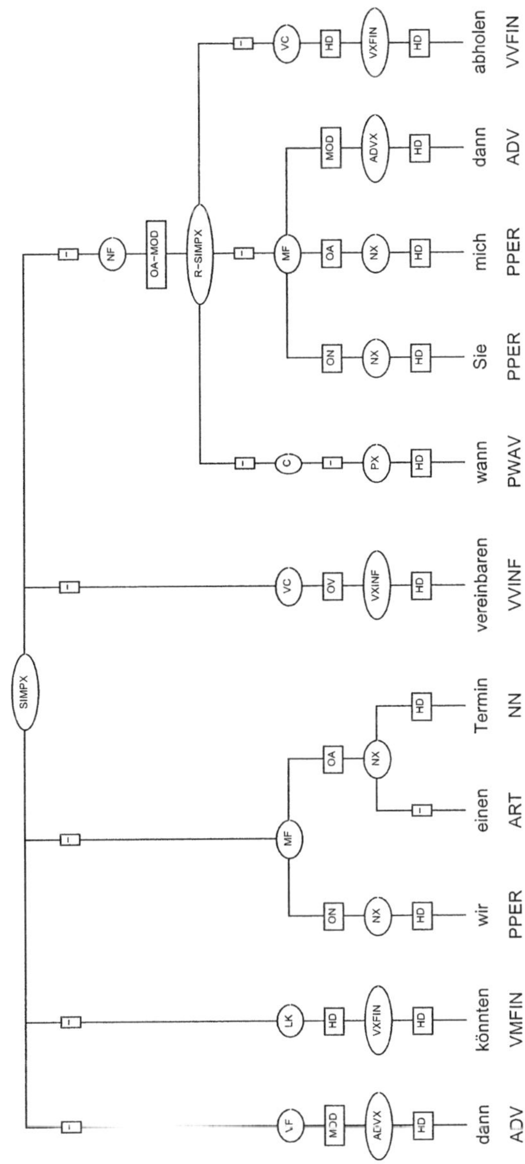

Fig. 5.15: *A comparable sentence from TüBa-D/S to the sentence in Figure 5.14.*

```
( (S
    (NP-SBJ-1 (DT The) (NN project) )
    (VP
      (VP (VBZ costs)
        (NP
          (QP ($ $) (CD 46.8) (CD million) )
          (-NONE- *U*) ))
      (, ,)
      (CC and)
      (VP (VBZ is)
        (VP (VBN intended)
          (S
            (NP-SBJ (-NONE- *-1) )
            (VP (TO to)
              (VP (VB boost)
                (NP
                  (NP (DT the) (NN company) (POS 's) )
                  (NN production) (NN capacity) )
                (PP-EXT (IN by)
                  (NP (CD 25) (NN %) ))
                (PP-DIR (TO to)
                  (NP
                    (NP (CD 34,500) (JJ metric) (NNS tons) )
                    (PP (IN of)
                      (NP (NN copper) (NN cathode) ))
                    (NP-ADV (DT a) (NN year) )))))))))
    (. .) ))
```

Fig. 5.16: *A sentence from the Penn treebank containing a trace.*

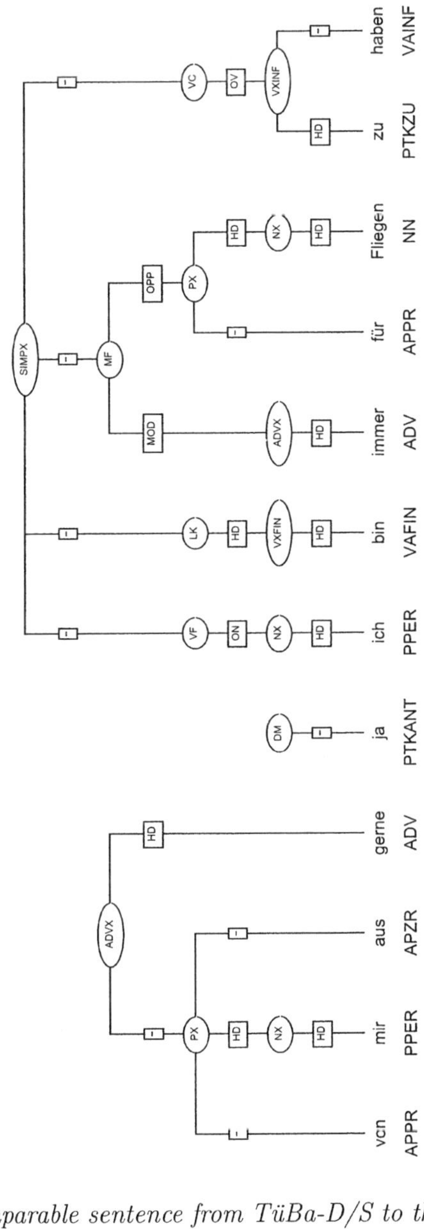

Fig. 5.17: *A comparable sentence from TüBa-D/S to the sentence in Figure 5.16.*

ities of including information on grammatical functions in standard rewrite rules. The simplest way would be to consider the categories of such a grammar as complex symbols consisting of the node label and the grammatical function of this node in relation to its mother node.

The complexity of the parsing algorithm is determined by the type of rules that it is designed to process, as already mentioned in Section 1.1. TüSBL (Kübler, 2002, 2003), however, uses complete tree structures in place of rules. It can be trained on any annotations that adhere to the same structural restrictions that hold for the annotations of the corpus for which it was developed (cf. Section 5.1.1).

The annotation scheme allows one extension to pure tree structures: the syntactic analysis may consist of more than one tree structure. This means, on the one hand, that there is no single root node. Instead there exist a set of nodes that can serve as root nodes. On the other hand, a single sentence (see Section 5.1.1 for a discussion of that term) may receive more than one tree structure, cf. for example the sentence in Figure 5.4. Such structures make the task of the parser more complex; in general, a parser can work on the hypothesis that its input is segmented into sentences such that each sentence is assigned exactly one tree structure spanning the input. The parser can be extended to assign partial structures in cases in which it cannot find a spanning analysis. If, however, the parser's input consists of possibly more than one sentence (or fragment), an additional task of the parser is to separate the input into sentences and fragments. That this task is not simple can be shown with the utterance in (20). The correct analysis into two separate trees is shown in Figure 5.18. Without any lexical co-occurrence data, it is impossible to decide that the noun phrase "kein Problem" cannot be the subject of the following sentence.

(20) kein Problem geht auf die Spesenrechnung
no problem goes on the expense account
'no problem it gets put on the expense account'

A more difficult problem constitutes those cases in which one sentence or fragment is "embedded" into another sentence. This can be the case if repetitions or corrections occur within a sentence. An example is given for the utterance in (21) in Figure 5.19. Here, the corrected phrase "vom zwölften" is projected to a prepositional phrase but not attached to the surrounding sentence. The words "bis zum", on the other hand, did not receive any annotation since they do not constitute a well-formed phrase.

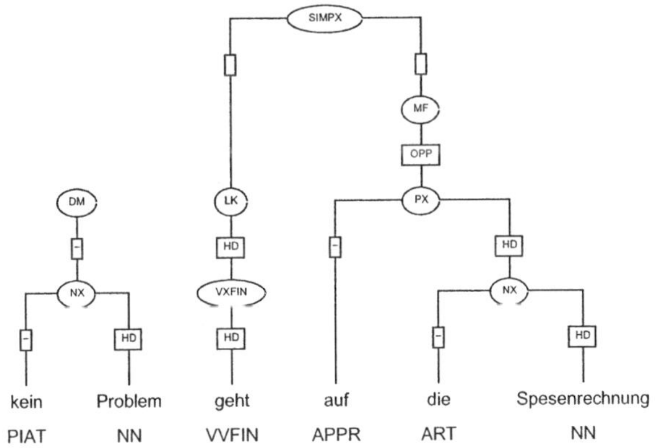

Fig. 5.18: *An utterance that must be analyzed as two separate trees.*

(21) wie wäre es vom zwölften bis zum nee vom
how would be it from the twelfth until to the no from the
elften bis zum vierzehnten Mai
eleventh until to the fourteenth May
'how would it be from the twelfth until the no from the eleventh until the fourteenth of May'

Another case of embedded trees is found in sentences which contain parentheses such as "denke ich". An example for such a case is shown in Figure 5.20 for the utterance in (22).

(22) das wäre ideal denke ich für anderthalb Tage
that would be perfect think I for one and a half days
'that would be perfect I think for one and a half days'

An extreme case of such parentheses can be found in utterances in which a complete sentence is embedded into another one, such as in the utterance in (23), for which the analysis is shown in Figure 5.21.

(23) ja dann sage ich da mal erkundige ich mich da mal was
well then say I there once ask I myself then once what
zu der Zeit so läuft
at that time so plays
'well then I will just say there I will just ask then about what is playing at that time'

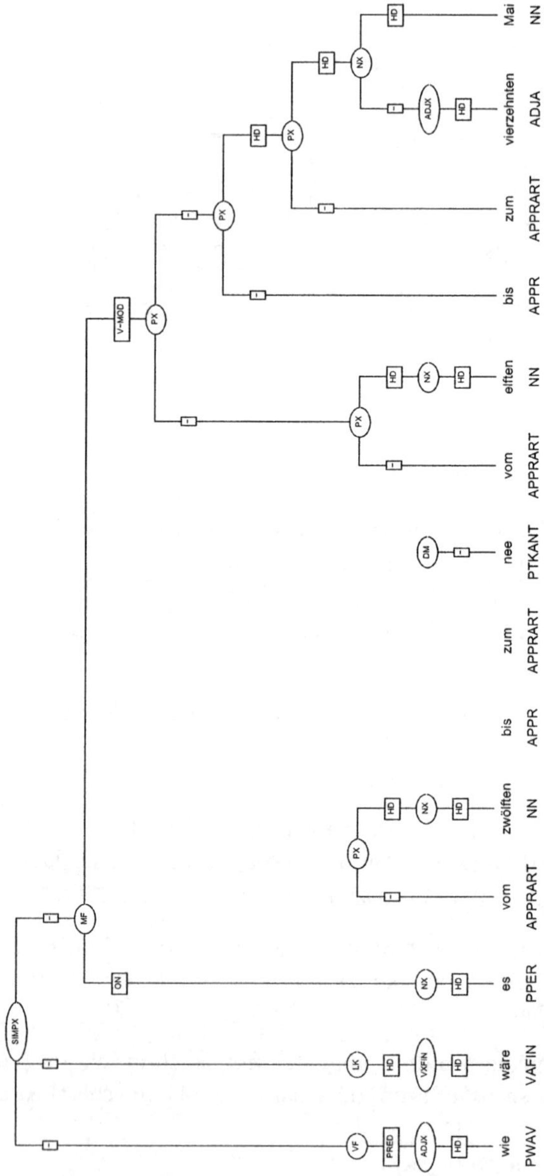

Fig. 5.19: *An utterance that contains an embedded correction.*

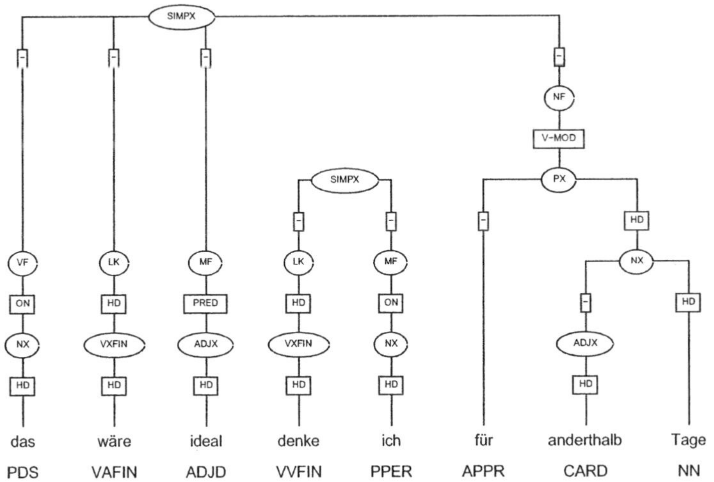

Fig. 5.20: *A sentence containing a parenthesis.*

In order to allow the parser to analyze such utterances, the algorithm needs to be extended so that it can exclude fragments of the input from the main analysis and analyze them separately. How this is realized in TüSBL, will be described in Section 5.7. There is another important reason for which this behavior of the parser was chosen: the same method can also be used to make the parser more robust and increase its coverage. There exist cases, for which the parser can find an analysis, i.e. a similar sentence in the instance base, only if one of the constituents is excluded from the analysis. Such cases are treated in the same way as cases for which parentheses and other embedded tree structures are the correct analysis (cf. Section 5.7).

Embedded tree structures such as discussed above also necessitate a representation format that deviates from the generally used bracketing format such as in the Penn treebank. In such a bracketing format, the utterance shown in Figure 5.21 would receive the structure shown in Figure 5.22. Here, the embedded structure cannot be distinguished from attached constituents without introducing a new label that signifies that this constituent is not attached to the surrounding tree[4]. Instead, the parser uses a pointer-based

[4] In the case that grammatical functions are also present in the bracketing, a root node could be marked by a specific label. Then unattached constituents could be distinguished by this label in their root nodes. But this would restrict the application of the parser to data that contain grammatical functions explicitly, which is true only for a

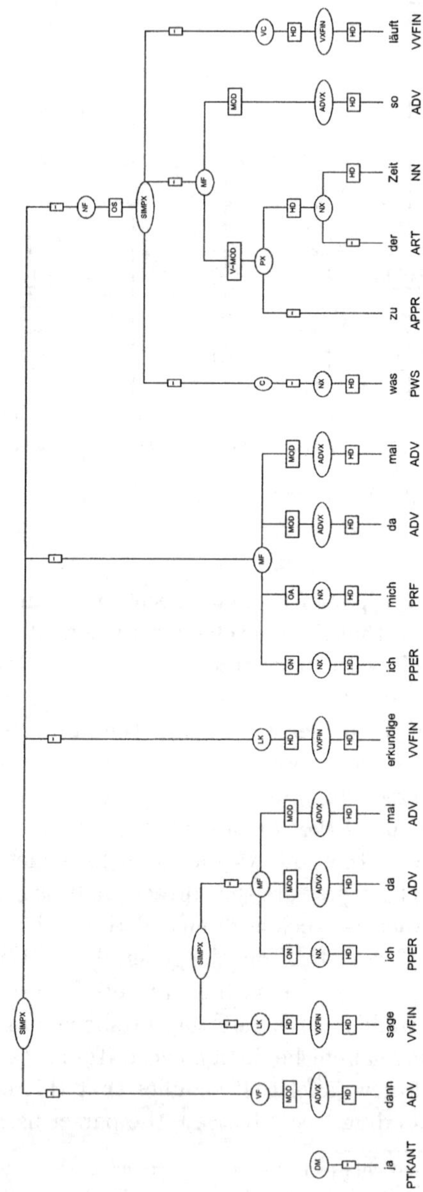

Fig. 5.21: *A sentence containing an embedded sentence.*

```
[DM
  [PTKANT ja]]
[SIMPX
  [VF
    [ADVX
      [ADV dann]]]
  [SIMPX
    [LK
      [VXFIN
         [VVFIN sage]]]
    [MF
      [NX
        [PPER ich]]
      [ADVX
        [ADV da]]
      [ADVX
        [ADV mal]]]]
  [VXFIN
    [VVFIN erkundige]]
  [MF
    [NX
      [PPER ich]]
    [NX
      [PRF mich]]
    [ADVX
      [ADV mal]]]
  [NF
    [SIMPX
      [C
        [NX
          [PWS was]]]
      [MF
        [PS
          [APPR zu]
          [NX
            [ART der]
            [NN Zeit]]]
        [ADVX
          [ADV so]]]
      [VXFIN
        [VVFIN läuft]]]]]
```

Fig. 5.22: *The bracketed version of the utterance in Figure 5.21.*

prev. word	**word**	next word	prev. POS	POS	next POS	class
NULL	das	geht	NULL	pds	vvfin	NP
das	geht	auf	pds	vvfin	appr	No-NP
geht	auf	die	vvfin	appr	art	No-NP
auf	die	Rechnung	appr	art	nn	NP
die	Rechnung	NULL	art	nn	NULL	NP

Table 5.1: *A toy world example for noun phrase recognition.*

format such as used in the NEGRA export format (cf. (Brants, 1997)). The pointer-based representation of the utterance in Figure 5.21 is shown in Figure 5.23. The first column contains the words or the nodes' ID numbers (for example #500), the second column contains the POS tags for words, or the node labels for tree nodes. The third column specifies the grammatical function of the word or node with respect to the dominating node. The fourth column contains the node ID of the mother node. A root node, such as "simpx" in the present example, is characterized by the missing function and mother node information. (For a more detailed description of the pointer-based representation cf. (Brants, 1997).)

5.2 Parsing as Classification

Memory-based learning in its pure form has been developed as a method for classification. An instance base of previously seen examples is used to find the most similar instance(s), and the most common class among these instances is then used to classify a new instance. In order to select the instance in the instance base which is most similar to the new instance to be classified, similarity metrics (cf. Section 2.1) are employed. These similarity metrics rely on the restriction that an instance is represented by a specific number of features, each feature containing a specific type of information. Thus, it is possible to assess the relevance of each feature for the classification, or in other words, to assess the seriousness of a divergence in feature values.

In the POS tagging example in Table 2.1, repeated here as Table 5.1, the information contained in the features is positional information. Information is given about the lexical word form and the POS tag of the corpus position to be classified, and of the previous and following corpus positions. If

minority of the treebanks available at present.

ja	PTKANT		500
dann	ADV	HD	501
sage	VVFIN	HD	502
ich	PPER	HD	503
da	ADV	HD	504
mal	ADV	HD	505
erkundige	VVFIN	HD	506
ich	PPER	HD	507
mich	PRF	HD	508
da	ADV	HD	509
mal	ADV	HD	510
was	PWS	HD	511
zu	APPR	-	521
der	ART	-	512
Zeit	NN	HD	512
so	ADV	HD	513
läuft	VVFIN	HD	514
#500	DM	–	0
#501	ADVX	MOD	515
#502	VXFIN	HD	516
#503	NX	ON	517
#504	ADVX	MOD	517
#505	ADVX	MOD	517
#506	VXFIN	HD	518
#507	NX	ON	519
#508	NX	OA	519
#509	ADVX	MOD	519
#510	ADVX	MOD	519
#511	NX	-	520
#512	NX	HD	521
#513	ADVX	MOD	524
#514	VXFIN	HD	522
#515	VF	-	527
#516	LK	-	523
#517	MF	-	523
#518	LK	-	527
#519	MF	-	527
#520	C	-	525
#521	PX	V-MOD	524
#522	VC	-	525
#523	SIMPX	–	0
#524	MF	-	525
#525	SIMPX	OS	526
#526	NF	-	527
#527	SIMPX	–	0

Fig. 5.23: *The pointer-based representation of the utterance in Figure 5.21.*

weighting shows that information about the POS tag of the corpus position to be classified, for instance, is more important than lexical information of the following word, a discrepancy in the first feature is much more serious than a discrepancy in the latter. Thus, instances matching in the POS tag of the focus word will be preferred to instances matching in the word form of the following word.

The calculation of similarity is only possible, however, because of the decision to use a windowing approach, i.e. a fixed length context. If one decides to use the complete sentence as context, the situation changes in a fundamental way: it is no longer possible to say that the fifth feature contains information about the POS tag of the focus word since the number of features depends on the length of the sentence[5].

POS tagging is a task that can easily be formulated as a classification task, and since the information necessary for classification is local and well-structured, it is also evident how to translate it into a feature representation. For syntactic parsing, the situation is less clear for several reasons:

- The type of information that needs to be induced in POS tagging is simple in that a 1:1 relation between words and POS tags is assumed. This makes linear processing possible. For syntactic parsing, however, the resulting structure is a graph which relates all words of a sentence to one another in a hierarchy. An example of such a resulting structure for the sentence in (24) is shown in Figure 5.24[6].

  (24) das ist schlecht da ich um zwölf Uhr ein
  that is bad because I at twelve o'clock a
  Arbeitstreffen hier in München habe
  work meeting here in Munich have
  'that is bad because I have a work meeting here in Munich at twelve o'clock'

- There is only a very restricted interdependence between the single decisions in POS tagging. In syntactic parsing, however, a considerable number of decisions depend on the complete structure of the tree induced up to that moment. In sentence (25), the annotation for which is shown in Figure 5.25, the prepositional phrase "wegen dieser

[5] It is certainly possible to introduce more global features which describe i.e. the number of words between the main verb and the focus word or whether the sentence contains an interrogative pronoun. But this means that the algorithm needs to abstract over some information in some form.

[6] A short description of the annotation scheme is given in Section 5.1.1, a more detailed description can be found in (Stegmann et al., 2000).

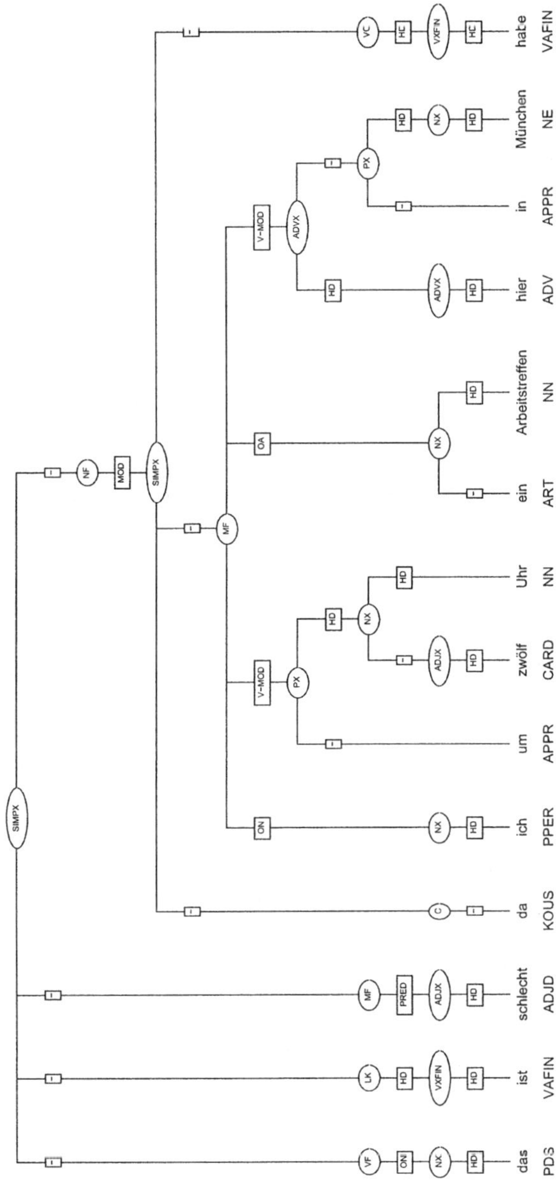

Fig. 5.24: *A sample syntactic structure.*

Filialgeschichte in Hannover" can only be correctly attached (via the label OA-MOD specifying the long-distance relationship) to the direct object "einen Termin" if the remaining words have already been analyzed concerning phrase structure, function-argument structure, and topological field information.

(25) wir müssen ja noch einen Termin vereinbaren wegen
we need well still a meeting arrange concerning
dieser Filialgeschichte in Hannover wir
this deal with the branch office in Hanover we
'we still have to arrange a meeting concerning this deal with the branch office in Hanover we'

- While in POS tagging, the inventory of POS labels is finite in size (and generally of a very restricted cardinality), and the labels are atomic, the resulting syntactic structure in parsing contains internal structure. Additionally, a combination of recursion (cf. the internal structure of the prepositional phrase PX in the final field NF in Figure 5.25) and unary branches may result in an infinitely large set of possible structures, even if the set of POS tags and syntactic labels is finite.

Previous approaches to syntactic parsing using memory-based learning techniques, such as (Argamon et al., 1998, 1999; Buchholz, 1998; Buchholz et al., 1999) (cf. Chapter 3 for a description of the different methods), approach the problem of parsing by splitting the complex problem into a number of subproblems, each of which can be formulated as a classification problem. One such problem might be formulated as "decide for each word whether it belongs to a noun phrase or not" (cf. the toy example in Figure 5.1). Such a cascaded approach is made feasible mostly by the extremely flat syntactic structure of the Penn treebank, from which training and test data were taken for the approaches mentioned above. Since the annotation scheme used in the syntactic annotation in Figures 5.24 and 5.25 is more complex and contains different types of information, the task of parsing with such an annotation scheme is to some degree more difficult than parsing with the Penn treebank annotation scheme. For these two trees, one would need levels for the following types of grouping:

On the phrase level:

- VXFIN
- ADJX
- NX (contains ADJX)
- PX (contains NX)

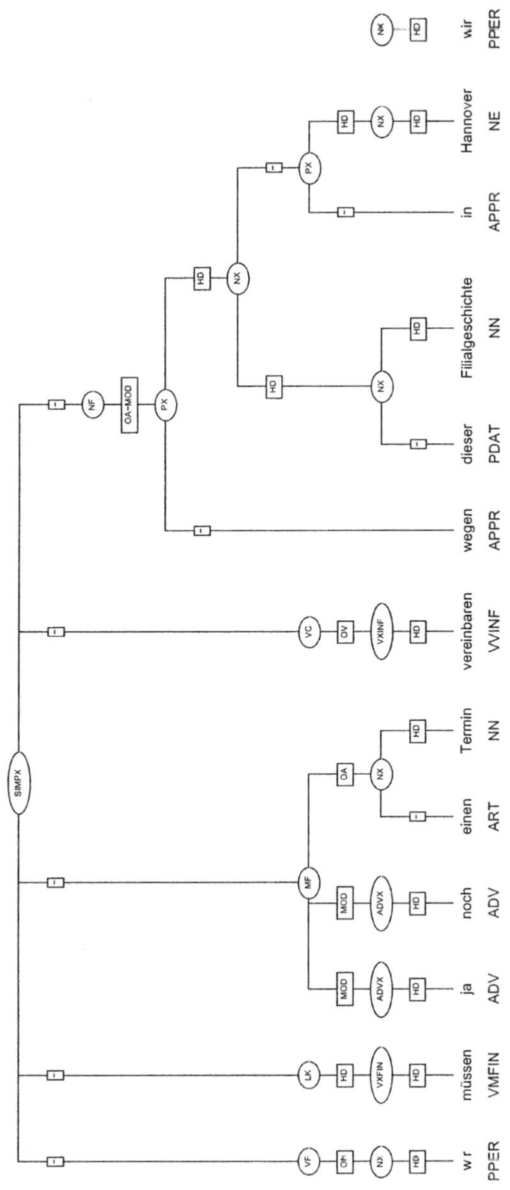

Fig. 5.25: *An example for a long-distance dependency analysis.*

- NX (contains PX)
- ADVX (contains PX)

On the topological field / clause level:

- C
- VF
- LK
- MF
- VC
- SIMPX
- NF (contains SIMPX)
- SIMPX (contains NF)

On the functional level:

- subject ON
- head of the sentence HD
- predicate PRED
- direct object OA
- verbal object OV
- modifiers MOD, V-MOD
- (long-distance) modifier of the direct object OA-MOD

It is evident that even for these two rather standard sentences, already 14 levels of recognition are needed, and at least one level for combining these independently recognized substructures. The repetition of certain levels is necessary to introduce recursive structures such as noun phrases postmodified by prepositional phrases. It is certainly possible to merge the recognition of adjective and adverbial phrases, for example, into a single level, but this will not alleviate the underlying problem of recursion. Additionally, it is a simple task to find more complex syntactic constructions which will extend the number of levels needed to cover the complete annotation scheme. These include very simple extensions such as prepositional or noun phrases containing adverbial phrases, for example in (26) or in (27), or noun phrases containing relative or subordinate clauses, as well as more complex phenomena such as coordination - which is possible at any level (cf. sentence (28) and Figure 5.26 for an example of a recursive noun phrase coordination), or extraposed fields, such as in sentence (29). Many coordination phenomena can be resolved by using information from intra-sentential punctuation. However, this is not possible for transliterated speech data since this type of information is not available.

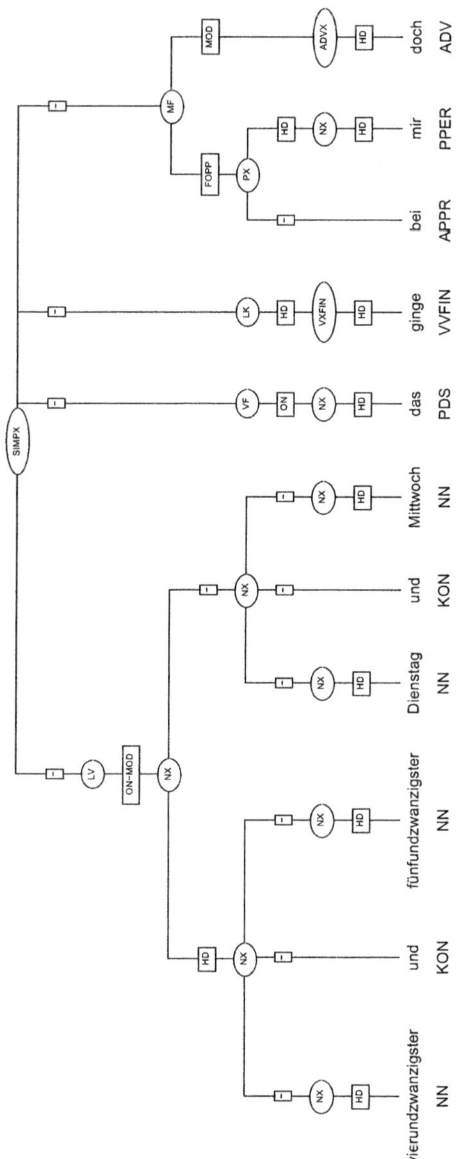

Fig. 5.26: *An example of a recursive noun phrase coordination.*

(26) erst am sechzehnten November
only on the sixteenth November
'not before November sixteenth'

(27) nur der Montag
only the Monday
'only Monday'

(28) vierundzwanzigster und fünfundzwanzigster Dienstag und
twenty fourth and twenty fifth Tuesday and
Mittwoch das ginge bei mir doch
Wednesday that would go with me certainly
'the twenty fourth and twenty fifth Tuesday and Wednesday that certainly works for me'

(29) Essen gehen könnten wir auf jeden Fall
eating go could we on any case
'we could go out to eat in any case'

Applying such a cascaded approach to a complex annotation scheme would lead to the following problems:

- Errors on early levels of recognition will mar the performance of later levels building on these ill-recognized structures. If for the sentence in Figure 5.24, the conjunction "da" would erroneously be grouped into an adverbial phrase, it would be impossible in a later step to annotate the subordinate clause since the adverbial phrase would be grouped with the matrix clause, and there is no other candidate for a C field.
- In order to make the annotation of complex noun phrases or prepositional phrases possible, each level of "embedding" needs to be implemented in a separate level in the cascade. From this approach it follows that a rather artificial upper limit on recursion needs to be defined during the design of the cascade. The limit is artificial since it is reflected in the levels of the cascade and therefore needs to be set during the development stage. At that time, however, the level of complexity that will be encountered in sentences during the testing and application stages is unknown.
- The system architecture is dependent on the annotation scheme. Thus, if the annotation scheme is extended, the ordering of levels might have to be changed, or a new level added. This is certainly a minor problem since the effort involved is marginal, but it still requires

manual adaptation, which will require the user to be at least familiar with the technical side of administrating the cascade of classifiers.

- Complex annotation schemes will result in a high number of independent levels in a cascade. As a consequence, the combination of these independent results will become more and more complex and error-prone. The subject classifier, for example, will decide for each noun phrase independently whether it might be a subject. This might result in none, two, or more suggested subjects. The same will hold for the classifiers for the direct and indirect objects. For this reason, it is necessary to have a final classifier to decide which of the suggestions will be accepted for the final annotation.
- The different classifiers need to be trained on data which are annotated on an appropriate level. For complex noun phrases, the training data need to be annotated for lower level noun phrases as well as for the target annotations. The higher the level is, however, the fewer training cases can be found in the data. Tjong Kim Sang (2001) performed a study on parsing the Penn treebank with a cascade of classifiers, modeling the approach of Brants (1999*a*). Tjong Kim Sang found that "the amount of available training data decreases at higher levels and therefore the precision of the recognition process decreases at higher levels" (Tjong Kim Sang, 2001, p. 183). The best F_β score was reached with 15 levels.

Another possibility to treat recursion with a cascade of classifiers is to attempt to learn all levels of a recursive phrase with a single classifier. In this case, the task of the classifier needs to be defined as finding all start and end points of all relevant phrases, for instance, NPs. This, however, leads to independent decisions concerning the start and end points. So in a next step, all such points need to be cleared which do not have a matching counterpart.

In order to avoid these problems, TüSBL (Kübler, 2002, 2003) uses another approach: instead of splitting the problem of syntactic parsing into subtasks, classes were defined as the complete syntactic trees, and the classification task was defined as selecting the most similar tree from the instance base of complete trees. This fundamental decision necessitates certain changes in the general approach:

- If complete trees are regarded as classes, a standard memory-based learning algorithm would only be capable of selecting the most similar tree for a new sentence. Therefore, only sentences that are already part of the instance base would receive a correct annotation. All other sentences would receive an approximation of a correct parse at best. This performance would be far from even the simplest rule-based parser. For this reason, the retrieved syntactic tree needs to be adapted to the input sentence. The (non-trivial) modification of classification results after retrieval does not conform with standard memory-based learning, and positions our approach closer to *case-based reasoning* (Kolodner, 1993).

- For TüSBL, classes have an internal structure, while in all previous approaches, classes consisted of atomic labels. Only the existence of internal structure makes adaptation at all possible. If we had atomic values, we would need to change the classification result to a completely different class, i.e., one would have to ignore the result given and redo the classification by other means. The tree structure allows simple modification, such as cutting phrases off the tree which might be present in the treebank sentence but not in the sentence to be classified. If the sentence in (30) is to be analyzed, but only the sentence in (31) can be found in the treebank, then the prepositional phrase dominating "am Donnerstag" needs to be removed from the tree structure of the latter sentence, cf. Figure 5.27.

  (30) wie sieht das bei Ihnen aus
  how looks that with you [verb particle]
  'how does that look on your side'

  (31) wie sieht das bei Ihnen am Donnerstag aus
  how looks that with you on Thursday [verb particle]
  'how does Thursday look on your side'

- Finding a complete parse tree in one step is a very difficult task. In order to minimize the error rate of the classifier, we have decided to use as much information to guide the selection process as is readily available. For this reason, Kübler (2002, 2003) uses as features all words of the input sentence, their POS tags, and, if necessary, information from a chunk parsing module (Abney, 1991, 1996) (cf. Sections 5.3.1 and 5.3.2 for a description of the chunk parser and its output structures) implemented as a preprocessing step. The chunk parsing step, however, should not be regarded as a first step in building the syntactic structure of the sentence, but rather as a source of more detailed information on the elementary structure of the sentence. This restricted use of the chunk parser output is due to inconsistencies between chunk structures and the tree structures, since chunks by definition end with

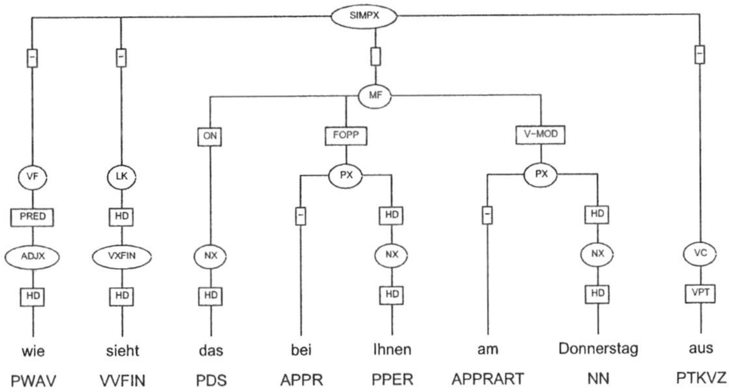

Fig. 5.27: *A tree from the treebank.*

the head of a sentence and contain less phrase internal structure than the tree annotations. More details on the differences in annotation will be given in Section 5.3.2.

- Since all words of the input sentence are used, the memory-based parsing system needs to cope with a flexible number of features. As a consequence, no standard weighting scheme could be used to describe the importance of a specific word in the sentence. Weighting, however, is a necessary extension of the basic algorithm, since otherwise too many features are used in the similarity calculation, and the parser would suffer heavily from data sparseness as well as from irrelevant features (cf. Section 2.3.2 for a discussion of the negative influence of irrelevant features on classification accuracy). If all words are given the same weight, sentences with the highest number of matching words, which in all likelihood would be conjunctions, determiners, prepositions, etc., would be found as the most similar to the input sentence. Therefore, instead of using the standard weighting schemes, Kübler (2002, 2003) decided to use the most basic metric, the overlap metric, combined with a weighting approach based on a cost model of modifying the tree if an element is missing. This approach is described in more detail in Section 5.7.
- Using trees as classes also leads to a very high number of such classes, approximately one per sentence. In general, the more instances there are for a specific class, the better defined the area is in the search space that the class occupies, and the easier it is to classify a new

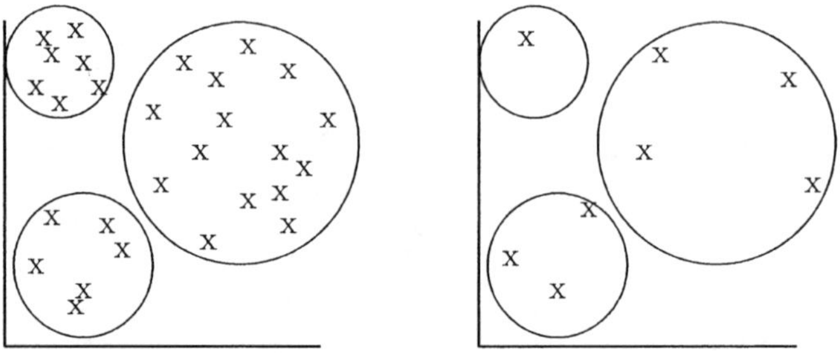

Fig. 5.28: *An example of a densely and a sparsely populated search space.*

instance. Figure 5.28 gives a graphic representation of one densely populated and one very sparsely populated search space. Clearly, it is more difficult to find a similar instance of the same class in the right search space than in the left one. Since in TüSBL's case the number of classes is almost as high as the number of training instances (for TüBa-D/S, there are 1.37 sentences per tree), a standard memory-based learning algorithm would be expected to perform poorly. For this reason, TüSBL uses a backing-off approach. If there is no match for a similar tree on the level using the most reliable information, i.e., the sequence of word forms, the system backs off to use less reliable information, which is more general and covers more instances, such as POS tagging or chunk sequences. If these backing-off strategies still do not manage to retrieve a syntactic tree for the complete input sentence, backing off to partial analyses is attempted. This step is generally successful, and the annotations thus found still contain more information than the chunk parses since the phrases receive internal structure and head/non-head information.

The use of complete trees instead of rules and backing-off to smaller tree fragments is reminiscent of DOP (Bod & Scha, 1996; Bod, 1998) (cf. Chapter 4), which uses tree fragments of arbitrary size instead of rules in a probabilistic parser. By using larger fragments, both approaches avoid to a high degree one problem very commonly encountered in analyses of standard probabilistic rule-based parsers: If a parse tree is constructed from rules, each decision of grouping different nodes into a higher node, or of expanding one node into its daughter nodes, is very local and independent from all

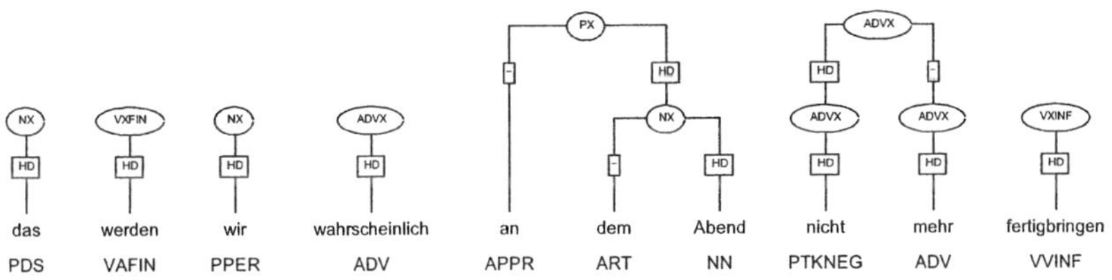

Fig. 5.29: *A partially annotated sentence.*

previous decisions. In sentence (32), a bottom-up stochastic parser needs to decide at the point in the parsing process shown in Figure 5.29 whether the first noun phrase "das" is the subject or the indirect object. For this decision, the parser does not have the information that the sentence contains another noun phrase "wir", which can only be nominative, and therefore must be the subject. The most recent probabilistic parsers (cf. for example (Collins, 1999; Charniak, 2000)) use extended probability models, which are conditioned on the heads of sibling phrases or on specific features of the mother node. These approaches, however, can only take a very limited amount of context into consideration, otherwise the number of parameters that need to be estimated from the training data is too high for estimation using the existing treebanks. Both DOP and memory-based parsing avoid these problems by taking maximal tree fragments into account, so that the decision concerning both noun phrases can be made at the same time if there is enough evidence from the training corpus.

(32) das werden wir wahrscheinlich an dem Abend nicht mehr
that will we probably on that evening not anymore
fertigbringen
get done
'we probably will not get it done with that evening anymore'

The similarity between DOP and memory-based parsing as sketched above, however, is restricted to the similarity on data structures. The processing methods are different in most accounts. While Bod uses a chart-based stochastic parser and an exhaustive search of fragment combinations, TüSBL is deterministic in that it attempts to find the largest fragment to cover an input sentence. Only if this search does not result in a spanning analysis, is the backing-off strategy invoked. Additionally, DOP is based on a probability model. TüSBL's model, in contrast, uses a much simpler mathematical model: the basic overlap metric combined with a weighting model based on a cost model. Thus, DOP is characterized by a very extensive search, resulting in high evaluation scores but also in a high processing load; memory-based parsing, on the other hand, is very efficient in processing costs, but since an extensive search is not attempted, it is to some degree heuristic in its search behavior.

5.3 Memory-Based Learning as Part of a Hybrid Parsing Architecture

This section gives an introduction to the internal organization of TüSBL (Kübler, 2002, 2003). Previous, and more restricted, versions of TüSBL (in a phase when, among other restrictions, it did not use any weighting mechanisms) were published in (Hinrichs, Kübler, Kordoni & Müller, 2000; Kübler & Hinrichs, 2000, 2001*a*,*b*).

TüSBL is designed as a cascade of several processing steps, in which the first step is invoked only when there are changes in the training data or in the chunk grammar:

- the learning component
- preprocessing:
  - POS tagging
  - tag fixing
  - chunk parsing (CASS)
- complete memory-based parsing

The learning component transforms a given treebank into the format of the instance base. This requires a reorganization of the training sentences and the calculation of the different weights. The complete process and the resulting data structure are described in Section 5.7. The learning component needs to be executed only when there is a change in the training corpus or in the preprocessing steps, since changes in the tagging or chunking scheme generally result in changed weights for the chunk structures.

In preprocessing, the output of a previous step serves as input for the following one. For POS tagging, the Stuttgart-Tübingen tagset (STTS) (Schiller et al., 1995; Thielen & Schiller, 1994) is used (for the complete list of POS tags and short descriptions cf. Appendix A). As POS tagger, TnT (Brants, 1998, 1999*b*, 2000) is used, because it has already been successfully used for tagging German texts using the STTS tagset (cf. (Brants, 2000, pp. 107)). TnT uses Markov Models combined with an elaborate smoothing method based on suffix trees. The tagger was trained on the POS tags of TüBa-D/S, on which TüSBL was evaluated (cf. Section 6), in order to avoid as many errors on the POS tagging level as possible. Even for POS tagging, it is necessary to train the tagger on data of the same domain as the test data, since each domain is characterized by different usages of words, etc. In speech transliterations, for example, the words "der" and "die" have a much higher probability of being demonstrative pronouns than in newspaper texts.

There are a small number of error types that constitute a majority of errors of all existing POS taggers for German: the distinction of subordinate conjunctions (KOUS) and prepositions (APPR), the distinction of predicative adjectives (ADJD) and adverbs (ADV), the distinction of prepositions (APPR) and verbal particles (PTKVZ), and the distinction of finite (VVFIN) and infinite verb forms (VVINF). These error types are a consequence of using only a very restricted amount of context for classifying a specific word. We will have a closer look at the problem of distinguishing finite and infinite verb forms since this distinction is crucial for the detection of clausal patterns in the chunk parser. The classification of the word "treffen" in sentence (33) is ambiguous between first and third person plural and infinitive, due to its suffix "-en".

(33)	wir	können	meinetwegen	uns	von	neun	bis	elf	Uhr	treffen
	we	could	as for me	us	from	nine	until	eleven	o'clock	meet

'as far as I am concerned we can meet from nine until eleven o'clock'

The correct choice, infinitive, can only be made if the POS tagger has access to the information that it has already encountered a finite verb in the clause. The two verb forms, however, are separated by the middle field in German, which in the present case consists of seven words, while most POS taggers only use a context of two to three preceding words. For this reason, the decision whether "treffen" is finite or infinite must be reached based on the local context of "bis elf Uhr", which in this case is not a very reliable indicator.

The chunk parser, however, needs exactly this type of information to detect left and right sentence brackets. For this reason, a new, underspecified POS label VVEN was introduced for these verb forms. This allows the POS tagger to avoid such tagging errors and the chunk parser to make more reliable predictions of the sentence brackets. TnT reached an accuracy of 97.79% on held-out data, averaged over a tenfold cross validation, when trained on the TüBa-D/S data which were modified as described above.

The next step in the cascade is the tag fixing component. This step is a prerequisite for the actual chunk parsing step – here, POS tags for specific words which are crucial for chunk parsing can be specialized (cf. Section 5.3.2 for examples of such cases). Tag fixing includes, among other things, the following cases: Possible measuring units (label: unit) for mass noun phrases are identified, specific copula verb forms (label: fcop) are distinguished from other auxiliaries, the most important intransitive verbs (label: noarg) are identified, and POS tagging errors are corrected for a few words which are crucial for chunk processing. The specialization of intransitive verbs is more in the nature of a very crude heuristic, but neither the POS tagger nor the parsers have access to morphological and subcategorization information. For this reason, this crude heuristic is used for the verb forms of the two verbs "glauben" and "denken", since these two words appear with a high frequency in TüBa-D/S, and many of the occurrences are in the form of parenthetical clauses such as in (34). Without subcategorization information, the chunk parser is unable to recognize the parenthetical character of the clause "glaube ich". As a consequence, the chunk parser would group "das Maritim glaube" into one clause since "glaube" is considered the left sentence bracket, and "ist" is the second finite verb and thus cannot be analyzed as the verb complex. Then the chunk parser would suggest another clause consisting of the remaining part, "ich ist mir schon bekannt".

(34) ja das Maritim glaube ich ist mir schon bekannt
yes the Maritim think I is to me already familiar
'yes I think I am familiar with the Maritim'

It might be argued that these changes in the POS tagging should be included in the tagging step. Since they do not exactly adhere to general linguistic principles but rather are based on the requirements of the subsequent processing step, it seems unwise to include them in the generally valid POS tagset. A typical output of the tag fixer for sentence (35) is shown in Figure 5.30. The first column contains the words of the sentence, the second column contains the tags after the tag fixing stage, and the third one the original POS tags from the POS tagger in cases for which the tag fixer changed the tag.

(35) wir können ja gleich am Montag dem vierten
we can well just on the Monday the fourth
losfahren
go ahead and leave
'we can go ahead and leave on Monday the fourth'

```
wir          pper
können       vmfin
ja           adv
gleich       adv
am           am        apprart
Montag       day       nn
dem          art
vierten      adja
losfahren    vven
```

Fig. 5.30: *The output of the tag fixer for sentence (35).*

The next two steps concern the actual syntactic analysis. The chunk parser will be described in more detail in the following section. The complete parsing step, which uses the chunk parsing output as features in the search for the most similar tree in the instance base, will be introduced in Sections 5.5 to 5.8.

5.3.1 *The CASS Chunk Parser*

We define a chunk parser as a cascade of deterministic finite-state transducers. The cascade can be interpreted as a sequence of levels where typically one type of chunk is bracketed per level. A chunk is, by definition, the non-recursive kernel of a phrase. This definition generally excludes postmodifications on any level to be attached during the chunk parsing step. This restriction is due to the deterministic nature of the chunk parser, which does not allow the disambiguation of phrases that might be postmodifiers of a preceding phrase or need to be attached at a higher level. For sentence (36), the chunk parser analysis is shown in Figure 5.31. Here, the chunk parser could not decide whether the two prepositional phrases "mit den Herren" and "von der GEMA" should be attached to the preceding noun phrases or whether they are adjuncts of the verb "ist".

(36) und Donnerstag ist ein Mittagessen mit den Herren von der GEMA
and Thursday is a lunch with the men of the GEMA
'and Thursday is lunch with the guys from GEMA'

The output of each transducer serves as the input for the next transducer. Finite-state transducers are incapable of capturing the notion of recursiveness, but recursion with a maximal number of embeddings can be

```
[kon und]
[simpx
  [nx2
    [day Donnerstag]]
  [fcop ist]
  [nx1
    [art ein]
    [nn Mittagessen]]
  [px
    [appr mit]
    [nx1
      [art den]
      [nn Herren]]]
  [px
    [appr von]
    [nx1
      [art der]
      [ne GEMA]]]]
```

Fig. 5.31: *The chunk parser's output, in which the attachment of the prepositional phrases is not disambiguated.*

simulated by a cascade of transducers. For TüSBL, Steven Abney's implementation of a chunk parser, CASS (Abney, 1991, 1996) was used.

CASS accepts the output of the tag fixer described in the previous section as input and passes this input through the cascade of finite-state transducers. On each level, specific structures as defined by a regular grammar for this level are recognized and replaced by the right-hand side symbol of the rule that was applied. This procedure necessitates a strict bottom-up approach, since it is impossible to introduce internal structure into a chunk once it is replaced by an atomic symbol. If no rule in a level can be applied to an input structure, the structure is passed to the next level in the cascade without any modification. This way of processing input sentences results in a very robust parser, since the parser cannot fail: if a transducer does not reach a final state when processing its input, the first symbol of the input string is shifted unchanged to the output, and the transducer resumes the analysis of the remaining input. This shifting of words is the default case for a transducer, since each transducer "fires" only on very specific linguistic phenomena. In the worst case, the output is passed through the cascade without modifications. This, however, happens in a very small number of cases, since the regular grammar is generally constructed in a way that it overgenerates slightly, and thus is also able to find at least partial analyses even for sub-standard input. The chunk grammar consists of rules of the form shown in (26).

$$nx3 \rightarrow art\, advmd?\, (adja \,|\, adjd) * \; h = mx \tag{26}$$

The righthand side defines the regular expression that describes the linguistic phenomenon to be grouped, the symbol on the lefthand side is the target category, in this case a type of noun phrase. In the regular expression, the question mark signifies an optional element, the Kleene star zero or more occurrences of the element, the Kleene plus one or more elements, and the symbol "|" a disjunction. All the elements used on the left hand side of the rule must have been introduced either through POS tagging (such as "art", "adja", and "adjd"), by tag fixing (such as "advmd"), or by previous stages of the cascade (such as "mx"). The rule in (26) gives one possibility for a noun phrase containing a mass phrase, which was recognized on the first level. This rule specifies possible premodifiers: an obligatory article (art), an optional degree adverb (advmd), and a sequence of zero or more adjectives. Since the POS tagger does not always reliably distinguish attributive and predicative uses of adjectives, both forms are permitted here ("$(adja \,|\, adjd)*$"). This definition of the rule leads to slight overgeneration,

```
[nx1 h=Anfang
  [nn h=Anfang Anfang]]
[simpx h=hätte
  [nx1 h=Juli
    [month h=Juli Juli]]
  [vafin h=hätte hätte]
  [nx4 h=ich
    [pper h=ich ich]]
  [advx h=noch
    [adv h=noch noch]]
  [nx1 h=Tage
    [mx h=Tage
      [card h=zwei zwei]
      [unit h=Tage Tage]]]
  [ptkvz h=frei frei]]
```

Fig. 5.32: *The chunk parser's output including head information.*

but since the context is restricted to obligatory elements of a noun phrase, the probability that errors are caused by overgeneration is negligibly small.

The mass phrase is additionally marked as the head of the phrase ("$h = mx$"). Head information is present in all rules. Figure 5.32 shows a sample chunk parse including head information[7] for sentence (37).

(37) Anfang Juli hätte ich noch zwei Tage frei
beginning July would have I still two days free
'at the beginning of July I would still have two days free'

In cases in which there exists an ambiguity concerning the coverage of a rule, CASS performs a left-most longest match, i.e., it always selects the left-most starting point for an analysis, and it prefers the longest analysis on one specific level.

The regular grammar used in TüSBL was written in such a way that the output structures can be processed in the memory-based parsing stage with the highest chances of finding a complete and correct analysis. This goal necessitates that the chunks be as similar in their definition to the treebank phrases as possible (for more examples cf. below). The grammar consists of

[7] In the following figures of chunk parses, we will mostly refrain from presenting head information in the chunk parses for reasons of legibility.

<table>
<tr><td>input
POS tags</td><td>da
da</td><td>muß
vmfin</td><td>ich
pper</td><td>leider
adv</td><td>zu
zu</td><td>einem
art</td><td>Treffen
nn</td><td>nach
appr</td><td>Köln
ne</td></tr>
<tr><td>gnp</td><td>da</td><td>vmfin</td><td>nx4</td><td>advx</td><td>zu</td><td colspan="2">nx1</td><td>appr</td><td>nx1</td></tr>
<tr><td>pp</td><td>da</td><td>vmfin</td><td>nx4</td><td>advx</td><td colspan="3">px</td><td colspan="2">px</td></tr>
<tr><td>simpx</td><td colspan="9">simpx</td></tr>
</table>

Fig. 5.33: *The chunk parser's analyses on the different levels for sentence (38). For representational clarity, only those levels in which a change of the annotation occurred are shown.*

the following levels[8]:

- gmeas-pattern, in which spelling phrases and mass noun phrases are analyzed
- time-pattern, in which mainly time expressions are analyzed
- gnp-pattern, in which most of the different types of noun phrases and adverbial phrases are treated
- pre-pp, which deals with complex prepositions such as "bis zum"
- pp-pattern, which treats prepositional phrases
- zrpp-pattern, in which postpositional phrases are analyzed
- vx-pattern, which analyzes verbal groups
- rel-clause, which groups relative clauses
- simpx-clause, which groups all chunks into clausal chunks.

Figure 5.33 shows the output of the different levels of the chunk analysis for sentence (38). The final output, in which the internal structures are shown as bracketing, is shown in Figure 5.34. It is evident that the chunk parse contains annotations on the chunk level, but it contains neither functional information nor specification of whether the second prepositional phrase "nach Köln" should be attached to the verb or to the preceding noun phrase.

(38) da muß ich leider zu einem Treffen nach Köln
then need I unfortunately to a meeting to Cologne
'unfortunately I have to go to Cologne for a meeting then'

The division of labor into a cascade of levels results in a determinism concerning decisions of previous levels. If a decision has already been made,

[8] The names of the different levels are generally due to their history rather than to the linguistic phenomena covered in these levels. For this reason, we will refrain from explaining the abbreviations.

```
[simpx
  [da da]
  [vmfin muß]
  [nx4
    [pper ich]]
  [advx
    [adv leider]]
  [px
    [zu zu]
    [nx1
      [art einem]
      [nn Treffen]]]
  [px
    [appr nach]
    [nx1
      [ne Köln]]]]
```

Fig. 5.34: *The chunk parser's restructured output of Figure 5.33.*

it cannot be undone at a later stage if the decision is found to be wrong. For this reason, a chunk analysis tends to be partial and does not attempt to resolve attachment ambiguities, the scope of coordination, etc. Examples of such chunk structures which deviate from complete analyses are given in the following section.

5.3.2 *CASS Output Structures*

The specific architecture which was chosen for CASS, namely a cascade of deterministic finite-state transducers which does not allow access to already analyzed structures, gives atypical results for specific linguistic phenomena. In this section, we will give examples of such phenomena, explain how the chunk annotation deviates from complete analyses, and give reasons why these deviations are necessary during chunk parsing. We will start with two phenomena, NP postmodifications and adverbial phrases, which are intra-clausal in their nature. Since they do not affect clause boundaries, their treatment has no direct influence on the memory-based parsing stage[9]. There, the clause-internal structure is re-analyzed in order to provide phrase-internal structure. The remaining phenomena, the treatment of final field constituents, of coordinations, of relative clauses, of subordinate clauses, and of parenthetical clauses, however, influence the positioning of clause boundaries. Therefore, special attention needs to be paid to the memory-based parsing module in order to assure a correct treatment of these deviations.

NP Postmodification. A sequence of noun phrases within a clause can either represent a complex noun phrase which is modified by the subsequent noun phrase or a sequence of two arguments. A deterministic parser, which has access only to POS tags, but not to the actual words, morphological information, or any subcategorization information, cannot resolve such ambiguities. TüSBL follows Abney (1991, p. 258), who proposes more generally not to analyze post-head modification. Figure 5.35 gives an example for a complex noun phrase containing a postmodifier: in sentence (39), the complex noun phrase "ein Glas Wein" was analyzed as two separate noun phrases without any attachment information. This analysis was chosen because the second noun phrase "Wein" could also constitute an argument of the verb "treffen". One needs to keep in mind here that the chunk parser does not know at this point in the analysis that the first noun phrase "ein Glas" is part of a prepositional phrase, since these structures will only be analyzed on a later level.

(39) wann wollen wir uns nach der Reise auf ein Glas Wein treffen
when want we us after the trip on a glass wine meet
'when should we meet after the trip for a glass of wine'

The only exception to this way of analyzing postmodified noun phrases is the analysis of date phrases. Only a very limited number of possible heads, i.e. the days of the week, have been tagged in the tag fixing step as "day". Here, the parser attaches possible dates to such noun phrases. In the sentence in (40), the chunk parser groups the complex noun phrase "Montag den sechsundzwanzigsten Juli" into a flat noun phrase, as shown in Figure 5.36.

[9] TüSBL uses the clauses recognized by CASS as its basic processing units. Therefore, it suffers more from unattached phrases than from clause-internal mis-attachments.

```
[simpx
  [nxq
    [pwav wann]]
  [vmfin wollen]
  [nx4
    [pper wir]]
  [prf uns]
  [px
    [appr nach]
    [nx1
      [art der]
      [nn Reise]]]
  [px
    [appr auf]
    [nx1
      [art ein]
      [nn Glas]]]
  [nx1
    [nn Wein]]
  [vven treffen]]
```

Fig. 5.35: *A sample chunk parse, for which the parser could not decide the attachment of the postnominal modifier "Wein".*

```
[simpx
  [nx4
    [pper ich]]
  [vmfin müßte]
  [px
    [am am]
    [nx2
      [day Montag]
      [art den]
      [adja sechsundzwanzigsten]
      [month Juli]]]
  [px
    [appr in]
    [nx1
      [ne Hannover]]]
  [vainf sein]]
```

Fig. 5.36: *An example of a complex noun phrase, in which the date expression "den sechsundzwanzigsten" could be attached.*

(40) ich müßte am Montag den sechsundzwanzigsten Juli in
I should on the Monday the twenty sixth July in
Hannover sein
Hanover be
'I should be in Hanover on Monday the twenty sixth of July'

Adverbial Phrases. The analysis of a sequence of adverbs into one or more adverbial phrases crucially depends on the semantics of these adverbs. The only way in which a chunk parser could make such a decision would be to use information on the actual word forms. Since CASS does not have this information, it can only group adverbs in the few cases for which the tag fixer has provided information: degree adverbs. Such an example is shown in Figure 5.37 for sentence (41). All other adverb sequences are resolved into adverbial phrases consisting of one word, cf. sentence (42) in Figure 5.38.

(41) ja bitte das wäre mir sehr recht
yes please that would be to me very all right
'yes please that would be quite all right with me'

```
[ptkant ja]
[ptkant bitte]
[simpx
  [nx1
    [pds das]]
  [vafin wäre]
  [nx4
    [pper mir]]
  [adjx
    [advmd sehr]
    [adjd recht]]]
```

Fig. 5.37: *An example of a complex adverbial phrase containing the degree adverb "sehr".*

```
[simpx
  [nxq
    [pwav wann]]
  [vafin hätten]
  [nx4
    [pper Sie]]
  [advx
    [adv denn]]
  [advx
    [prop dafür]]
  [advx
    [adv mal]]
  [nx1
    [nn Zeit]]]
```

Fig. 5.38: *An example of a sequence of adverbial phrases.*

(42) wann hätten Sie denn dafür mal Zeit
when would have you well for that once time
'when would you have time for that'

Final Field Constituents. The chunk grammar described in this section was mainly developed for parsing the TüBa-D/S corpus of spontaneous speech (cf. Section 5.1.1 for more details). For this reason, it assumes no sentence-internal punctuation. This type of punctuation, however, is the only information on the scope of clauses. Since this information is not available in the parser, it was decided to end a clause with its verbal complex, since any phrase following the verbal complex might also constitute the initial field or middle field of the next clause, such as in sentence (43), where the subject of the second clause might be analyzed as a final field constituent of the first clause. In such cases, it is much more difficult for the memory-based parser to correct the clause boundaries than it is to attach the remaining constituents.

(43) ich würde sagen wir nehmen am Freitag morgen den Flug
I would say we take on the Friday morning the flight
'I would say let us take the flight on Friday morning'

The strategy of not attaching possible final field constituents results in unattached phrases, which, in a complete analysis, would be grouped in the final field. Figure 5.39 gives an example for such a shortened clause in sentence (25), repeated here as (44).

(44) wir müssen ja noch einen Termin vereinbaren wegen dieser
we need well still a meeting arrange concerning this
Filialgeschichte in Hannover wir
deal with the branch office in Hanover we
'you know we still have to arrange a meeting concerning this deal with the branch office in Hanover we'

Coordinations. Coordination is a difficult phenomenon for any linguistic theory, and consequently also for parsing. Parsing spontaneous speech is especially difficult, because sentence-internal punctuation, which might give an indication of the scope of a coordination, is missing from the data. The chunk parser needs to decide deterministically at a very early stage whether a conjunct introduces a coordination on the phrase or on the clausal level. An example for such an ambiguity can be found in sentence

```
[simpx
  [nx4
    [pper wir]]
  [vmfin müssen]
  [advx
    [adv ja]]
  [advx
    [adv noch]]
  [nx1
    [art einen]
    [nn Termin]]
  [vven vereinbaren]]
[px
  [appr wegen]
  [nx1
    [pdat dieser]
    [nn Filialgeschichte]]]
[px
  [appr in]
  [nx1
    [ne Hannover]]]
```

Fig. 5.39: *An example of an unattached final field.*

(45), in which the parser needs to decide if "drei Hotels und das eine" is a coordinated noun phrase without having access to topological field information. In such cases, the potential for erroneous decisions is very high. For this reason, the chunk parser does not annotate coordinated structures, but leave resolving such scope ambiguities to the later processing step except for truncated words. Figure 5.40 shows examples of the treatment of different types of coordinations in sentence (46). It is evident that only the truncated noun "Schwimm–" was (correctly) attached to the following noun "Dampfbad". Both the first and the third conjunction remain unattached.

(45) also ich kenne jetzt da drei Hotels und das eine ist das Hotel
well I know now there three hotels and the one is the hotel
Royal
Royal
'well I know three hotels there and the one is the Royal hotel'

(46) das Hotel Loccumer-Hof ist gleich beim Bahnhof anscheinend
the hotel Loccumer-Hof is right at the train station apparently
und es gibt ein Schwimm– und Dampfbad und eine Pianobar
and there exists a swimming– and steam bath and a piano bar
'the hotel Loccumer-Hof apparently is right at the train station and there is a swimming pool and a sauna and a piano bar'

Relative Clauses. Similar to coordinations, the analysis of relative clauses suffers from the missing sentence-internal punctuation. In German, the word forms of relative pronouns coincide with those of articles, which can also be used as demonstratives, a very frequent phenomenon in spontaneous speech. For this reason, the POS tagger is incapable of recognizing relative pronouns, and the chunk parser cannot recognize relative clauses without a correct analysis of the relative pronoun and access to topological field information. Therefore, the analysis of sentences containing a relative clause whose relative pronoun was not recognized as such by the POS tagger generally results in clause fragments. For example, the chunk analysis for the sentence in (47) is shown in Figure 5.41, wherein the verb of the relative clause "stattfindet" could only be analyzed as the beginning of a new clause, since it is considered the second finite verb after "könnte", and there exists no indication of a subordinate clause.

```
[simpx
  [nx1
    [art das]
    [nn Hotel]
    [ne Loccumer-Hof]]
  [fcop ist]
  [advx
    [adv gleich]]
  [px
    [apprart beim]
    [nx1
      [nn Bahnhof]]]
  [advx
    [adv anscheinend]]]
[kon und]
[simpx
  [nx4
    [pper es]]
  [vvfin gibt]
  [nx1
    [art ein]]
  [nx1
    [trunc Schwimm--]
    [kon und]
    [nn Dampfbad]]]
[kon und]
[nx1
  [art eine]
  [nn Pianobar]]
```

Fig. 5.40: *The chunk analysis for different types of coordination.*

```
[simpx
  [nx2
    [adja siebenundzwanzigster]]
  [vmfin könnte]
  [nx4
    [pper ich]]
  [advx
    [adv natürlich]]
  [px
    [appr nach]
    [nx1
      [pposat meinem]
      [nn Zahnarzttermin]]]
  [nx1
    [art der]]
  [px
    [appr um]
    [time
      [card acht]
      [uhr Uhr]]]]
[simpx
  [vvfin stattfindet]
  [advx
    [adv dann]]
  [ptkvz weg]]
```

Fig. 5.41: *The chunk analysis for a sentence containing a non-recognized relative clause.*

(47) siebenundzwanzigster könnte ich natürlich nach meinem
twenty seventh could I naturally after my
Zahnarzttermin der um acht Uhr stattfindet dann weg
dentist appointment which at eight o'clock takes place then away
'I could leave of course on the twenty seventh after my dentist appointment which takes place at eight o'clock'

Subordinate Clauses. The recognition of subordinate clauses is only possible if the subordinating conjunction was recognized during the POS tagging step. Since there exists an ambiguity class of conjunctions and prepositions, for example for the word "seit", and there is no sentence-internal punctuation available which might give some indication for a conjunction, this is not a trivial task. If the conjunction is tagged as "appr", clause boundaries might not be detected, such as in Figure 5.42 for sentence (48).

(48) ich wäre schon in fünfzehn Minuten am Bahnhof
I would be already in fifteen minutes at the train station
während ich zum Flughafen fast eine Stunde brauche
while I to the airport almost one hour need
'I would be at the train station in fifteen minutes while I need almost an hour to the airport'

(49) fünfzehn Uhr würde ich vorschlagen wenn wir uns da
fifteen o'clock would I suggest if we ourselves there
treffen
meet
'fifteen o'clock I would suggest if we meet there'

Correctly recognized subordinate clauses are not attached to the matrix clauses (cf. sentence (49) and Figure 5.43). This is mainly due to processing reasons in the memory-based parser.

Parentheses. There are two different types of parentheses which are not attached to the surrounding clauses: repeated phrases and parenthetical clauses, such as the matrix clauses in long-distance wh-movements. Repeated phrases cannot be recognized as such by the chunk parser – this recognition would only be possible if the function-argument structure of the clause were analyzed and a spurious argument found. This, however, is beyond the capabilities of a deterministic chunk parser. Therefore, such

```
[simpx
  [nx4
    [pper ich]]
  [vafin wäre]
  [advx
    [advmd schon]]
  [px
    [appr in]
    [nx1
      [mx
        [card fünfzehn]
        [unit Minuten]]]]
  [px
    [am am]
    [nx1
      [nn Bahnhof]]]
  [px
    [appr während]
    [nx4
      [pper ich]]]
  [px
    [zu zum]
    [nx1
      [nn Flughafen]]]
  [cdql fast]
  [nx1
    [art eine]
    [nn Stunde]]]
 [simpx
  [vvfin brauche]]
```

Fig. 5.42: *An example of a mis-recognized subordinating conjunction.*

```
[simpx
  [time
    [card fünfzehn]
    [uhr Uhr]]
  [vafin würde]
  [nx4
    [pper ich]]
  [vven vorschlagen]]
[simpx
  [kous wenn]
  [nx4
    [pper wir]]
  [prf uns]
  [da da]
  [vven treffen]]
```

Fig. 5.43: *An example of a correctly recognized subordinate clause.*

noun phrases are included in the surrounding chunk clause (cf. the chunk annotation of sentence (50) in Figure 5.44).

(50) da kenne ich ja ein da kenne ich ein Restaurant ein sehr
there know I well a there know I a restaurant a very
gutes Restaurant in der Mitte
good restaurant in the middle
'I know I know of a restaurant a very good restaurant in the middle of the city there'

The phenomenon of parenthetical clauses in TüBa-D/S is generally restricted to inclusions, such as "glaube ich". Since in most of these cases, the tag fixer changes the verb's tag to "noarg", the chunk parser is capable of recognizing such structures. An example is sentence (51) whose chunk annotation is shown in Figure 5.45. In order to facilitate further processing in the memory-based parsing step, the parentheses are included in the surrounding clause during chunk parsing.

(51) also mindestens zwei Treffen denke ich müßten wir noch abhalten
so at least two meetings think I should we still hold
'well we should hold I think at least another two meetings'

```
[simpx
  [da da]
  [vvfin kenne]
  [nx4
    [pper ich]]
  [advx
    [adv ja]]
  [nx1
    [art ein]]
  [da da]]
[simpx
  [vvfin kenne]
  [nx4
    [pper ich]]
  [nx1
    [art ein]
    [nn Restaurant]]
  [nx1
    [art ein]
    [advmd sehr]
    [adja gutes]
    [nn Restaurant]]
  [px
    [appr in]
    [nx1
      [art der]
      [nn Mitte]]]]
```

Fig. 5.44: *An example of a parenthetical noun phrase, "ein Restaurant", which is analyzed in the TüBa-D/S treebank as a parenthesis.*

```
[advx
   [adv also]]
 [nx1
   [cdql mindestens]
   [card zwei]
   [nn Treffen]]
 [sub-simpx
   [noarg denke]
   [nx4
     [pper ich]]]
 [simpx
   [vmfin müßten]
   [nx4
     [pper wir]]
   [advx
     [adv noch]]
   [vven abhalten]]
```

Fig. 5.45: *The chunk analysis for a sentence containing a parenthetical clause.*

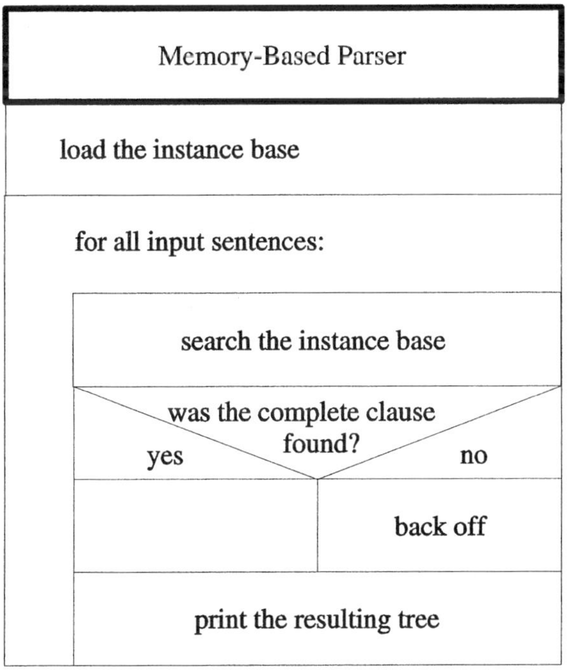

Fig. 5.46: *An overview of MBP's architecture.*

5.4 An Overview of the Architecture of the Memory-Based Parser

The memory-based parsing component of TüSBL, *MBP*, accepts the output of the CASS chunk parser as its input. The input sentences are parsed individually by CASS and then passed to MBP along with their chunk analysis. We will give here an overview of the complete memory-based parser. The individual modules will be described in more detail in the following sections. An overview of the architecture of MBP is shown as a Nassi-Shneiderman diagram in Figure 5.46.

As a first step before starting the syntactic analysis, the memory-based parser needs to read the instance base and the weights for omitting POS tags and chunks. The instance base is stored in the memory as a prefix trie (for more details cf. Section 5.5.2). After this initialization, the syntactic analysis starts. Since the sentences that the parser receives often consist of more than one sentence in the traditional sense, MBP uses the clause boundaries found by CASS to segment each input sentence into clauses – or maximal chunks if CASS was unable to attach these chunks to a clause. Each of these clauses, including its chunk annotation, is then passed to the memory-based search module, which attempts to find the clause in the instance base. If this search does not fully succeed, i.e., if there are at least parts of the clause that have not been found in the instance base, these parts are passed to the backing-off module where they are further processed and receive a syntactic annotation. In the worst case, the annotation will consist of the chunk annotation converted into the output structure. The syntactic tree structures of the individual clauses of a sentence are combined and printed in a pointer-based format that can be used as input for the NEGRA annotation tool *Annotate* (Brants & Skut, 1998; Plaehn, 1998).

5.5 The Learning Task

Memory-based learning is a well-documented approach to machine learning, as shown in Section 2. The algorithms for MBL and weighting are well developed, but there is no theory yet (neither for MBL nor for any other machine learning approach) which explains how to find the optimal feature and parameter settings for a specific problem. Existing empirical evaluations only give very selective answers. Moreover, recent results by Banko & Brill (2001*a*,*b*) have shown that even for a relatively simple learning task, the extension of the training set by orders of magnitude results in a significantly improved performance of all algorithms that were tested. Banko and Brill used the task of confusion set disambiguation, i.e. the task of choosing the correct word from a set of homophones, for example (to, two, too). For this task, the gold standard consists of the correct word and its context of pure text. Therefore, any collection of text can serve as a training corpus for the supervised learning task. Thus, the acquisition of a corpus that goes beyond the standard one million words is possible. Banko and Brill tested several machine learning techniques on training corpora of increasing size, starting from one million words and ending with one billion words. The accuracy results (cf. Figure 5.47[10]) show that there is a significant improvement when going from the smallest to the largest training set. And since the learning curves still rise at one billion words, this suggests that there is still room for improvement if there were more training data available.

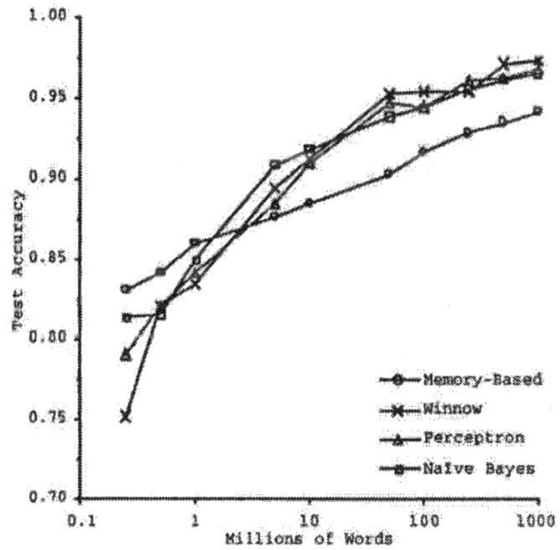

Fig. 5.47: *The learning curve for confusion set disambiguation (Banko & Brill, 2001*b*, p. 27).*

Comparative analyses in machine learning (cf. for example (van den Bosch & Daelemans, 1993; Daelemans, Zavrel, Berck & Gillis, 1996; Mooney, 1996; Escudero et al., 2000)) indicate that even more training data are necessary for more complex learning tasks, i.e. for tasks for which the search space is greater in size as well as in the number of dimensions. For learning syntactic annotation, one might expect that the size of a training set that comes even close to optimal conditions should be orders of magnitude greater than the one for a relatively simple task such as confusion set disambiguation. The cost of producing such an annotated training set, however, grows exponentially with the complexity of the task. While for confusion set disambiguation, the cost is restricted to the collection of texts, collecting a corpus for POS annotation is more cost-intensive since every word needs to be annotated with the correct POS tag and manually checked for correctness[11]. Creating a gold standard for syntactic annotation

[11] It is also possible to use purely automatically annotated corpora for training. But the errors contained in such training data may encourage certain error types to which the program to be trained might not be susceptible if trained on manually corrected data. If the POS tagger that produces the annotated training data is, for example, incapable of distinguishing between demonstrative and relative pronouns in German, any POS tagger which is trained on these data will only have distorted data available on this distinction. Thus, it will not be able to make any correct generalizations, even if it

is again more cost-intensive since for such a treebank, the annotations are much more extensive and complex. For this reason, syntactically annotated and manually corrected treebanks generally do not reach a size of more than one million words. The Tübingen treebanks for Spoken German and English (Stegmann et al., 2000; Kordoni, 2000) cover approximately 38 000 and 30 000 sentences respectively, and the NEGRA treebank (Skut et al., 1998) contains 20 000 sentences.

The combination of the findings of Banko & Brill (2001*a*,*b*) and the severely limited size of available treebanks for training seem to suggest that machine learning approaches that do not rely on extracting rules, but larger fragments instead are predestined to fail. One possibility of alleviating this problem lies in increasing the amount of information used for classification. For memory-based learning, this strategy translates into using a large number of features. It is, however, easy to see that for a small instance base, there is an area of conflict between too many features in order to retrieve the correct instance and not enough information to make the correct choice.

Another question that needs to be answered is how to decide which features are relevant for the problem of syntactic annotation. There exist theoretical and empirical analyses that indicate that the complexity of correct classification in lazy learning is exponential in relation to the number of irrelevant features. Langley & Iba (1993) show that the probability of a nearest neighbor algorithm correctly classifying a test instance decreases significantly depending on the number of irrelevant features used for classification. Figure 5.48[12] shows the curve for a classifier using two relevant features plus an increasing number of irrelevant features in a noise-free instance base. The lines represent theoretical learning curves, the error bars show experimental results. Wettschereck (1994) corroborated these findings by empirical tests. He found that adding irrelevant features decreased performance considerably (cf. Figure 5.49). This effect can be counterbalanced to some degree by choosing larger values for k, i.e. for the number of nearest neighbors that vote on the class of a test instance.

Daelemans & Hoste (2002) and Daelemans et al. (2003) show in empirical investigations that an interdependence of feature selection and parameter optimization exists. They tested two different machine learning algorithms on several classification tasks, first with default parameter settings, then with optimized parameter settings, and finally with a combination of feature selection and parameter optimization. They found that both param-

were theoretically capable when learning on perfect data.

[12] Copyright (1993), reprinted with permission from Elsevier.

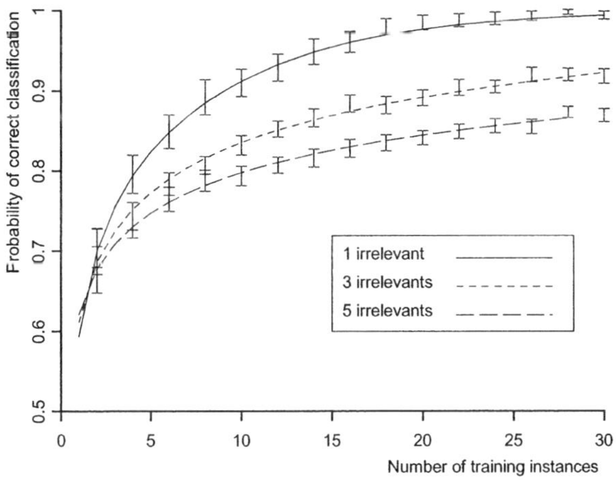

Fig. 5.48: *Predictive accuracy of a nearest neighbor classifier with an increasing number of irrelevant features (Langley & Iba, 1993, p. 893).*

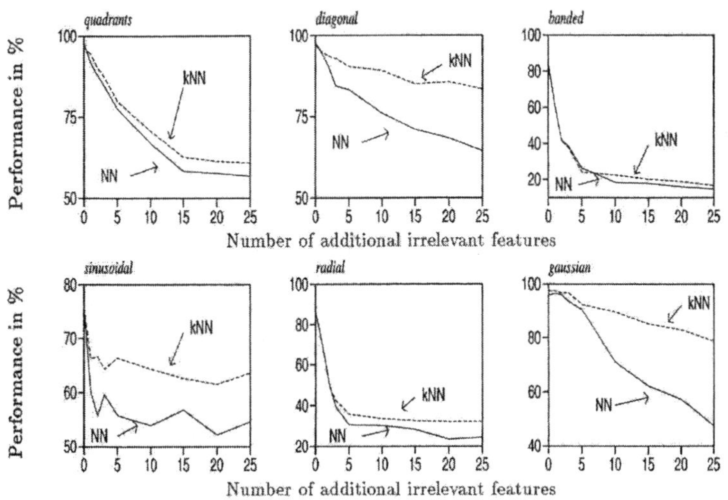

Fig. 5.49: *The influence of irrelevant features on nearest neighbor classification (Wettschereck, 1994, p. 38).*

eter optimization and the combination of feature selection and parameter optimization give major improvements compared to the results with default parameters. Additionally, results based on default settings as well as results based on optimizing either features or parameters do not allow a reliable comparison of learning algorithms since the performance of the different algorithms profit from optimization to different degrees. The differences based on optimization were larger than the difference between algorithms. These results show that it is impossible to evaluate machine learning algorithms reliably without first having optimized the selected feature sets combined with optimizing algorithm parameters. Unfortunately, such a combined optimization can be very costly as all combinations need to be tested. Previous results of Kool, Daelemans and Zavrel (Kool, Daelemans & Zavrel, 2000; Kool, Zavrel & Daelemans, 2000) show that standard search techniques for exploring large search spaces such as *genetic algorithms* do not always lead to improved results for word sense disambiguation. However, the application of genetic algorithms resulted in improved classification accuracy (Daelemans et al., 2003).

In the light of the above results, it is difficult to envisage a successful approach to such a complex task as parsing including function-argument structure. On the one hand, there does not exist an extensive enough treebank for training a memory-based learner. On the other hand, there exists a dichotomy of not having enough information for a reliable classification and too many irrelevant features making a correct classification less probable. For these reasons, TüSBL approaches the traversal of the search space in a different manner: since the parser needs all available information in order to perform such a complex task, it is given access to all possibly useful information but not necessarily at the same time. The types of information available to the parser are ordered according to their reliability: the types of information that are the least likely to contain erroneous data are accessed first. If the search based on these features does not prove successful, the parser backs off to less reliable types of information. During the later steps in the parsing architecture, the parser will in some cases provide only partial analyses. This adheres to the basic assumptions of *robust parsing* that if there is not enough information available for a complete and spanning parse, a partial analysis is preferred.

In the following section, we will look at the types of information which are available from preprocessing and will give examples for which these types of information will be relevant in parsing. We will then describe the first and most important level of processing, the search on the word level.

We assume (cf. Section 5.4 for an overview of the complete architecture of the memory-based parser MBP) that the input sentence is split into single clauses according to the clausal boundaries found by the chunk parser, and the single clauses are processed individually by the search component. If, however, the search module finds the complete sequence of words, but the last node found in the trie is not a leaf node, the parser attempts to attach the following clause(s). All further processing is postponed until the backing-off component. The modules of the backing-off component will be described in Section 5.8.

5.5.1 *The Different Types of Information*

The literature reviewed in Chapter 3 as well as the research discussed above very clearly demonstrate the importance of feature selection for the success of a memory-based learning approach. Therefore, one needs to be very careful in selecting the features for MBP.

The simplest solution to the choice of features would be to use the set of all words as the feature set. The words themselves do not contain any errors[13]. If the weighting approach described in Section 5.7 is used, weights can be assigned to words in the training data so that the parser might retrieve similar sentences from the instance base that contain one word which is not present in the test sentence and which does not have a significant influence on the tree structure. When parsing the new sentence (52), the parser might retrieve the sentence in (53) from the instance base and delete the spurious word "gar" and its dominating node (node 504 in Figure 5.50) from the corresponding tree.

(52) da sieht es bei mir nicht schlecht aus
there looks it with me not bad [verb particle]
'there it does not look bad at my end'

[13] This ignores typographical errors and the possibility that the string of words might be the output of a speech recognizer. The former case presents problems for any parser that uses lexical information, but is not specific to our approach. The latter would result in serious problems for a parser since typical errors of speech recognizers include, for example, the omission of auxiliaries. In this case, the parser would have to be modified to parse a word lattice rather than only the best hypothesis of the speech recognizer. Additionally, it would need a module to select the most probable path through the word lattice based on the syntactic analysis. This constitutes a complex problem in itself, which goes beyond the scope of the present book.

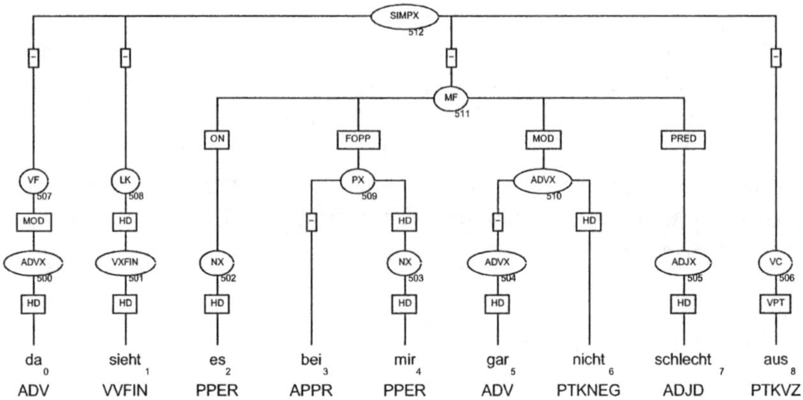

Fig. 5.50: *A tree from the instance base containing the spurious word "gar".*

(53) da sieht es bei mir gar nicht schlecht aus
there looks it with me at all not bad [verb particle]
'there it does not look bad at all at my end'

This approach, however, would have no means of differentiating between minor and major mismatches in the features since standard weighting methods cannot be used due to the flexible number of features. Thus, the sentence pairs (54) vs. (55) and (56) vs. (57) would be considered equally similar. However, there would be no difference in the corresponding trees for the first pair, but for the second one the differences would be extensive (cf. Figures 5.51 and 5.52). For both trees, the initial field consists of a prepositional phrase "px". The internal structure of these phrases, however, is different: in the first tree, the px contains a postposition "über". In the second tree, the px contains the more standard preposition (in the position of the article in the first tree), but it is modified by an adverbial phrase "dann", which takes the position of the postposition in the first tree.

(54) das halte ich für eine wunderbare Idee
that hold I for a wonderful idea
'I think that is a wonderful idea'

(55) das halte ich für ne ausgezeichnete Idee
that hold I for a excellent idea
'I think that is an excellent idea'

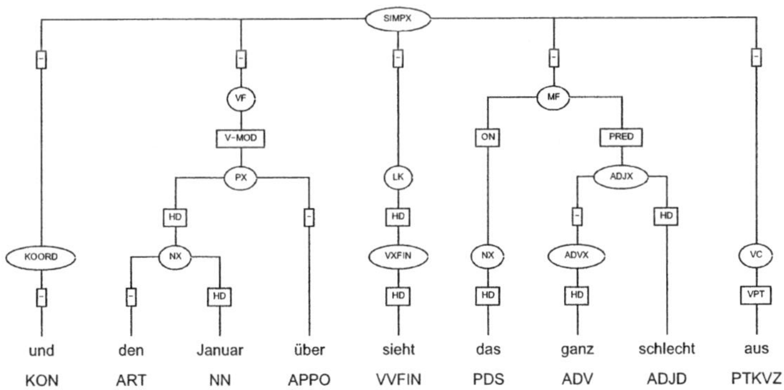

Fig. 5.51: *The syntactic tree for sentence (56).*

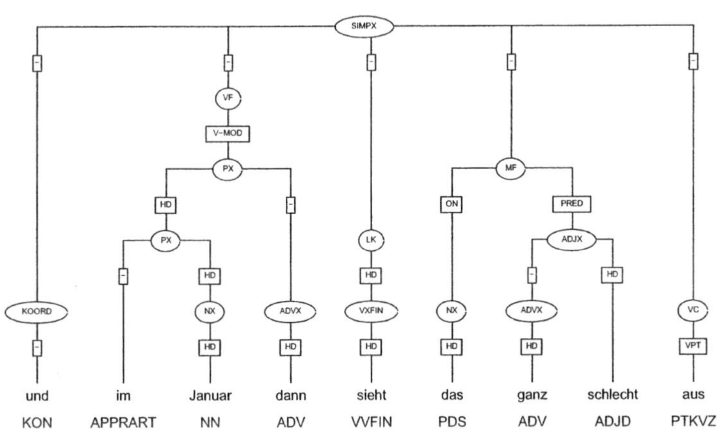

Fig. 5.52: *The syntactic tree for sentence (57).*

(56) und den Januar über sieht das ganz schlecht aus
and the January long looks that very bad [verb particle]
'and all January long it looks very bad'

(57) und im Januar dann sieht das ganz schlecht aus
and in the January then looks that very bad [verb particle]
'and in January then it looks very bad'

In order to capture the differences between the sentence pairs described above, it is necessary to introduce part-of-speech information. This type of information is relatively easy to obtain and reasonably reliable. POS taggers are available "off the shelf", and the training data (i.e. word-POS pairs) can be extracted from the treebank that is also used for training the memory-based parser. The POS tagger used for TüSBL, TnT (Brants, 1998, 1999*b*, 2000), reached an accuracy of 97.79%. This means that in general, one out of 50 words receives a wrong POS tag, which should give a reliable basis for further processing. This picture, however, is somewhat optimistic. It is generally the case that there is a specific subset of POS tags which are crucial for further syntactic processing. For the STTS, for example, there are ambiguity classes whose correct disambiguation does influence further syntactic processing significantly. Whether a sentence-initial "aber" (but) receives the POS tag "kon" (coordinating conjunction) or "adv" (adverb) and whether "üblich" in sentence (58) receives "adv" or "adjd" (adverbial adjective) has only minor influence on the analysis of the remaining sentence. These error types, however, are rather infrequent. The more frequent error types are those that disrupt the clause structure, such as erroneous classifications of relative pronouns as demonstratives or articles, the misrecognition of subordinating conjunctions as prepositions, or the confusion of finite and infinite verb forms (cf. Section 5.3.2 for examples of such mistagged words and the consequences for chunk parsing).

(58) ich denk mir wie üblich wieder
I think to me as usual again
'I think again as usual'

Since such POS tagging errors can disrupt the parsing process, POS information should be considered less reliable than the information on the word level itself. For this reason, POS information is only used when the words themselves do not provide enough information to find a similar syntactic tree.

Another type of information that is related to the word level is the ordering information. If the parser used the words of a sentence as a set, it

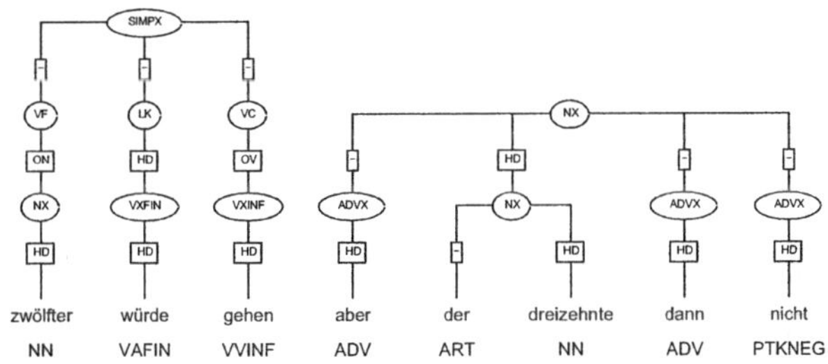

Fig. 5.53: *The syntactic tree including phrasal negation.*

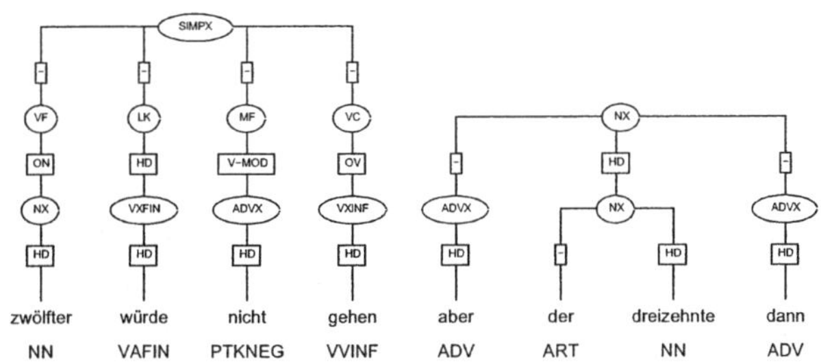

Fig. 5.54: *The syntactic tree including clause negation.*

could not decide, for example, the scope of a negation. While permutations in word order concerning arguments do not cause structural changes apart from exchanging the phrase-internal structures, changing the sequence of words concerning the placement of negations necessitates changes in the syntactic trees. The change from sentence (59) to (60) results in non-trivial changes in the syntactic tree. Figure 5.53 shows the syntactic tree for the first sentence with the scope of the negation restricted to the second date, and Figure 5.54 shows the tree for the second sentence and the clause negation.

(59) zwölfter würde gehen aber der dreizehnte dann nicht
twelfth would work but the thirteenth then not
'the twelfth would work but not the thirteenth then'

(60) zwölfter würde nicht gehen aber der dreizehnte dann
twelfth would not work but the thirteenth then
'the twelfth would not work but then the thirteenth'

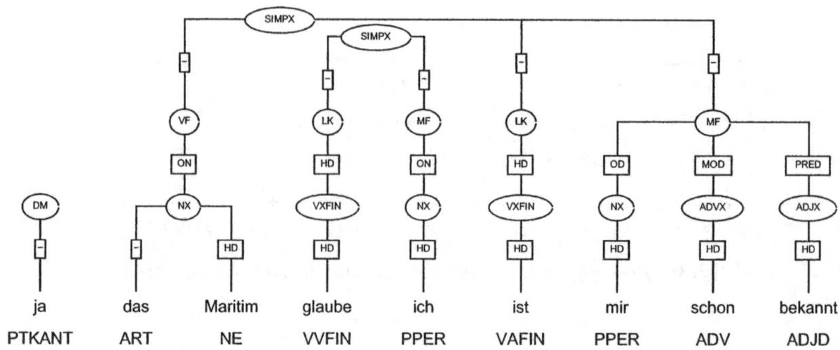

Fig. 5.55: *A syntactic analysis for a sentence including a parenthesis.*

The following two types of information can be taken from the chunk parser output: chunk information and information on clause boundaries. Chunk information is necessary for the treatment of parentheses, for example. Parentheses, as shown in Section 5.3.2, are included in the chunk analysis of the surrounding sentence. In the treebank, however, these parentheses are not attached (cf. Figure 5.55). In order to analyze the sentence correctly, the parser, which only has access to the separate trees for the parenthesis and for the remaining sentence in the instance base, needs to recognize the parenthetical character of the words "glaube ich" and exclude them from the analysis of the sentence. This information can be accessed in the output of the chunk parser (cf. Figure 5.56). In the case of parenthetical clauses, the chunk to be left out can be recognized by its label. In the more general case of parentheses consisting of repeated noun phrases, etc., the parser needs to be able to leave out complete chunks if the search for the complete sentence was unsuccessful.

The other type of information that can be extracted from the chunk parser output is information about the clause boundaries of an input sentence. This information is essential for processing transliterated speech since in this case, the sentence boundaries are rather tentative, and the chances of MBP of finding the complete sequence are low. The chunk parser output for sentence (61) is shown in Figure 5.57. From the chunk parse, the memory-based parser uses the clause segmentation to split up the input into three subclauses which are processed independently if possible. The only exception to the independent treatment of chunk parser clauses occurs if there

```
[ptkant ja]
[nx1
  [pds das]
  [ne Maritim]]
[sub-simpx
  [noarg glaube]
  [nx4
    [pper ich]]]
[simpx
  [fcop ist]
  [nx4
    [pper mir]]
  [advx
    [adv schon]]
  [adjx
    [adjd bekannt]]]
```

Fig. 5.56: *The chunk analysis for the sentence containing a parenthetical clause.*

is evidence that the next clause needs to be attached to find a complete sentence (cf. Section 5.5.2 for more details).

(61) die Ausstellung ist auch Samstag von zehn bis neunzehn Uhr
the exhibition is also Saturday from ten to nineteen o'clock
geöffnet und dann könnten wir uns überlegen ob wir am
opened and then could we us consider whether we on
Samstag abend noch etwas unternehmen wollen
Saturday evening still something do want

'the exhibition is also open on Saturday from ten a.m. to seven p.m. and then we could think about whether we want to do something on Saturday night'

From all preprocessing steps, the following types of information are available: sequential word information, POS tags, chunks on the phrase level, and clause boundaries. Figure 5.58 gives an overview of all types of information for sentence (62).

```
[simpx
  [nx1
    [art die]
    [nn Ausstellung]]
  [fcop ist]
  [advx
    [adv auch]]
  [nx2
    [day Samstag]]
  [px
    [appr von]
    [nx1
      [card zehn]]]
  [px
    [bis bis]
    [time
      [card neunzehn]
      [uhr Uhr]]]
  [adjx
    [adjd geöffnet]]]
[kon und]
[simpx
  [advx
    [adv dann]]
  [vmfin könnten]
  [nx4
    [pper wir]]
  [prf uns]
  [vven überlegen]]
[simpx
  [kous ob]
  [nx4
    [pper wir]]
  [px
    [am am]
    [nx2
      [day Samstag]]]
  [advx
    [adv abend]]
  [advx
    [adv noch]]
  [pis etwas]
  [vven unternehmen]
  [vmfin wollen]]
```

Fig. 5.57: *The chunk parser's analysis for a "sentence" in transliterated speech.*

words	die	werden	vermutlich	zuhaben	am	Abend	meinen	Sie	nicht
POS	pds	vafin	adv	vven	apprart	nn	vven	pper	ptkneg
chunks	nx1		advx		px			nx4	
clause	simpx				simpx				

Fig. 5.58: *The types of information available for sentence (62).*

(62) die werden vermutlich zuhaben am Abend meinen Sie
those will probably have closed at the evening think you
nicht
not
'they will probably be closed in the evening do you not think'

5.5.2 *Searching the Instance Base*

In the previous section, we described which types of information are available from the preprocessing steps. In this section, we will explain in which form these types of information are used in the main search routine. This search routine mainly uses the most reliable type of information – the sequence of words.

The Representation of the Instance Base. Since word order within a clause was found to be important for the retrieval of the most similar tree, the data structure on which the search is performed needs to reflect this information. For this reason, the instance base is organized along a representation of sequences of words that can be searched efficiently: a prefix trie. The sentences are stored as a tree in which every word is represented as a node. Sentences that start with the same sequence of words share the same path through the tree to the last common word. After this node, the tree splits into two subtrees, each of which represents one sentence. For the sentences in Table 5.2, which is a small extract of the actual instance base, the corresponding prefix trie is shown in Figure 5.59. The last words of the sentences, i.e. the leaf nodes, are marked by circles. In the sample of the instance base, there is one example of a sentence, sentence (63), which is a complete prefix of sentence (64). The presence of the former sentence in the instance base can only be recognized by the marking of the leaf nodes of sentences.

dann mache ich Ihnen die Tickets fertig
dann mache ich das mit der Flugverbindung
dann mache ich den Flug fest
dann machen Sie das
dann machen Sie das doch bitte
dann machen wir am elften die Konferenz
daran habe ich auch schon gedacht
darf ich Ihnen einfach mal einen Vorschlag machen vom Termin her
darf ich Sie mal eben sprechen

Table 5.2: *A small sample of sentences from the instance base.*

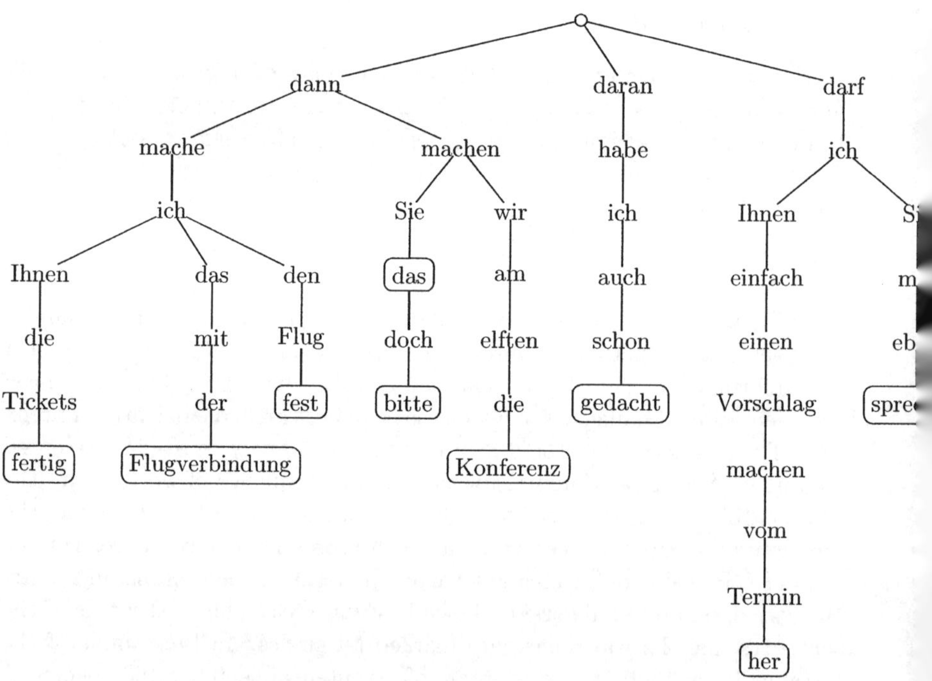

Fig. 5.59: *The prefix trie for the sentences in Table 5.2.*

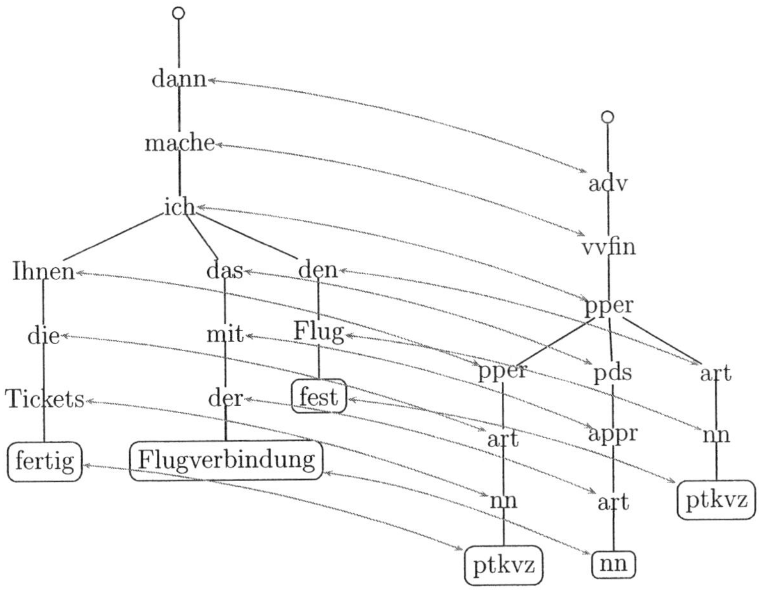

Fig. 5.60: *The combined tries for words and POS tags.*

(63) dann machen Sie das
then do you that
'then do that'

(64) dann machen Sie das doch bitte
then do you that certainly please
'then please certainly do that'

The POS tags are stored in the same type of data structure, in a parallel trie. Both tries are connected so that the parser can access the POS tag of a word and vice versa. Via this POS tag node, the parser can also access the list of POS tags which can occur at that position in a sentence, given the same prefix. Figure 5.60 shows a small portion of the instance base. If the parser searches for an equivalent of the input sentence (65) in the instance base in Figure 5.60, it will reach the word "ich", but will not find the next word in the instance base. Then the parser will continue the search on the POS tag level. There, it will find the POS tag of "die", "art", and afterwards the POS tag of "Buchungen", "nn". After this node, the parser can return

#	adv	hd	500;
#	vvfin	hd	501;
#	pper	hd	502;
#	pds	hd	503;
#	appr	-	507;
#	art	-	504;
#	nn	hd	504;
#500	advx	mod	505;
#501	vxfin	hd	506;
#502	nx	on	509;
#503	nx	hd	508;
#504	nx	hd	507;
#505	vf	-	510;
#506	lk	-	510;
#507	px	-	508;
#508	nx	oa	509;
#509	mf	-	510;
#510	simpx	;	

Table 5.3: *The pointer representation of the syntactic tree for sentence (66).*

to the word level and then match the last remaining word and be thus able to parse the whole sentence.

(65) dann mache ich die Buchungen fertig
then make I the reservations ready
'then I will finish the reservations'

The leaf nodes of both the word trie and the POS tag trie additionally contain the corresponding syntactic tree describing the sentence. The syntactic trees, which are not shown in Figures 5.59 and 5.60 for representational reasons, take the form of a pointer structure, which is very similar to the NEGRA export format used by the NEGRA annotation tool *Annotate*. The corresponding tree annotation for sentence (66) is shown in Table 5.3. The first column contains a wild card character (#) for the word or the sentence id numbers (for example #500), with the second column containing the POS tags for words or the node labels for tree nodes. The third column specifies the grammatical function of the word or node with respect to the dominating node, and the fourth column contains the node id

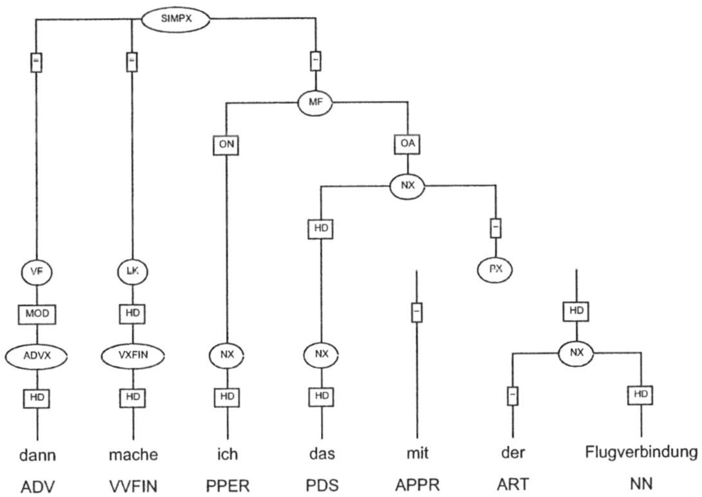

Fig. 5.61: *The graphical representation for the tree structure in Table 5.3.*

of the mother node. A root node, such as "simpx" in the present example, is characterized by the missing function and mother node information. The respective graphical representation of the tree is shown in Figure 5.61.

(66) dann mache ich das mit der Flugverbindung
then do I that with the flight connection
'then I will do that with the flight connection'

The pointer-based representation of the tree structure was necessary to represent the complete set of phenomena that occur in the parsing process. The use of a bracketing structure such as the one employed in the annotation of the Penn treebank would have been easier to process as well as more economical in terms of storage requirements. It is, however, restricted to the representation of pure trees. Treelike structures such as parenthetical clauses or "embedded" phrases cannot be represented in such a format (cf. Section 5.1.3). Therefore, a pointer-based representation was chosen, which allows the representation of such structures since each mother–daughter dependency is encoded separately. The word order is implicit in the ordering of the entries and does not coincide with the structure of the nodes governing the words.

The Search in the Instance Base. The module that performs the search on the word level covers all aspects of searching that involve the word trie. An overview of the module is given in Figure 5.62. If a new sentence is passed to MBP, the first step is to search the instance base, i.e. traverse the trie. In the trivial case, the sentence is included in the training data, then the parser reaches a leaf node and a clausal boundary in the chunk structure at the same time. The syntactic tree can then be retrieved from the leaf node, the words being inserted instead of the wild card characters, and the resulting tree structure proposed as the syntactic analysis of the sentence.

In the majority of cases, however, there will be no identical sentence contained in the instance base. In these cases, the search in the trie will reach a point where there is no further daughter node that corresponds to the next word in the input sentence. Then the search module attempts to omit some part of the input sentence or of the sentence in the instance base. Possible omission functions are:

- omit one word in the trie
- match the next word on the POS tag level
- omit one phrase in the trie
- omit one word / POS tag in the input sentence
- omit one chunk in the input sentence

The weights assigned to such omissions are determined during the learning phase of the parser. They are assigned to words or chunks based on the cost of modifying the remaining tree structure if the omitted part is extracted from the sentence. The weighting scheme is explained in more detail in Section 5.7.

If the parser reaches a point in the search where it needs to omit, all of the above mentioned omission functions are applied, and all possible omission that meet the conditions are collected. They are then sorted according to their respective weight and stored in an agenda. For each item , the agenda saves the current state of the parser at the point when the omission function was called, as well as information on which element is suggested for omission. Every time the search for elements to be omitted is completed, the best item from the agenda is selected, the state of the parser is adjusted to the state represented by the item, and the search continues from that point. The agenda can be used to perform either a best-first search or a beam search. In the first case, all possible omission items are allowed in the agenda, whereas in the second case only a fixed number of items is allowed

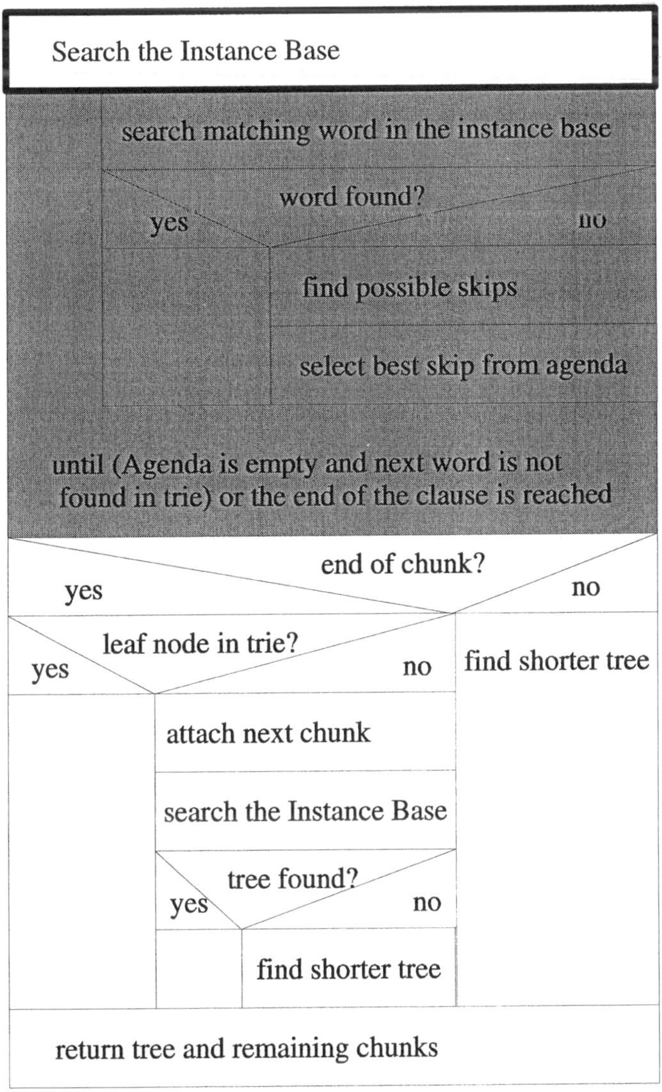

Fig. 5.62: *An overview of the search in the word trie.*

in the agenda at any time. Thus, the new item is only inserted if it has a lower weight than the item with the highest weight in the agenda. In this case, the item with the highest weight is removed from the agenda. The agenda is discarded when the parser leaves the search module.

Omitting one word in the trie is necessary, for example, when analyzing sentence (67). This sentence is not included in the instance base, the most similar sentence being sentence (68). Thus, the search module traverses the trie down to the word "Hamburg" but cannot find the next word. Instead it encounters the possible following words "ja" and "jetzt".

(67) ich kenne mich in Hamburg nicht so gut aus
I know myself in Hamburg not so well [verb particle]
'I do not know my way around Hamburg very well'

(68) ich kenne mich in Hamburg jetzt nicht so gut aus
I know myself in Hamburg now not so well [verb particle]
'now I do not know my way around Hamburg very well'

The *omit one word* function tests whether one of these words has a successor in the trie that is identical to the succeeding word in the input sentence. For the first possibility, the only successor is "aus", but for the second word, the search succeeds, and the sentence receives the analysis of sentence (68), from which the word "jetzt" and its dominating node are removed[14]. Omitting one word in the trie is only successful if the word immediately after the omitted word is identical to the next word in the input sentence. It therefore becomes impossible for the parser to match the first word and omit the remaining words.

The next possible action in the omission module is switching to the trie for POS tags (cf. above for an example). This move only succeeds if there is an identical POS tag under the node of the last word that was found in the word trie. However, it does not depend on the condition that the next word after this current word needs to be found as a successor of the POS tag. Thus, a sequence of more than one word matched on the POS level can lead to a leaf node and the desired analysis. But the return to the word trie is associated with a lesser weight than if the parser remained in the POS tag trie.

[14] This example, as well as most of the following examples, is quite simple. The sentences have been chosen so that it is easy to follow the description of the search strategy. Most "real-world" examples, for which these strategies are invoked, are more complex, and the sentences can often only be parsed by a combination of these strategies.

Omission of a phrase in the trie is similar to the *omit one word* function, the only difference being that a complete phrase is omitted instead of only one word. For this omission function, it needs to be determined which phrases of a syntactic tree are considered to be candidates for omitting. On the one hand, allowing the omission of too complex phrases (or fields) needs to be avoided since this would modify the tree structure to a very high degree. If, on the other hand, the phrases are chosen at a very low level, there is a risk that phrases whose presence requires adaptations in the tree are deleted. In the tree in Figure 5.63, for example, there are three different possible levels on which a phrase could be omitted: the prepositional phrase with root node 511, the noun phrase with root node 510, and the noun phrase with root node 504 plus the prepositional phrase with root 509. If the parser was allowed to omit the prepositional phrase "nach Hannover", the resulting complex noun phrase would not be correct, since then the "nx" node 510 would not be necessary. This projection is only necessary for postmodified noun phrases. For this reason, the set of phrases that may be omitted is defined as the set of maximal phrases that contain at least one lexical item. For the tree in Figure 5.63, the following phrases would belong to this set: "adjx" (500), "vxfin" (501), "nx" (502), "vc" (503), and "px" (511).

Equivalent to omitting one word in the word trie, the parser can also omit a word in the input sentence. This strategy is useful for transliterated speech data because such data contain a considerable number of repetitions and hesitations. Such words are not included in the sentences in the instance base as they are not attached to the tree structure. Since for such cases, the actual words themselves are less relevant, the weights for this omission action are computed on the POS level instead of the word level. Additionally, the resulting weights are generally based on more occurrences than if they were based on lexical information.

The last omission function allows the omission of a complete (maximal) chunk in the chunk structure. By maximal chunk, we refer to the chunks directly included in the "simpx" structure but not those that are embedded in a deeper level. This type of omission is only possible if the current word in the input sentence is contained in a clause "simpx" in the chunk parse. If the chunk parser cannot group the phrasal chunks into clauses, these (maximal) chunks are processed individually by MBP. Omitting chunks within such maximal chunks is not possible.

There still remain instances when the parser will not be able to find complete analyses only by using the omission functions presented above. In

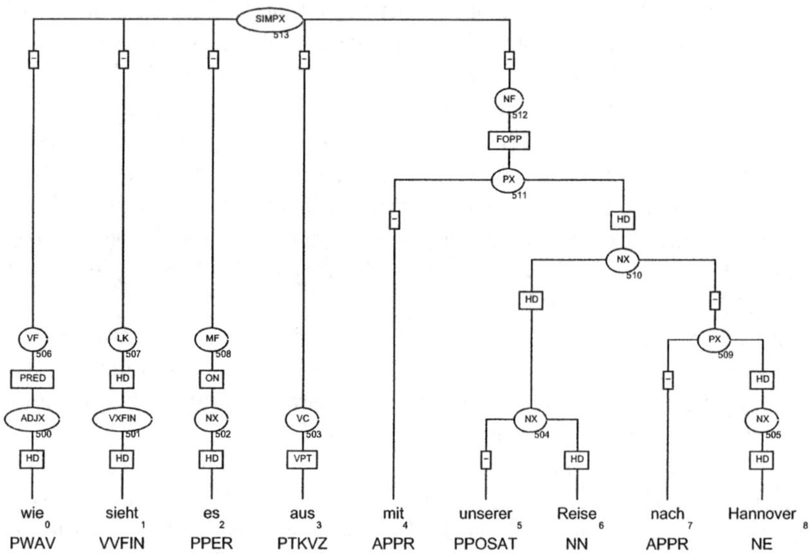

Fig. 5.63: *Omitting a complete phrase in the syntactic tree.*

```
[kokom als]
[simpx
  [nx1
    [nn nächstes]]
  [vafin hätten]
  [nx4
    [pper wir]]
  [advx
    [adv dann]]
  [advx
    [adv noch]]
  [nx1
    [pposat unsere]
    [nn Projektbesprechung]]]
```

Fig. 5.64: *The chunk parser could not group "als nächstes" into a noun chunk.*

these cases, when all possibilities of excluding parts of the input sentence and of the trie structure have been tried and no matching sentence was found, the search module tests whether the last word that was found in the trie represents a clause boundary in the chunk parse, i.e. the end of a "simpx" chunk was reached, but this does not coincide with the end of a sentence in the instance base. If this is the case, there is a possibility that this clause boundary is not correct. Therefore, the search module attempts to attach the next clause(s) from the chunk parse. For sentence (69), the chunk parser is unable to analyze the first noun phrase "als nächstes" as a constituent (cf. Figure 5.64). As a consequence, the particle of comparison "als" cannot be attached to the clause because the chunk grammar only allows one chunk in the initial field.

(69) als nächstes hätten wir dann noch unsere Projektbesprechung
as next would have we then still our project meeting
'as the next point we still have our project meeting'

This error is rectified in memory-based parsing, where the search in the instance base shows that the word "als" can only be the beginning of a sentence, but it cannot appear alone. Thus, the following chunk is attached, and the complete sentence is retrieved from the instance base (cf. Figure 5.65).

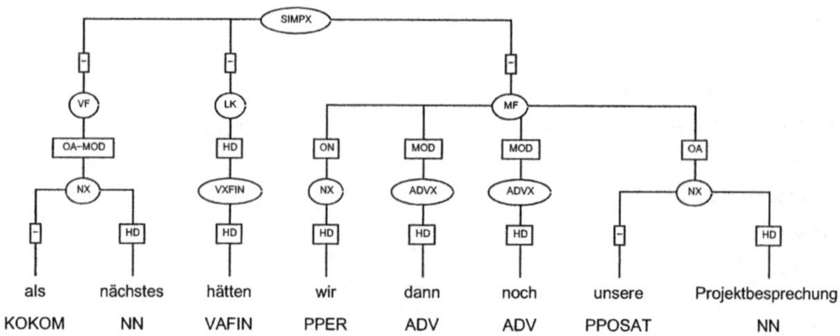

Fig. 5.65: *The output of the memory-based parser, in which the particle of comparison has been attached.*

If attaching the next chunk does not result in reaching a leaf node in the trie, the search module retraces its steps through the trie in order to search for a leaf node higher up in the trie. If such a leaf node can be found, this can be taken as an indication that the chunk parser suggested a clause that also contains chunks from the next clause. In such cases, the shorter clause hypothesis is accepted, and the remaining chunk sequence is again passed to the search module for further processing.

If there are still parts of the clause for which no counterpart in the instance base could be found, the search module returns the not yet analyzed chunk sequence to the main routine. These chunks are treated as if they were the next chunks to be found, i.e. the parser will first try to find them in the instance base. If this search does not succeed, the backing-off module is invoked.

5.6 A Sample Parse

In this section, we will demonstrate for the input sentence (70) how the parsing process proceeds. The sample parse is simplified in that only a small portion of the instance base is considered, since otherwise the representation would become too complex. However, we will use the weights calculated for these sentences in one of the tests (cf. Section 6.4.1).

(70) wie sieht das ab dem fünfundzwanzigsten aus
how looks that from the twenty fifth [verb particle]
'how does that look from the twenty fifth on'

```
[simpx
  [nxq
    [pwav wie]]
  [vvfin sieht]
  [nx1
    [pds das]]
  [advx
    [adv denn]]
  [px
    [appr ab]
    [nx3
      [art dem]
      [adja fünfundzwanzigsten]]]
  [ptkvz aus]]
```

Fig. 5.66: *The chunk parser's output for the sentence in (70).*

The first step is preprocessing: POS tagging, tag fixing, and chunk parsing. After preprocessing, the information in Figure 5.66 is available to the memory-based parsing module (MBP).

After preprocessing, MBP accesses the instance base. The relevant portion of the instance base containing sentences (71), (72), and (73) is shown in Figure 5.67.

(71) wie sieht das aus
how looks that [verb particle]
'how does that look'

(72) wie sieht das bei Ihnen aus
how looks that with you [verb particle]
'how does that look at your end'

(73) wie sieht das denn ab dem fünfundzwanzigsten aus
how looks that so from the twenty fifth [verb particle]
'well how does that look from the twenty fifth on'

MBP finds the first three words of the input sentence, "wie sieht das", in the trie. The path through the trie is shown as dashed arcs in Figure 5.68. After having reached the word "das", the parser cannot find the next word, "ab" in the instance base. Therefore, the omission module is invoked. It finds the following possibilities for omission:

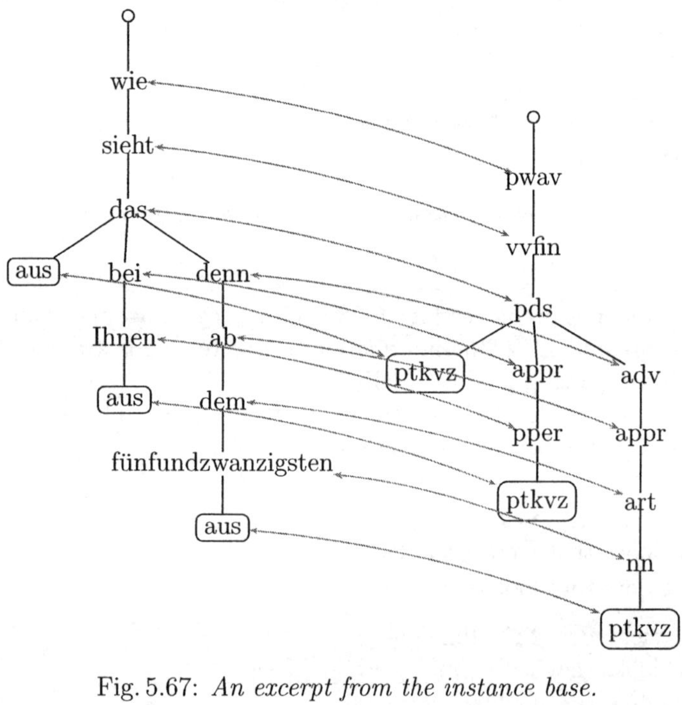

Fig. 5.67: *An excerpt from the instance base.*

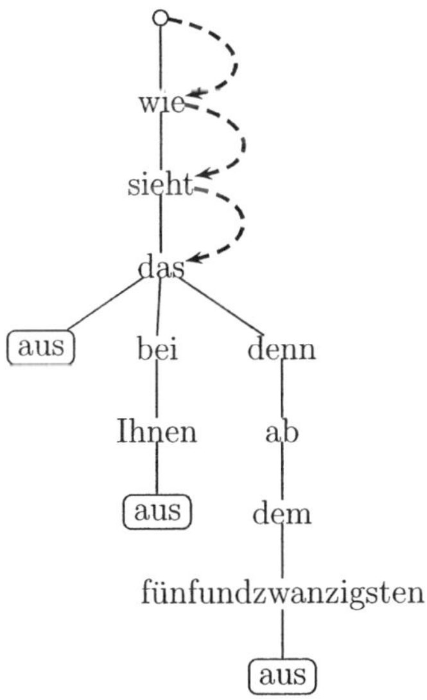

Fig. 5.68: *The first steps through the instance base.*

1. switch to the POS level, to the POS tag "appr" of the word "bei"; weight: 0.5
2. omit the word "denn" in the trie and continue at the word "ab"; weight: 1
3. omit the chunk "ab dem fünfundzwanzigsten" in the input sentence and attempt to find the word "aus" next; weight: 1

The moves in the instance base connected to these omission possibilities are shown as dotted lines in Figure 5.69. The possibilities are sorted by weight or, if the weights are the same, by the order in which the different omission possibilities are ordered, and then are stored in the agenda. In our example, switching to the POS level is associated with the smallest weight, and is thus the preferred omission method. The other two possibilities both have been assigned the maximal weight, 1, but the ordering of omission possibilities prefers the omission of a word in the instance base to omitting a complete phrase in the input sentence.

Since switching to the POS level was assigned the lowest weight, in other words the lowest cost, this possibility is retrieved from the agenda, and the parser switches to the POS tag "appr". The next task then is to

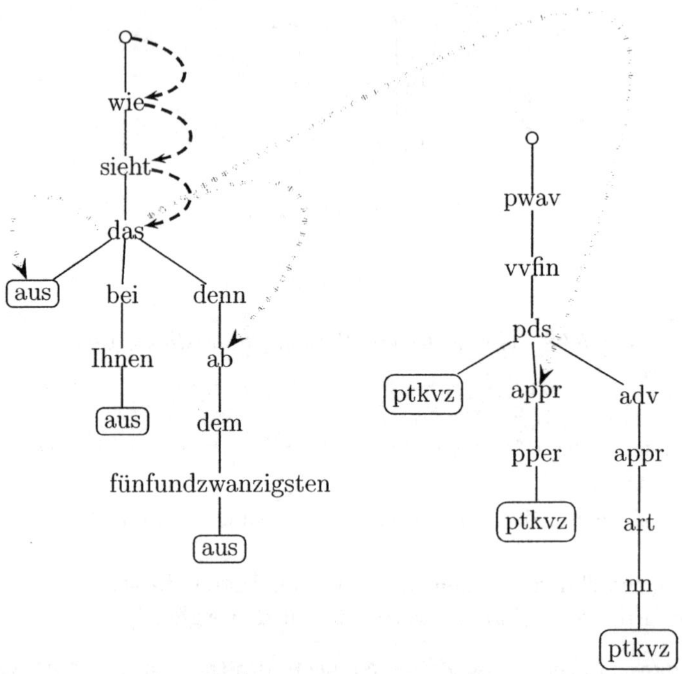

Fig. 5.69: *The different omission possibilities after having reached the word "das" in the trie.*

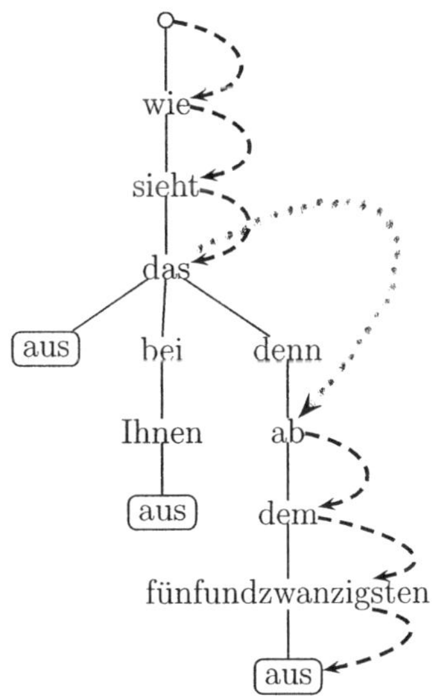

Fig. 5.70: *The parser's path through the instance base.*

find either the word "dem" or the POS tag "art". However, the only possible continuation after "appr" is the word "Ihnen", or respectively the POS tag "pper". Thus, the parser discards the first hypothesis, returns to the word "das" in the trie, and retrieves the next hypothesis. As a consequence, it omits the word "denn" and continues to match the following words. This choice allows MBP to match the remaining words of the clause to words in the instance base. The complete path through the trie is shown in Figure 5.70.

As the last word in the clause corresponds to a leaf node in the instance base, the search is at an end, and the parser retrieves the tree structure attached to this leaf, deletes the redundant word and its mother node, and converts the structures into the output format. The resulting tree is shown in Figure 5.71, with the deleted word and node marked in gray.

5.7 Feature Weighting with a Flexible Number of Features

We have seen in Section 5.5 which types of omission are available to the memory-based parser. It is clear that for all types of omission there are

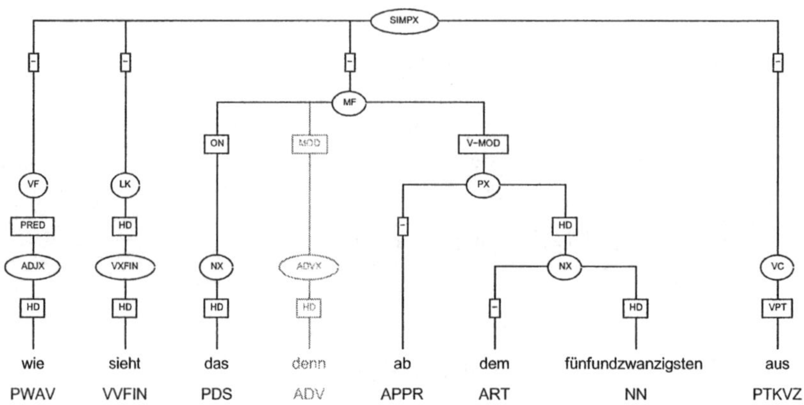

Fig. 5.71: *The result of the sample parse. The omitted word and node are marked in gray.*

elements that can be more harmful if they are removed from the sentence than others. If the parser, for example, decides to omit the adverb "noch" in the input sentence (74), it is definitely less harmful to the complete analysis than leaving out the word "Flieger" in sentence (75). For this reason, the parser needs a weighting scheme to be able to differentiate between important and less important parts of a sentence.

(74) im August könnte ich noch am sechsundzwanzigten
in the August could I also at the twenty sixth
'in August I could also on the twenty sixth'

(75) es gehen stündlich Flieger ab München
there go hourly planes from Munich
'there are planes departing hourly from Munich'

The weights are calculated off-line during the learning phase based on the training data. Basically, there are two different places in which the parser can omit: in the word trie or in the input sentence. In the trie, the parser can omit either one word or a complete phrase. In the chunk parsed input sentence, the parser can omit either one word or a complete chunk. The weights based on omitting a word or a phrase in the trie can be extracted directly from the training data (cf. Section 5.7.2). This type of information is not readily available from the training data for the weights for omitting a word or a chunk in the input sentence since phrases in the treebank do not always coincide with chunks (cf. Section 5.3.2). Therefore, the sentences from the treebank are extracted and preprocessed in the same way as if they were input sentences for the parser. Thus, the preprocessing information to which the parser has access during the actual parsing step is simulated during training. Based on this preprocessing information, the weights for omitting words or chunks in the input sentence are calculated.

As explained in Section 5.2, the weighting approach cannot be based on existing weighting schemes for memory-based learning because the parser uses a flexible number of features. Instead, the weighting scheme is based on a combination of two different types of information:

1. How often the original sentence containing the element, (i.e. the word, phrase, or chunk to be omitted) can be found in the training data in relation to how often the same sentence without this element can be found.
2. To what degree does the tree change if the element is omitted?

Thus, we have four different types of omission: omitting a word or phrase in the sentence from the instance base, and omitting a word or chunk in the input sentence. If they are all combined with both types of weighting, this would result in eight different values. However, not all of these combinations of types of omission and types of information are possible and meaningful. Only four out of the eight possible weighting schemes are meaningful and need to be calculated. For the four different types of weights, different types of weighting information is available: the first type of information, frequency information, is available for both the elements from the trie and from the chunk parse, but it is only meaningful in the chunk parsed data (cf. Section 5.7.2). The second type of information, structural change in the tree, is only available for the two omission functions concerning omitting words or phrases in sentences from the instance base as these elements are connected to the gold standard information. For the elements which are omitted in the chunk parse, however, we cannot calculate differences in the annotation because the chunk parse is by definition flat and does not contain attachment information. Therefore, the deletion of a word or phrase from the input sentence will at most result in very minor differences in the chunk parse. The difference in the chunk parses for sentences (76) and (77) is limited to the missing internal mass phrase in the noun phrase (cf. Figure 5.72). If the verb was left out, the chunk parser would not group the single chunks into the "simpx" clause, but there would be no difference in the chunks.

```
[simpx                              [simpx
  [vven sagen]                        [vven sagen]
  [nx4                                [nx4
    [pper wir]]                         [pper wir]]
  [advx                               [advx
    [adv mal]]                          [adv mal]]
  [nx1                                [nx1
    [mx                                 [card zwei]]
      [card zwei]                     [advx
      [unit Stunden]]]                  [adv vorher]]]
  [advx
    [adv vorher]]]
```

Fig. 5.72: *The two chunk parses for the sentence with and without the word "Stunden".*

(76) sagen wir mal zwei Stunden vorher
say we just two hours before
'let us say two hours before'

(77) sagen wir mal zwei vorher
say we just two before
'let's say two before'

In the sections below, we will explain how the weights for the two different sources of knowledge are calculated.

5.7.1 *Weights for Omission in the Input Sentence*

For omission in the input sentence, there are two different weights to be calculated from the sentences in the training data: the weights for omitting a POS tag, and the weights for omitting a maximal chunk. As already mentioned in Section 5.5.2, the module uses POS tag weights instead of word weights. This is due to the fact that the main phenomena which need to be covered with this omission method are repetitions and hesitations, i.e. words that should not be included in the final syntactic tree. For these cases, the actual word forms are less informative that the POS tags. Additionally, POS tag weights can be estimated on more occurrences than word weights.

Both weights are extracted from the information which preprocessing provides for the sentences in the training data. For the POS tag weights, the sentences are extracted without annotation from the training data. These sentences are then POS tagged by a POS tagger, which was trained on the training data. Based on these POS tag sequences, the weights are calculated. Using the POS tags of a tagger instead of using the POS tags from the training data ensures that the weights will be calculated on the same kind of input that will receive the weights in actual parsing.

For the chunk weights, the output of the POS tagger is chunk parsed by the chunk parser using the same grammar that will be used in actual parsing afterwards. From these chunk parses, the sequence of labels of the maximal chunks is extracted for all clauses which are marked as "simpx". Additionally, each such label also contains the head word. Sentence (78), with the chunk annotation shown in Figure 5.73, will result in the chunk sequences:

> simpx(könnte): nx4(ich) vmfin(könnte) nx4(mir) vven(vorstellen)

and

> simpx(bin): kous(daß) nx4(ich) adjx(hungrig) fcop(bin)

The two prepositional chunks at the end of the sentence are not represented since they could not be grouped into a clause.

(78) ich könnte mir vorstellen daß ich dann sehr hungrig bin nach
I could myself imagine that I then very hungry am after
einer nach einem ausgiebigen Arbeitstag
a after a extensive workday
'I could imagine that I will be very hungry then after a long workday'

The training algorithm loops over the sentences and the POS tags and chunk labels respectively. It then calculates the number of times the sentence appears in the training data with and without the current element X. The weight of this element X, is calculated as follows:

$$weight(X) = 1 - \frac{\frac{freq(SoX)}{freq(SwX)}}{freq(SoX) + freq(SwX)} \quad (27)$$

where SoX is the sentence not containing the current element X and SwX is the sentence containing the element. This calculation is performed on the sequence including the heads and once again solely on the basis of the chunk labels.

The weights for the sentence in Figure 5.73 are given in Table 5.4. The weight in the second column is based on the comparison of chunk labels only

```
[simpx h=könnte
  [nx4 h=ich
    [pper h=ich ich]]
  [vmfin h=könnte könnte]
  [nx4 h=mir
    [pper h=mir mir]]
  [vven h=vorstellen vorstellen]]
[simpx h=bin
  [kous h=daß daß]
  [nx4 h=ich
    [pper h=ich ich]]
  [advx h=dann
    [adv h=dann dann]]
  [adjx h=hungrig
    [advmd h=sehr sehr]
    [adjd h=hungrig hungrig]]
  [fcop h=bin bin]]
[px h=nach
  [appr h=nach nach]
  [nx1 h=einer
    [art h=einer einer]]]
[px h=nach
  [appr h=nach nach]
  [nx1 h=Arbeitstag
    [art h=einem einem]
    [adja h=ausgiebigen ausgiebigen]
    [nn h=Arbeitstag Arbeitstag]]]
```

Fig. 5.73: *The chunk parse for sentence (78).*

chunk	weight	head	weight
nx4	0.94	ich	1.00
vmfin	1.00	könnte	1.00
nx4	0.94	mir	1.00
vven	0.98	vorstellen	0.50
kous	1.00	daß	1.00
nx4	0.98	ich	1.00
advx	0.91	dann	1.00
adjx	0.95	hungrig	1.00
fcop	0.91	bin	1.00

Table 5.4: *The weights for the sentence in Figure 5.73.*

, and the weight in the fourth column is calculated on the basis of the chunk labels plus the head word of the respective chunk. For the first element, "nx4", for example, the weight in column two is based on the frequency of the POS tag sequence

vmfin nx4 vven kous nx4 advx adjx fcop

as compared to the sequence:

nx4 vmfin nx4 vven kous nx4 advx adjx fcop

For the weight in the fourth column, the sequence

vmfin(könnte) nx4(mir) vven(vorstellen) kous(daß) nx4(ich) advx(dann) adjx(hungrig) fcop(bin)

is set in proportion to the sequence:

nx4(ich) vmfin(könnte) nx4(mir) vven(vorstellen) kous(daß) nx4(ich) advx(dann) adjx(hungrig) fcop(bin)

It is obvious that all chunks in both clauses are considered relevant, the only exception being the weight for the last POS tag of the first clause, based on the calculation including head information. This is due to the fact that this clause occurs only once in the training data, and there is also one clause "ich könnte mir" in the data.

Clause (79) gives a more typical example for the weights that are calculated. The chunk parse for the clause is shown in Figure 5.74, the corresponding weights are shown in Table 5.5.

(79) wenn Ihnen das wirklich nichs ausmacht
if to you that really nothing matters
'if it really does not matter to you'

```
[simpx h=ausmacht
  [kous h=wenn wenn]
  [nx4 h=Ihnen
    [pper h=Ihnen Ihnen]]
  [nx1 h=das
    [pds h=das das]]
  [advx h=wirklich
    [adv h=wirklich wirklich]]
  [pis h=nichts nichts]
  [vvfin h=ausmacht ausmacht]]
```

Fig. 5.74: *The chunk parse for clause (79).*

chunk	weight	head	weight
kous	1.00	wenn	1.00
nx4	0.50	Ihnen	1.00
nx1	1.00	das	1.00
advx	0.14	wirklich	0.20
pis	0.09	nichts	1.00
vvfin	0.50	ausmacht	1.00

Table 5.5: *The weights for the sentence in Figure 5.74.*

It is obvious that, in general, there are more cases where the comparison based on chunk labels leads to weights of less than the maximal weight than cases where the comparison is based on chunk labels and their head words. In the calculation of the chunk label weight for the chunk containing the substituting indefinite pronoun "pis", for example, the algorithm also considers clauses such as (80), (81), or (82), whose chunk parses consist of the same sequence of maximal chunks. Another typical effect of weighting that can be shown in this example is that adverbial phrases tend to receive lower weights, i.e. they are less important for the clausal structure. This is in keeping with linguistic intuition. It could be argued here that from the linguistic point of view, there are different categories of adverbial modifiers, some of which cannot be so easily deleted because of their semantic contribution. One example for such a modifier would be the negation particle "nicht" (not). However, it is important to keep in mind that the parser does not delete words from the output but only irrelevant chunks from the structural analysis.

(80) ob ich das noch finde
if I that still find
'if I can still find it'

(81) wie ich das jetzt sehe
as I that now see
'just as I see it now'

(82) ob ich das Wochenende dort verbringe
if I the weekend there spend
'if I should spend the weekend there'

5.7.2 *Weights for Omission in the Instance Base*

There are three different types of weights that are calculated on the basis of the sentences in the instance base. Firstly, there are weights for omitting a word for which the identity (except for the element to be omitted) of two sentences is determined based on the comparison of words. Then we have weights for omitting a word for which the identity is based on the comparison of POS tags (subsequently referred to as the weight of omitting POS tags). The third type of weights are weights for omitting a complete phrase. In order to make the search for identical sentences as efficient as possible, the sentences from the training data are stored in a prefix trie very similar to the one used for memory-based parsing (cf. Section 5.5.2). The only additional information that is needed is the information about phrase boundaries. Thus every node does not only contain the word form and its POS tag but also a link to its phrase node if this word constitutes the first word of a phrase. The trie structure enables the training algorithm to search for the modified sentence only in the subtree whose root node is the last word before the omitted element.

Sentences that occur more than once in the training data are represented only once in the trie. Since the weights reflect the degree of structural change in the tree if one element is omitted, the relative frequency of sentences in the training corpus is not relevant. The calculation of the weights depends solely on the structure of the respective trees. For the weights for omitting a single word (as opposed to omitting a POS tag) and for omitting a phrase in the sentence, at most one sentence can occur in the instance base which is identical to the original sentence without the omitted element. For the search based on POS tags, however, there might be more than one sentence with the POS sequence without the omitted element, and their respective trees may differ to different degrees. Because of this, the latter calculation differs from the former two.

The weights for omitting words and for omitting phrases are based on the comparison of two trees. These weights are calculated by the function

$$weight(word) = weight(phrase) = 1 - \frac{nr\_ident\_nodes}{nr\_all\_nodes} \qquad (28)$$

where *nr_all_nodes* is the number of non-terminal nodes in the tree of the original sentence. The leaf nodes, i.e. the words, are not considered in the calculation since their identity has already been established, and we are interested in the structural changes above the leaf nodes. *nr_ident_nodes* is the number of nodes that can be found in the tree of the original sentence as well as in the tree of the sentence where the element is omitted. The identity of nodes is determined by the comparison of whether both nodes are non-terminal nodes, whether their categories (i.e. constituent labels) are identical, and whether they have the same daughters. The identity of daughters is based on identical categories and functions.

If the trees are completely different, the weight is 1; if the trees are identical, the weight is 0. If the algorithm does not find any sentence for comparison, the weight also receives the maximal value 1. If the two trees for sentence (83) are compared, the omitted element being "immer", there are seven nodes (cf. Figure 5.75).

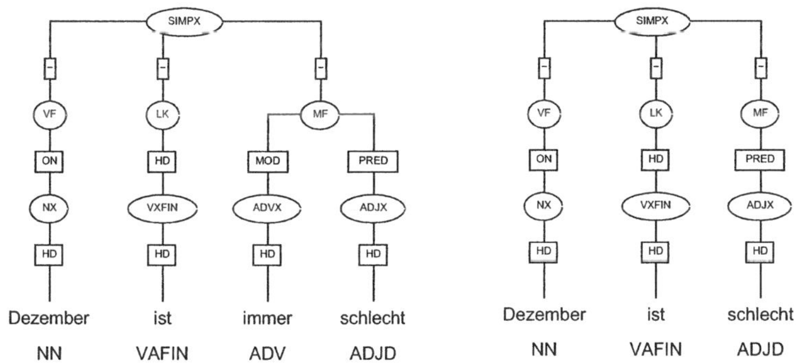

Fig. 5.75: *The original tree including the word to be omitted, "immer", and the tree without the omitted word.*

(83) Dezember ist immer schlecht
December is always bad

Nodes that dominate the omitted word or that have unary subtrees dominating the omitted word are not counted. For this reason, the node "advx" immediately dominating the word "immer" does not count. All of these nodes are also included in the second tree, therefore the weight for "immer" is calculated as follows:

$$weight(\text{“immer”}) = 1 - (7/7) = 0 \tag{29}$$

Figure 5.76 gives an example of two trees for which the change in structure is considerable if in sentence (84) the verb "beträgt" is omitted.

(84) Fahrtdauer beträgt viereinhalb Stunden
travel time is four and a half hours

This reduces the structure from a complete clause to a complex noun phrase. The original tree contains 6 non-terminal nodes (not counting the nodes "vxfin" and "lk" since they only have unary daughters and dominate the omitted word). Out of these, 3 of the non-terminal nodes match nodes in the other tree. This results in the following weight:

$$weight(\text{“beträgt”}) = 1 - (3/6) = 0.50 \tag{30}$$

For the calculation of the weights based on omitting a POS tag, the training algorithm needs to take into account that there may be more than

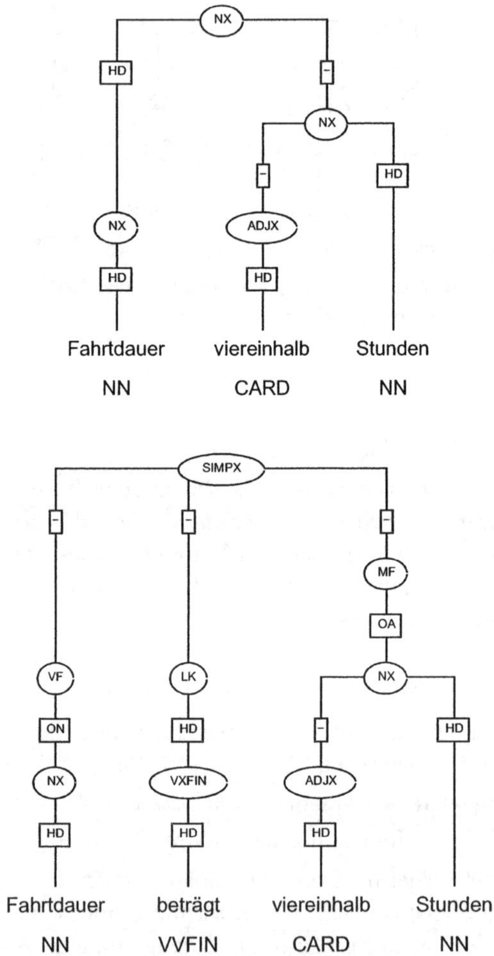

Fig. 5.76: *Two trees whose word sequence differs only in the word "beträgt". The structure, though, changes from a clause to a noun phrase.*

one sentence in the instance base that are identical in their POS sequence to the original sentence except for the omitted POS tag. It is, however, possible that these sentences are assigned structurally different trees. If the word "Februar" is omitted in sentence (85), the resulting POS tag sequence is:

nn vafin adv adjd

There are 21 different sentences that share this POS sequence. As for the syntactic structure, they fall into two different categories. there are sentences where the adverb is attached on the field level, as in (86), and sentences where the adverb is attached to the adjectival phrase, as in (87). The tree structure of the original tree (85) is shown in Figure 5.77, and the trees for the two sentences (86) and (87) in Figure 5.78.

(85) Anfang Februar ist auch gut
beginning February is also good
'beginning of February is also good'

(86) Flug ist immer besser
flight is always better
'flying is always better'

(87) siebzehnter wäre ganz prima
seventeenth would be really great

In order to account for the comparison of the original tree to possibly several different trees, Equation 28 needs to be modified:

$$weight(tag) = \frac{\sum_{trees} 1 - \frac{nr\_ident\_nodes}{nr\_all\_nodes}}{nr\_trees} \tag{31}$$

Here, the differences between comparing the original tree to more than one tree are added up and then divided by the number of trees that share the same POS tags sequence as the original sentence where the word is omitted.

For the POS tag of the word "Februar", for example, in Figure 5.77, there are two different trees to consider. The first, with the adverb attached high, shares 8 out of 9 non-terminal nodes with the original tree, the only different node is the complex noun phrase 505. For the second sentence, 6 out of 9 nodes coincide with the original tree structure. As well as the differing node in the first sentence, there are different attachments for the middle field node 507, and the adjectival phrase 504. This results in the following partial weights: $1-(8/9) = 0.1111$ for the first tree, and $1-(6/9) = 0.3333$ for the second tree. The first tree is found 9 times in the instance base, the

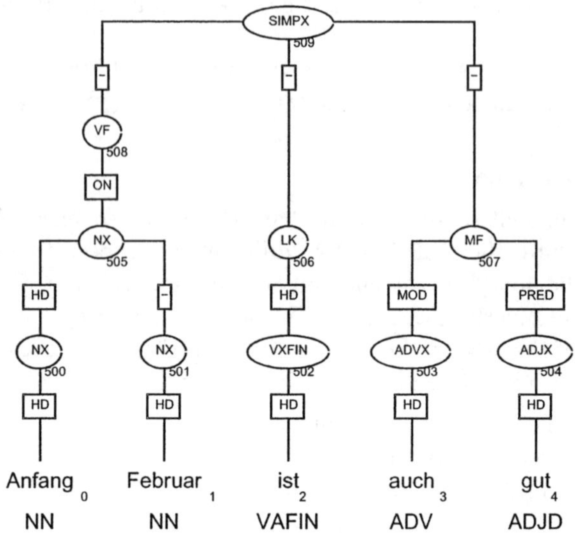

Fig. 5.77: *The original tree containing the word "Februar", which is the target for omission.*

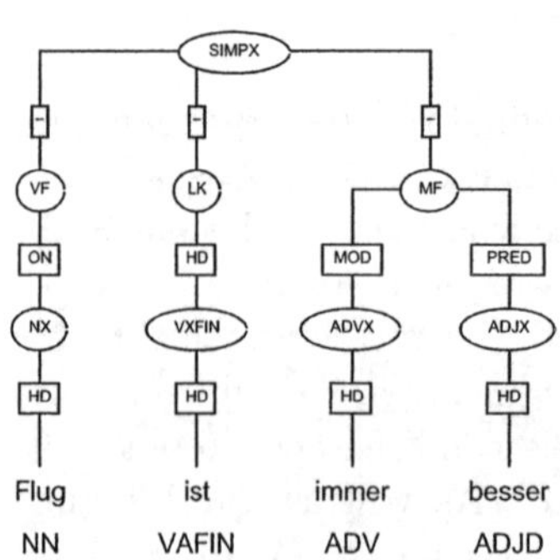

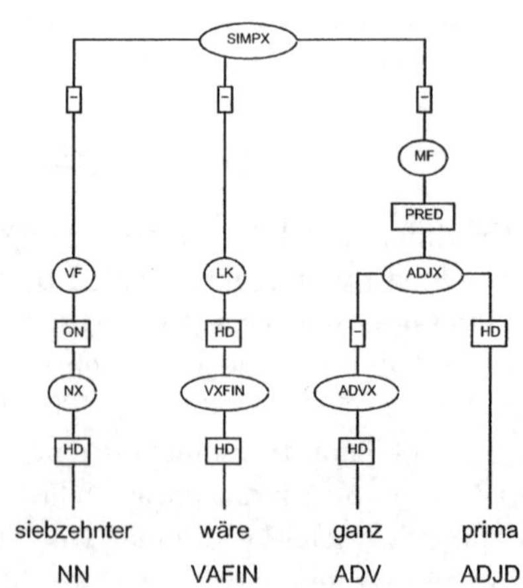

Fig. 5.78: *Two trees sharing the same POS tag sequence.*

second one 14 times. This results in the following weight for the POS tag "nn":

$$weight(nn) = ((9 \times 0.1111) + (14 \times 0.3333))/23 = 0.2464 \qquad (32)$$

5.8 The Backing-Off Approach

The backing-off module receives as input the chunks that could not be assigned a tree structure during the search in the instance base. It attempts to find syntactic analyses based on less reliable information than the word sequences, which are the major source of information during the search in the instance base. Figure 5.79 gives an overview of the backing-off module. There are two basic types of chunk structures which can serve as input for backing-off: the first is a complete (maximal) chunk, the second is the remainder of a maximal chunk, from which some subchunks were found and annotated during the search in the instance base.

If the input consists of a remainder of chunks not yet annotated after the search in the instance base, there exists the possibility that the clause proposed by the chunk parser includes subchunks from the following clause. The remaining chunk sequence may still then be found in the instance base (possibly necessitating the attachment of the next maximal chunk). Therefore, the first step is to send the remaining chunks as a proposed clause to the module that searches the instance base. The other steps in backing-off are employed only if this does not succeed. For sentence (88), the chunk parser analyzes the second verb as belonging to the first clause so that the second clause could not be found (cf. Figure 5.80). The memory-based parser, however, can analyze the first three words as a clause, but the remaining verb needs to be analyzed separately. In backing-off, the parser finds a possibility of attaching the next chunks, and the second clause can also be found in the instance base and thus be analyzed correctly (cf. Figure 5.81).

(88) dann habe ich beginnen wir doch auch schon morgens
then have I start we really also already in the morning
'then I have – let us do already start in the morning then'

If the complete clause is passed to the backing-off module, the first strategy is executed: the search in the word trie starting from the last word that was found. The search will access all subtrees in the trie branching off from this word. If a leaf node is found, the syntactic tree is retrieved and

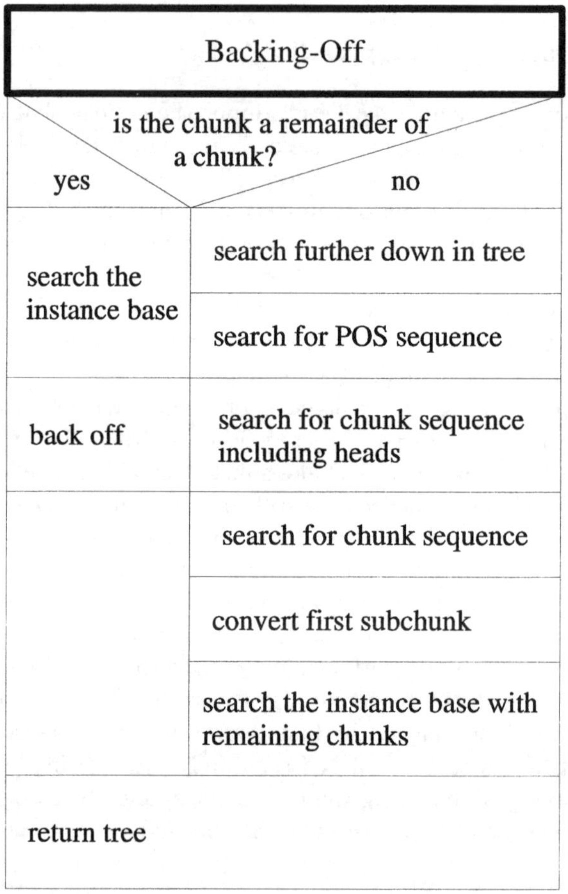

Fig. 5.79: *An overview of the backing-off module.*

```
[simpx
  [advx
    [adv dann]]
  [vafin habe]
  [nx4
    [pper ich]]
  [vven beginnen]]
[nx4
  [pper wir]]
[advx
  [adv doch]]
[advx
  [adv auch]]
[advx
  [adv schon]]
[advx
  [tod morgens]]
```

Fig. 5.80: *A chunk parse in which the second verb is erroneously attached to the first clause.*

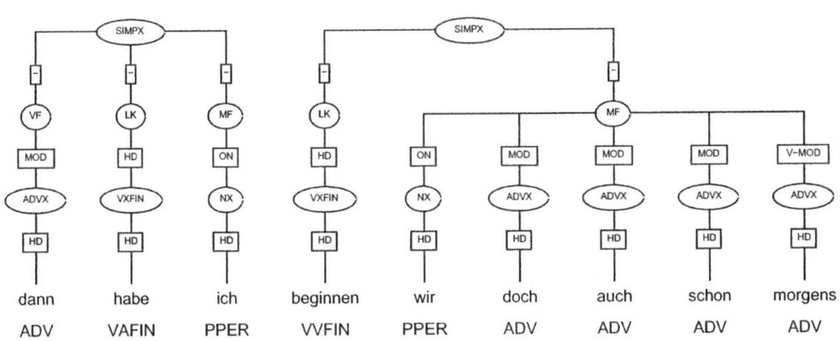

Fig. 5.81: *The syntactic analysis in which the clause boundaries have been corrected.*

all additional words are deleted along with their dominating nodes from the tree. The search is restricted to a specific number of words in order to avoid an exhaustive search which might result in a very long tree from which the majority of words need to be cut off. The default setting for the number of words is 3.

The next step in backing-off, searching for the POS tag sequence, is only executed if the previous step was not successful. The search for the sequence of POS tags can be executed in the already existing POS tag trie in the instance base. By using the trie, the search can be performed more efficiently than a brute force search through the tree structures. It is, however, not the most efficient way of searching since the POS tag trie in the instance base is parallel to the word trie. It is therefore not guaranteed that all sentences that start with the POS tag "adv", for example, are represented by a single node in the trie. The reason for the parallelism of word and POS tag trie lies in the main use of these tries in searching the instance base using weighted omission. If the POS tag trie were organized in such a way that identical POS tags at identical positions in the sentence were collapsed into one node, it would be impossible to switch from the word level to the POS tag level and back. This problem is exemplified by the two sentences (89) and (90) in Figure 5.82: if the adverb in both sentences were represented as one node in the POS tag trie, it would be impossible to say to which node in the word trie the parser should return.

(89) ich kann dann ab dem neunzehnten
I can then from the nineteenth
pper vmfin adv appr art nn
'I can after the nineteenth then'

(90) ich kann gar nicht klagen
I can at all not complain
pper vmfin adv ptkneg vvfin
'I cannot complain at all'

Since creating a second POS tag trie for searching POS tag sequences would consume too much memory in comparison to the gain in processing time, the parser therefore executes the latter search also on the POS tag trie of the instance base at the cost of slightly higher processing times.

The next step after an unsuccessful search for the POS sequence is the search for the sequence of chunks of the sentence. During training, chunk weights are calculated and the weighted chunk sequences are stored in a trie. This trie is now used for finding an identical chunk sequence in the training

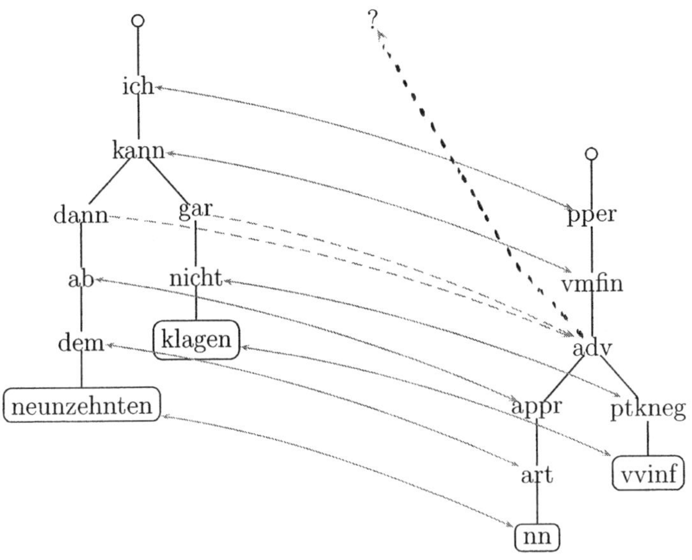

Fig. 5.82: *A modified POS tag trie in which the adverbs of both sentences are represented by one node.*

data. The search is conducted in two steps. In the first step, identity is defined as having identical chunk labels and identical chunk heads. Only if this strategy fails to retrieve a tree, the second step is performed, in which identity is established based only on the chunk labels, and not on the chunk heads. Thus, sentence (91) is identical in its chunk sequence, including the head words of the chunks, to sentence (92) as well as to sentence (93): they all share the following chunk sequence:

nx4(ich) vvfin(buche) nx1(Flüge)

(91) ich buche die Flüge
I book the flights
'I will book the flights'

(92) ich buche alle Flüge
I book all flights
'I will book all flights'

(93) ich buche alle unsere weiteren Flüge
I book all our further flights
'I will book all our further flights'

If only the chunk labels are compared, i.e. if the chunk sequence is "nx4 vvfin nx1", sentence (91) is also identical to sentence (94) or to sentence (95).

(94) ich kläre das
I clear up that
'I will clear that up'

(95) es gibt einen konkreten Anlaß
it gives a concrete reason
'there is a concrete reason'

If the search for an identical chunk sequence succeeds, the corresponding tree is used as the most similar tree and is then adapted to the input sentence. Since the parser searches for sequences of maximal chunks, the input sentence and the sentence from the instance base may have different structures within the chunks. The input sentence (96), for example, is identical in its chunk sequence, including the chunks' head words, to sentence (97).

(96) ab Donnerstag bin ich wieder hier
from Thursday am I again here
'from Thursday on I will be back'

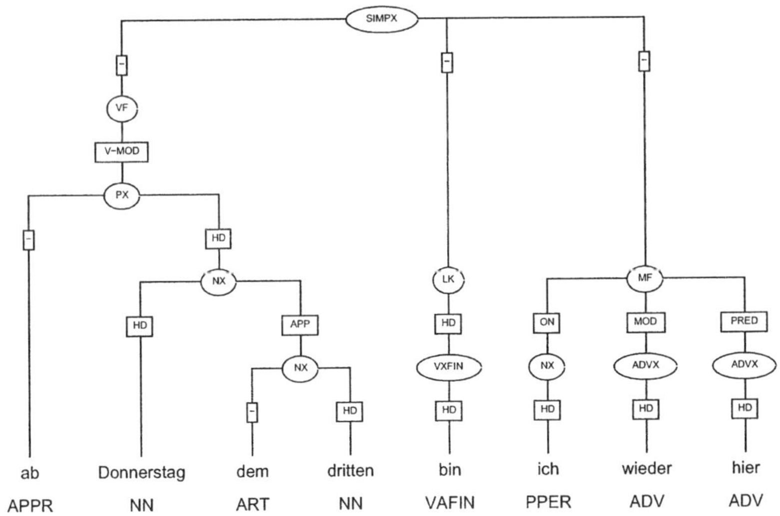

Fig. 5.83: *The analysis for sentence (97).*

(97) ab Donnerstag dem dritten bin ich wieder hier
from Thursday the third am I again here
'from Thursday the third I will be back'

The prepositional phrase in sentence (97), however, contains a complex noun phrase (which is analyzed as a single noun chunk by the chunk parser). Thus the tree structure, which is shown in Figure 5.83, is more complex than the correct tree structure for sentence (96). For this reason, the phrases that correspond to the chunks with the differing structure need to be replaced by phrases that match the input structure. So, in the example above, for example, the subtree of node NX with yield "Donnerstag dem dritten" needs to be replaced by a noun phrase tree for "Donnerstag". The new analysis for the latter phrase is copied from a tree in the instance base containing this phrase. The analysis for sentence (96) thus results in the tree structure shown in Figure 5.84.

If all of the methods described above fail to find an analysis for a chunk, the first subchunk is split off and converted into the pointer-based representation. The remaining chunk structure is again presented to the module that searches in the instance base, and if this search does not result in an analysis, the chunk structure is passed through the steps in backing-off.

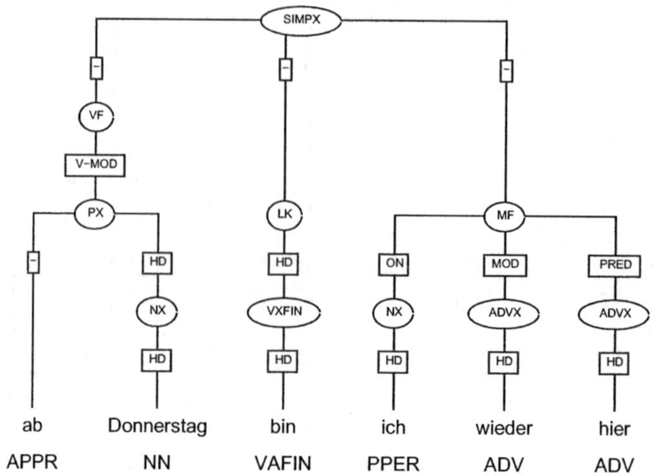

Fig. 5.84: *The analysis for sentence (96).*

Almost all of the search strategies described in Section 5.5 as well as in this section are deterministic. The only exceptions are the search for a longer tree and the search for the POS sequences. Both search strategies, however, are invoked only in the cases where there was no result from the search in the instance base. Additionally, the search for a longer tree is restricted by the maximal number of additional words in such a tree, and the search for POS tags is restricted by the structure of the POS tag trie. As a consequence, the resulting parser shows a very efficient behavior in the annotation of large amounts of data (cf. Section 6.4.3 for a detailed analysis).

5.9 Summary

In this chapter, we introduced a *memory-based parsing* algorithm, MBP. Since the definition of full parsing including function-argument structure as classification is not straightforward, we first of all considered the most widely used approach of cascaded classifiers, where each classifier is responsible for recognizing only specific linguistic phenomena. However, it is clear that such an approach is only feasible if the target annotation is relatively flat and contains only severely restricted recursive structures. In light of this, an approach that considers the complete tree structure as the goal of one classification step was introduced.

This decision necessitates certain modifications of the basic memory-based learning approach: classification results cannot be directly used as the parser's final output. If these were used, the parser could only correctly annotate sentences that are part of the training corpus. Therefore, the tree found by the memory-based algorithm must be adapted to fit the input sentence. This procedure is only possible because the classes, i.e. the syntactic trees, contain internal structure, allowing the parser to omit parts of the annotation.

Going from the sequence of words directly to the complete syntactic annotation is an extremely complex task. For this reason, it is necessary to base the decision about the most similar sentence on as much information as is available. MBP therefore uses a POS tagger, a tag fixer, and a chunk parser as preprocessing steps, and extracts information on word sequences, POS tag sequences, and chunk sequences from the resulting annotations. The former two types of information are stored in two interlinked prefix tries so that they can be searched efficiently.

If the search in the instance base does not result in a complete match, the parser will invoke an omission module, which tests whether it can find a similar sentence in the instance base either by reverting to the POS tag trie, by omitting a word or a phrase in the instance base, or by omitting a word or a chunk in the input sentence.

An important component in any memory-based learning system is the weighting of features as the use of irrelevant features can easily lead to a significant decrease in classification accuracy. Since MBP uses a flexible number of features, the exact number depending on the number of words in a sentence, it is impossible to use standard weighting approaches. Therefore, a weighting scheme is introduced which is based on the cost of modifying the syntactic tree to match the input or on modifying the input in order to find a match in the instance base. The cost of modifying a tree structure is based on the number of differences between the original and the modified tree, the cost of modifying the input sentence is based on the frequencies of both the original and the modified sentence. Both types of weights are extracted from the training data in the learning module.

In cases where the parser cannot find any sentence in the instance base judged to be sufficiently similar to the input sentence, the parser resorts to a backing-off strategy. During this phase, different types of information are used that are less reliable than the word or POS tag sequences. The backing-off strategy involves the search for a longer tree that can be shortened to match the input sentence, the search for the POS tag sequence without any access to lexical information, the search for chunk sequences, and the search for subchunks if the complete chunk could not be found.

By using the strategies described in this chapter, the memory-based parser MBP assigns a syntactic analysis to any input sentence. Thus, the parser is very robust. In cases for which no complete analysis could be found, the parser resorts, in keeping with the general approach to robust parsing, to assigning incomplete information to the input sentences. Since (almost) all of the search strategies described in this chapter are deterministic, the resulting parser is not only robust, but also very efficient.

Chapter 6
Empirical Evaluation

The evaluation of NLP systems serves mainly two aims: firstly, the evaluation should give an indication of the quality of the system when performing on previously unseen data, therefore serving as an indication of how well the system will perform in actual applications. Secondly, the evaluation needs to allow the comparison of different systems that perform the same task.

An evaluation is, in general, performed on test data, i.e. data that are of the same domain as the training data but that were not used in training. These data along with their syntactic annotation constitute the *gold standard* against which the parser's analyses are judged.

The evaluation methodology of parsers has become an important issue in recent years (cf. (Carroll et al., 1998) for an overview). The simplest measure, which is at the same time to most difficult to achieve, is the *exact match*. This measure counts the number of parser analyses that are identical to the gold standard. However, parsers often differ from such gold standards, especially when they are based on manually written grammars or when they adhere to specific grammar formalisms different to the one underlying the annotations of the gold standard. For this reason, an evaluation metric is needed that makes it possible to reliably compare different parsers even if they assign different linguistic analyses to specific phenomena. Additionally, the evaluation metric needs to assign at least some merit for partially correct analyses.

In 1991, the workshop "PARSEVAL" resulted in the proposal of the PARSEVAL evaluation metrics based on recall and precision (Black et al., 1991). Although these measures were initially a compromise for all those involved in the workshop, they have since become a standard for evaluating parsers.

During the last decade, however, it has become evident that these measures tend to favor specific types of annotation, while, at the same time, harshly punishing specific error types. Since these measures were designed with regard to parsing architectures that have complete parses as their goal, they pose a problem for robust, partial parsing approaches such as TüSBL, which have become more frequent during the last few years.

We will introduce the PARSEVAL measures in more detail in Section 6.1. The evaluation of TüSBL is then described in more detail. A short description of the test settings for all the tests are given in Section 6.2 and an overview of the parser's time and memory requirements in Section 6.3. Since the PARSEVAL measures are still considered the standard metrics for evaluating parsers, we will conduct an evaluation of TüSBL based on these metrics in Section 6.4. Section 6.5 will provide an analysis of the errors that TüSBL makes. We will then present problematic cases for partial parsers when the PARSEVAL measures are used, using TüSBL as an example, and propose a different approach to evaluating such parsers based on a dependency-based representation of the gold standard and the parser output. The new approach will be described in Section 6.6, and in Section 6.7, TüSBL's analyses will be evaluated based on dependencies, and the two evaluation approaches will be compared. The chapter finishes with conclusions, presented in Section 6.8.

6.1 Standard Evaluation Metrics

There are four different metrics defined by PARSEVAL:

Exact Match. The exact match is the percentage of sentences whose analysis is identical to the one in the gold standard, i.e. in the treebank. This metric is very strict since every analysis with only one wrong label will be counted as "not identical" and thus as a complete failure. In most contexts, however, this metric is not very informative as most systems that use syntactic processing as one step are built robustly enough to successfully process partial or partially correct data.

Crossing Brackets. This is a measure of how many constituent boundaries proposed by the parser violate the boundaries of the constituents in the gold standard. Thus, if the parser gives an analysis of a sentence "a b c d" that assigns a constituent to the sequence "b c" and the gold standard includes a constituent "c d", this would constitute a crossing bracket error. However, if the gold standard only contains a constituent "b c d", no crossing bracket error will be given. This measure enables the evaluation of parsers whose grammar does not coincide with that of the gold standard. In order to illustrate the extent of this problem, Black et al. (1991) report that, for the sentence "The famed Yankee Clipper, now retired, has been assisting as a batting coach.", the grammars of different major parser builders only had the following constituents in common: "[as [a batting coach]]".

Recall. Recall is the percentage of non-terminal nodes in the gold standard that were also found by the parser. If the treebank analysis contains $nr_{treebank}$ non-terminal nodes, and the parser finds $nr_{correct}$ of those non-terminal nodes, recall is defined as follows:

$$recall = \frac{nr_{correct}}{nr_{treebank}} \tag{33}$$

Labeled recall takes into account the syntactic categories of the constituents as well. Thus, instead of counting the number of correct constituents only on the basis of their yield, now the comparison for correctness also includes the comparison of the labels of the respective nodes. If there are $nr_{correct\_label}$ nodes in the parser's analysis that coincide with treebank nodes in yield and label, labeled recall is defined as follows:

$$labeled\,recall = \frac{nr_{correct\_label}}{nr_{treebank}} \tag{34}$$

Precision. Precision is the percentage of non-terminal nodes in the parser's analysis that are correct (i.e. that also appear in the gold standard). If the parser's output contains nr_{parser} non-terminal nodes, and $nr_{correct}$ of those are correct with regard to the treebank analysis, precision is defined as follows:

$$precision = \frac{nr_{correct}}{nr_{parser}} \tag{35}$$

Labeled precision is not only based on the comparison of the yield of a node but also on the comparison of the labels attached to those nodes. If there are $nr_{correct\_label}$ nodes that are correct concerning the yield of the node and the label, labeled precision is defined as follows:

$$labeled\,precision = \frac{nr_{correct\_label}}{nr_{parser}} \tag{36}$$

F$_\beta$ Measure. There is an additional metric, the F$_\beta$ measure, which is a combination of precision and recall. For many applications, there is a trade-off between precision and recall: if precision increases, recall will drop, and vice versa. The F$_\beta$ measure gives a clearer picture of a system's performance than using the mean, especially in cases where precision and recall differ significantly. The F$_\beta$ measure can also be used for optimizing a system. For this, it is often necessary to have a single number rather than two different ones. F_β is defined as follows:

$$F_\beta = \frac{(\beta^2 + 1) \times precision \times recall}{\beta^2 \times (precision + recall)} \tag{37}$$

We will follow the standard practice in parsing literature and will set $\beta = 1$ so that both precision and recall equally influence the F_β measure.

6.2 TüSBL's Test Settings

For the evaluation of TüSBL, the TüBa-D/S treebank as described in Section 5.1.1 was used as gold standard. From the treebank, approximately 67 000 trees were extracted. In order to minimize the effects of benign data splitting, *ten-fold cross validation* (Weiss & Kulikowski, 1991) was used: the set of ca. 67 000 trees was randomly split into ten folds. From these annotated trees, the sequences of words were extracted. With these data, ten experiments were performed, each using one of the folds for testing and the remaining nine folds for training. The results given in the remainder of the chapter were averaged over the results of the ten test runs.

For every test run, the sentences extracted from the treebank annotations were first sent through preprocessing, i.e. POS tagging using TnT (Brants, 1998), tag fixing, and chunk parsing using CASS (Abney, 1996). Using the information from preprocessing, the memory-based parsing module, MBP (cf. Section 5.4) assigned complete analyses to the sentences. From the results, we calculated *labeled precision* and *labeled recall*, both based solely on syntactic categories, as well as *(function-) labeled recall* and *(function-) labeled precision*, based on syntactic categories and grammatical functions. For the latter metrics, we additionally calculate the percentage of unattached constituents, which have the correct constituent label but no function label. An example of such a parser output is shown in Figure 6.1 for sentence (98).

(98) bei Ihnen dann
with you then
'for you then'

When recall is calculated for the analysis shown in Figure 6.1, based on syntactic categories as well as grammatical functions, "0:advx" is compared to "-:advx". Consequently, the node "advx" counts as incorrect since it does not have a grammatical function. Therefore, this needs to be recorded

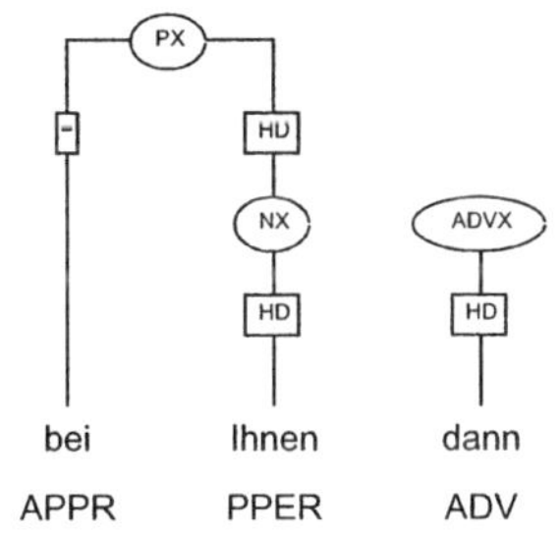

Fig. 6.1: *TüSBL could not attach the final adverb to the noun phrase.*

separately since the information provided by the parser for this constituent is incomplete but not incorrect.

In Section 5.1.2.2, we argued that grammatical functions constitute one of the most important types of information in a parser's analysis. Since many components, for example in machine translation or question answering, that build on syntactic analysis use this type of information, we will evaluate the quality of the grammatical functions that the parser assigned to constituents. For this measure, we will only consider such constituents that have been assigned a grammatical function and then count the percentage of correct grammatical functions. Thus, this measure will not give an indication of how many constituents have been assigned such functions but rather an indication of how good the assigned grammatical functions are.

In Sections 6.4.3 through 6.4.5, we will look at the performance of different components of the parser. However, significance information will not be presented for the different results. Although significance tests have been widely used in comparative machine learning experiments, there are several unsolved problems that make the application of such tests rather hazardous. Such tests generally assume the independence of the separate members of the test set, but Church & Mercer (1993) present evidence that this is not always true. Yeh (2000) points out that the most widely used tests, such as the paired *t*-test, additionally assume independence of the techniques to be compared. He suggests the use of the*sign test* for recall and *randomization tests* for precision and recall, but the machine learning community has shown no tendency to accept this procedure.

	training (∼ 67 000 sentences)	test (6 697 sentences)
time	447 sec.	115 sec.
memory	81.8 MB	51.7 MB

Table 6.1: *The time and memory requirements of TüSBL.*

6.3 TüSBL's Time and Memory Requirements

It is well known that memory-based learning in general is very efficient in training but costs in CPU time and memory during the actual classification step are considerable. This is due to the fact that training consists of only storing the training instances, while the task of generalizing over the instances is performed during classification. Thus, all the training instances need to be kept in memory to allow fast access. This is not suitable for parsing, which is often used in systems that interact with humans, where efficiency is a major design criterion.

Memory-based parsing in TüSBL does not exhibit these characteristics that are generally attributed to memory-based learning. The training step is more extensive because during this step the weights for omitting words, phrases, or chunks need to be calculated. Parsing, on the other hand, is a very efficient process since it is mostly deterministic. The parser forgoes a complete search of the search space, instead applying a best-first search strategy. In order to minimize the loss in quality, it uses a wider context than most other parsing algorithms.

The time and memory requirements of TüSBL on an Athlon 1700+ (256 MB memory) are shown in Table 6.1. The numbers for training were obtained when all sentences were used for training. The numbers for testing were obtained for one of the folds from the ten-fold cross-validation setting. TüSBL parsed the 6 697 sentences of one of the folds in 115 seconds; in other words, it parsed more than 58 sentences per second.

6.4 Constituency-Based Evaluation of TüSBL

6.4.1 *Evaluating TüSBL*

In this section, TüSBL will be evaluated as a complete system. This evaluation will give an insight into how well the system performs on unseen data from the same domain as the training data.

labeled recall (syntactic categories)	82.45%
labeled precision (syntactic categories)	87.25%
F_1	84.78
labeled recall (incl. functional categories)	71.72%
labeled precision (incl. functional categories)	75.79%
F_1	73.70
unattached constituents in recall	7.14%
unattached constituents in precision	7.60%
functional recall of attached constituents	95.31%
functional precision of attached constituents	95.21%
F_1	95.26

Table 6.2: *TüSBL's results.*

The results of the evaluation of TüSBL are shown in Table 6.2. The first three metrics concern recall, precision, and the F_β measure based on the syntactic categories of the constituents (ignoring the functional labeling), while the next three figures give the performance of the parser when a combination of syntactic and functional labels are evaluated. These measures, though, do not make a distinction between whether a constituent receives the wrong grammatical function or whether the constituent could not be attached by the parser. In both cases, the combination of syntactic and functional labels for the gold standard and the parser's output are not identical and are thus counted as incorrect. An unattached constituent leads to at least one other incorrect constituent since the node that should dominate this constituent consequently shows the wrong yield. For this reason, we also give the percentage of unattached constituents, i.e. the percentage of root nodes which have an equivalent non-root node in the gold standard. These numbers show that a considerable number of constituents could not be attached.

The numbers for precision are considerably higher than for recall for both the syntactic evaluation and the evaluation on both syntactic and functional labels. This, in combination with the high percentage of unattached constituents, is an indication that the parser could not find a spanning analysis for sentences in all cases. If such a spanning analysis was found, the parse is reliable.

The last two lines in Table 6.2 give an evaluation of the functional labeling of constituents that could be attached to a higher constituent. We have

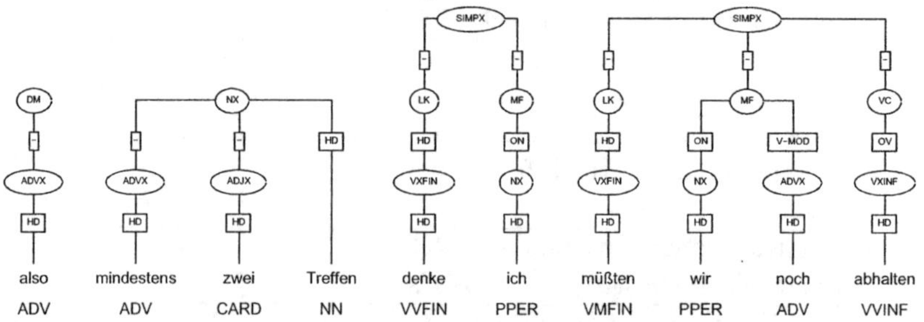

Fig. 6.2: *An example of a sentence for which MBP could only find a partial analysis.*

previously explained in all cases that unattached phrases result in low precision numbers since the unattached root node does not contain the correct grammatical function. Figure 6.2 gives an example for a partial analysis of sentence (99).

(99) also mindestens zwei Treffen denke ich müßten wir noch abhalten
so at least two meetings think I should we still hold
'so I think we still need to have at least two more meetings'

Here, the parser could not attach the noun phrase "mindestens zwei Treffen" to the remainder of the sentence "müßten wir noch abhalten". When analyzing precision based on syntactic categories and grammatical functions, the root node of the noun phrase would count as incorrect since it does not carry the grammatical function OA, which it would be assigned if it were attached. Consequently, in the analysis shown in the last two lines in Table 6.2, only nodes that are dominated by another node are counted, i.e. non-root nodes. Therefore, the root node of the noun phrase is not considered in the calculation, and for this example, the only incorrect grammatical function is V-MOD, which should correctly be analyzed as MOD.

The good results for the evaluation of functional labels with regard to attached constituents show that if the parser was able to find a spanning analysis rather than separate analyses on the phrasal level, the quality of the assigned grammatical functions is very high. Since, for this evaluation, the parser was trained on a rather small data set, it is expected that the parser will find similar instances for a higher proportion of the input sentences if it is trained on a sufficiently larger data set. In this case, the proportion of sentences reliably analyzed on the functional level will also increase, considerably improving the performance.

task	accuracy	standard deviation
POS tagging	96.9%	0.52
grammatical functions	95.2%	0.29
phrasal categories	92.1%	1.37

Table 6.3: *The results for parsing based on Markov Models (Brants, 1999*b*, pp. 107, 118, 127).*

In the following three sections, we will take a closer look at the performance of the different system components.

6.4.2 *Comparison to Other Parsers Evaluated on TüBa-D/S*

There exist two parsers that have been trained and tested on TüBa-D/S data: the parser of Brants (1999*b*) and of Ruland (2001). In this section, the performance of TüSBL will be compared to these two parsers. It is, however, important to point out that both evaluations have been performed on an older and smaller version of TüBa-D/S.

The parsing approach employed by Brants (1999*b*) is based on Markov Models, which can be used for classification tasks in sequential text processing. Brants shows that this technique, which is generally used for POS tagging, can also be employed for automatically annotating higher levels of linguistic knowledge. Since Markov Models are used for the task of classification, Brant's main evaluation of the technique is performed for partial annotation, which can easily be formulated as classification tasks: POS tagging, grammatical function assignment, and phrasal category assignment. The results of Brant's parser for TüBa-D/S data (which, at the time of the evaluation, consisted of approximately 15 000 sentences) are shown in Table 6.3.

A combination of these partial parsers can also be used for interactive annotation, where the parser suggests a new node in the syntactic tree, and the human annotator confirms the choice if it is correct, or corrects the suggested grouping if it is not. In order to evaluate the quality of such an interactive parser, Brants (1999*b*) simulated the human annotator by comparing the suggested phrase to the gold standard. If the phrase is correct, it is added to the annotation, otherwise it is corrected to model the nearest correct phrase. The parser also has the option of not suggesting any phrase. If this situation occurs, one correct phrase is selected randomly from the gold standard and added to the parsing results, and the simu-

only prob. LR parser	exact match	46.3%
	labeled precision	90.2%
	labeled recall	83.5%
	no analysis	3.4%
complete system	exact match	53.8%
	labeled precision	90.8%
	labeled recall	84.0%

Table 6.4: *The results of the hybrid parser (Ruland, 2001).*

lated interactive annotation continues. The evaluation of this approach on TüBa-D/S shows that the parser suggested a new phrase in 99.9% of the cases. Out of these suggested phrases, 91.9% were structurally correct, i.e. they covered the correct daughters, and 88.7% were correct in structure and in the assigned label. These results, however, cannot be directly compared to TüSBL's results shown in the previous section because the simulation of an interactive annotation, errors of the parser were corrected immediately so that the following decision could be based on the correct annotation, whereas for TüSBL no such correction was possible.

The parser presented by Ruland (2001) is a hybrid parser that combines a stochastic LR parser with a tree transformation component. The tree transformations are based on Brill's *transformation-based error-driven learning* (Brill, 1993), they allow the replacement of complete subtrees by other tree structures. Ruland defines the term *replacement* as an operation which is inverse to substitution in predicate logic. This component enables the parser to correct errors that go beyond the local context of decisions in the LR parser. This parser was trained on approximately 20 000 sentences of an earlier version of TüBa-D/S. The results are shown in Table 6.4.

While these results are clearly better than TüSBL's results, a direct comparison between these numbers is difficult since the two parsers have been evaluated on two different versions and two different sizes of TüBa-D/S. Additionally, Ruland selected 1 000 sentences from the treebank as test set and used the remaining sentences as training material. An increase in training data, however, does not seem very promising for Ruland's parser as the training for these 20 000 sentences required approximately 14 days and resulted in a parsing table of 200 MB (p.c. T. Ruland). TüSBL, however, seems to be more robust: it could assign analyses to all sentences, while the LR parser could not find an analysis for 3.4% of the sentences. TüSBL is

labeled recall (syntactic categories)	67.37%
labeled precision (syntactic categories)	74.27%
F_1	70.65
labeled recall (incl. functional categories)	30.03%
labeled precision (incl. functional categories)	33.06%
F_1	31.47
unattached constituents in recall	3.43%
unattached constituents in precision	3.79%
functional recall of attached constituents	98.55%
functional precision of attached constituents	98.55%

Table 6.5: *The results for the word-based search.*

also faster in parsing: Ruland reports an average of 425 milliseconds per sentence for the stochastic LR parser, meaning that it can parse 2.4 sentences per second, while TüSBL reaches an average of 58 sentences per second.

6.4.3 *The Evaluation of the Word-Based Search Module*

The search in the instance base is the backbone of TüSBL; the analyses found by this component should be the most reliable. In order to test whether this assumption is true, the system was configured so that only the search in the instance base was enabled. Both the omission function and the backing-off module were disabled. Sentences that could not be found by the search in the instance base are separated into the first maximal chunk, which is then converted into the output structure, and the remaining sentence, which is then presented to the search module again. The results of TüSBL when using only the instance base search without omission and backing off are shown in Table 6.5.

A comparison of recall and precision between Table 6.5 and Table 6.2 shows that both precision and recall have dropped to less than half in the evaluation of syntactic plus functional labels. The numbers for syntactic constituents only are also lower, but the difference is less pronounced. This indicates that a large number of sentences could not be found in the instance base. For all these sentences, only the chunk parser's information was available. While the analysis on the constituent level may be correct, the chunk parser does not provide functional information, which results in the dramatically lower precision and recall numbers when the functional analysis is evaluated as well.

labeled recall (syntactic categories)	72.02%
labeled precision (syntactic categories)	77.97%
F_1	74.88
labeled recall (incl. functional categories)	42.65%
labeled precision (incl. functional categories)	46.14%
F_1	44.33
unattached constituents in recall	3.63%
unattached constituents in precision	3.94%
functional recall of attached constituents	97.91%
functional precision of attached constituents	97.90%

Table 6.6: *The results for the word-based search including omission.*

The analysis of the functional labels of the constituents attached in a tree structure show that this information is extremely reliable. The numbers here are approximately 3% higher than those for the complete system. This corroborates our hypothesis that the analyses found by the search in the instance base should be very reliable. It is, however, obvious that backing-off strategies which allow the analysis of the remaining sentences are necessary.

6.4.4 *Evaluating the Word-Based Search Including Skipping*

The next module to be evaluated is the extended word-based search, which also allows the omission of words or chunks in the input sentence, or of words or phrases in a sentence from the instance base. The expectation is that this extension of the algorithm will allow TüSBL to parse more sentences without resorting to the conversion of chunk structures into the output format. Thus, recall should be increased. The results of TüSBL when using only the instance base search including omission but without backing off are shown in Table 6.6.

The first two sections in Table 6.6 show that both precision and recall are considerably increased when the omission module is used. The differences are especially evident for the evaluation based on syntactic and functional labels, where the numbers increase by more than 30%. It is clear that recall should increase, but one might expect a slight drop in precision since the omission of parts of the sentences introduces a factor of uncertainty. The increase in precision can be explained by the improvement of the structures that were found. Chunk structures do not necessarily coincide with phrase structures in the gold standard, and the chunk information does not contain

labeled recall (syntactic categories)	82.95%
labeled precision (syntactic categories)	87.96%
F_1	85.38
labeled recall (incl. functional categories)	70.52%
labeled precision (incl. functional categories)	74.73%
F_1	72.56
unattached constituents in recall	8.36%
unattached constituents in precision	8.81%
functional recall of attached constituents	94.63%
functional precision of attached constituents	94.51%

Table 6.7: *The results for the backing-off module in a stand-alone architecture.*

functional information. Thus, the increase in precision shows that more (parts of) sentences were found by the search in the instance base, and fewer sentences had to be converted directly from chunk information.

The comparison of precision and recall for functional information with regard to attached constituents between Table 6.5 and Table 6.6 shows that there is a slight drop in performance, but that the grammatical functions that were found are still very reliable. This confirms our hypothesis that omitting words, phrases, or chunks changes the syntactic structure of a sentence only to such a degree that the original syntactic analysis is still valid.

6.4.5 *Evaluating the Backing-Off Module*

The results for precision and recall in Table 6.6 give a clear indication that a backing-off module is indispensable for this memory-based parser. However, different strategies are possible for the backing-off module (cf. for example (Streiter, 2001*a*) where the reparsing of substructures is used as a backing-off strategy). This leads to the question of the quality of the backing-off module itself, which can be tested by using the module in a stand-alone architecture. The results of TüSBL when only using only backing-off are shown in Table 6.7.

The results for precision and recall show that the backing-off module alone reaches approximately the same quality as the complete parser (cf. Table 6.2). The comparison of the percentage of unattached constituents, however, shows that fewer constituents could be attached by the backing-off

recall (syntactic categories)	85.15%
precision (syntactic categories)	89.34%
F_1	87.19
recall (incl. functional categories)	76.00%
precision (incl. functional categories)	79.65%
F_1	77.78
functional recall of attached constituents	96.56%
functional precision of attached constituents	96.48%
F_1	96.52

Table 6.8: *MBP's results in the leave-one-out test with 5 000 cycles.*

module than by the complete parser. Precision and recall on the functional labels of the attached constituents is also lower. These results show that the backing-off module is a valuable approach to parsing if used in a stand-alone architecture. However, if it is used as fall-back strategy after using the instance-based search, the results are more reliable, especially in cases where the correct annotation of grammatical functions is important for further tasks that build on the syntactic analysis.

6.4.6 *Leave-One-Out Evaluation*

In order to determine the influence of the rather limited amount of training data, an additional leave-one-out evaluation for 5 000 sentences was performed. For this test, one sentence was randomly removed from the treebank, the parser was trained on the remaining treebank and tested on the single sentence. Since training requires approximately six minutes, this test had to be restricted to 5 000 cycles. The results in Table 6.8 are quite promising. It is obvious that both precision and recall increased significantly, which indicates that the performance of the parser would increase even further if more syntactically annotated training data were available.

6.5 Error Analysis

In this section, we will give an overview of the types of errors that occur in TüSBL's analyses. Since the correctness of the parser's output depends to a very high degree on the sentences in the instance base, it is impossible to list the linguistic constructions that the parser is capable of parsing correctly. It possible that the parser will parse a complex input sentence while failing to

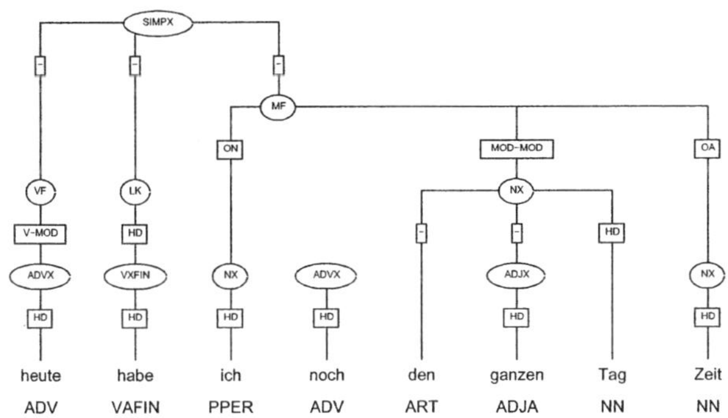

Fig. 6.3: *A sample analysis where the adverb "noch" could not be attached.*

attach the correct analysis to the subsequent simple sentence. Depending on the sentences in the instance base, the parser might find a similar sentence for the complex sentence but not for the simple one. Additionally, it is difficult to give a frequency ranking of the parser's error types since they also depend on the instance base. For this reason, we will restrict ourselves to a description of the most common error types that were found in a manual inspection of the sentences that the parser did not analyze correctly.

6.5.1 *Unattached Constituents*

One of the main characteristics of TüSBL is that if the parser cannot find an analysis for the complete sentence, it will attempt to omit parts of the sentence. This behavior leads to the presence of unattached words or phrases, which is a common phenomenon in spontaneous speech. However, not all of those cases represent phenomena of spontaneous speech – the parser uses the same mechanism for robustness. Sentence (100) is one of the sentences that could not be analyzed correctly during the ten-fold cross-validation. It was assigned the analysis shown in Figure 6.3. A comparison with the gold standard in Figure 6.4 shows that the adverb "noch" could not be attached to the syntactic tree.

(100) heute habe ich noch den ganzen Tag Zeit
today have I still the complete day time
'today I still have time throughout the day'

In general, the omission of an adverb will not lead to any problems in further processing. The error in the analysis of sentence (101), though, will

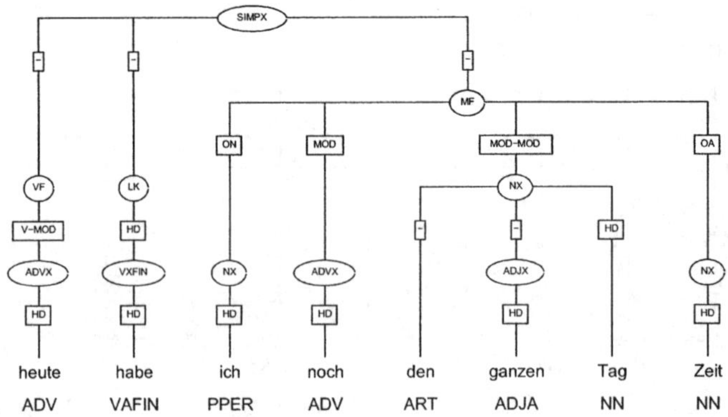

Fig. 6.4: *The gold standard for sentence (100).*

certainly be more difficult, for translation as well as for question answering. The comparison of the parser's analysis in Figure 6.5 and the gold standard in Figure 6.6 shows that, for this sentence, the participle "erledigt" could not be attached to the remaining sentence. In this case, the omitted word was assigned a higher weight, but the analysis in Figure 6.3 was still the best analysis available.

(101) dann haben wir auch das erledigt
then have we also that done
'we also have done that then'

6.5.2 *Errors as Consequences of Unattached Constituents*

In cases where the parser cannot find a similar sentence starting at the beginning of the input sentence, the first constituent is converted from the chunk annotation to the output format, and the parser attempts to find an analysis for the remaining sentence. In some cases, this leads to unexpected analyses. Sentence (102) is an example of such an incorrect analysis.

(102) da liegen wieder diverse Wochenenden dazwischen
there lie again various weekends in between
'there are various weekends in between again'

For this sentence, the parser could not find analyses for the first two words, "da" and "liegen", as shown in Figure 6.7. The remaining sequence of words was then analyzed as a complex noun phrase. Figure 6.8 shows the

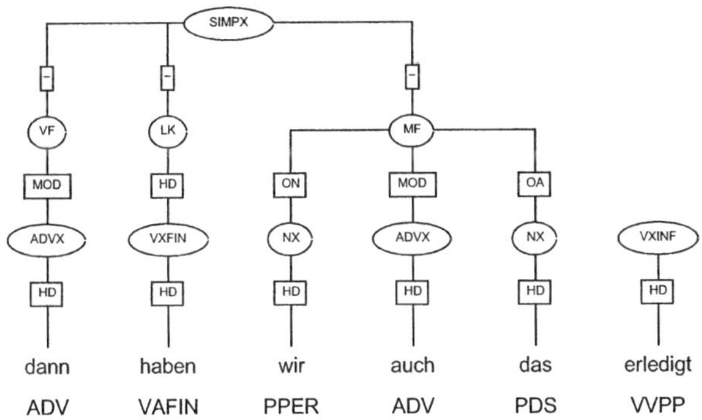

Fig. 6.5: *A sample analysis where the last chunk could not be attached.*

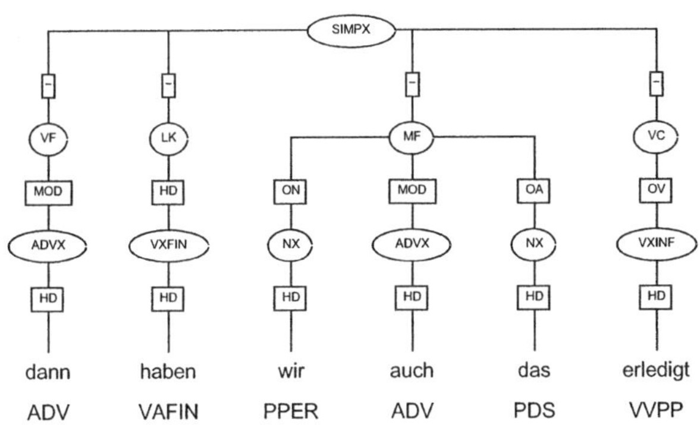

Fig. 6.6: *The gold standard for sentence (101).*

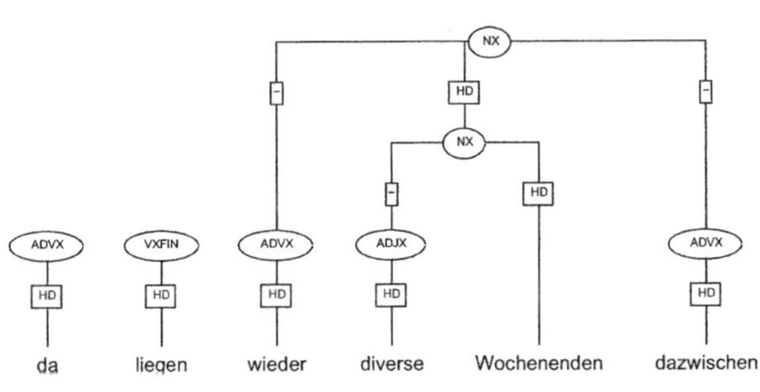

Fig. 6.7: *A sample analysis where the first two constituents were not found.*

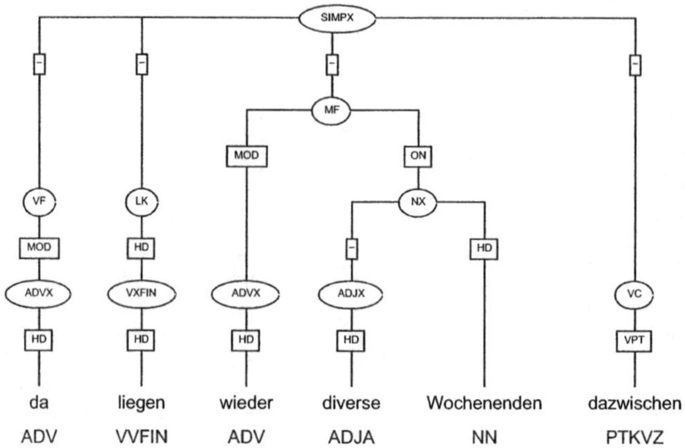

Fig. 6.8: *The gold standard for sentence (102).*

correct analysis. Here, the adverb "wieder" is analyzed as a modifier of the verb "liegen", and "dazwischen" as verb particle. It should be noted that the structure of the noun phrase in Figure 6.7 is only possible for unattached noun phrases. Thus, if the parser had been able to find a clausal analysis for the sentence, the adverb would have had to be attached to the middle field directly. Also, the verb particle could not have been attached to the noun phrase. Here, the POS tagger had assigned the POS tag PROP to "dazwischen". Only the memory-based module changed the POS tag to ADV. The error occurred because the chunk parser analyzed the word as an adverbial chunk and then the memory-based component found the resulting chunk sequence "advx nx1 advx" in the instance base.

6.5.3 *Incorrect Grammatical Functions*

The evaluation in Section 6.4.1 shows that the assignment of functional labels to constituents is very reliable if the constituents can be attached to a tree. There are, however, still errors concerning grammatical functions. An example is shown here for sentence (103).

(103) am dreizehnten August bin ich unterwegs
on the thirteenth August am I away
'on the thirteenth of August I am on a business trip'

Figure 6.9 shows that the adverb "unterwegs" was erroneously interpreted as a modifier (MOD) instead of as the predicate (PRED) of the verb

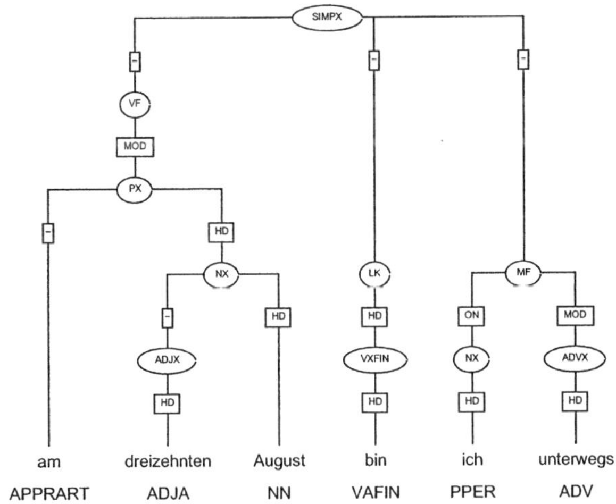

Fig. 6.9: *A sample analysis where two of the constituents received the wrong grammatical function.*

"bin", as shown in Figure 6.10. This error is due to the fact that an adverbial phrase is a very unlikely candidate for a predicate. Only approximately 7% of all predicates in the treebank consist of an adverbial phrase.

A more common error is found in the analysis of sentence (104). In the parser's analysis, as shown in Figure 6.11, the prepositional phrase "in den Februar" was interpreted as a modifier (MOD) where it should have been analyzed as the prepositional object (OPP) of the verb, as shown in Figure 6.12. Thus, the parser could not distinguish between complements and adjuncts here. This analysis was found by the backing-off step which searches for the sequence of chunks, where the parser selected the analysis of sentence (105) which was judged to be the most similar sentence in the instance base.

(104) sollen wir die in den Februar legen
should we those in the February put
'should we put those in February'

(105) kann ich die in diesem Fall benutzen
can I those in this case use
'can I use those in this case'

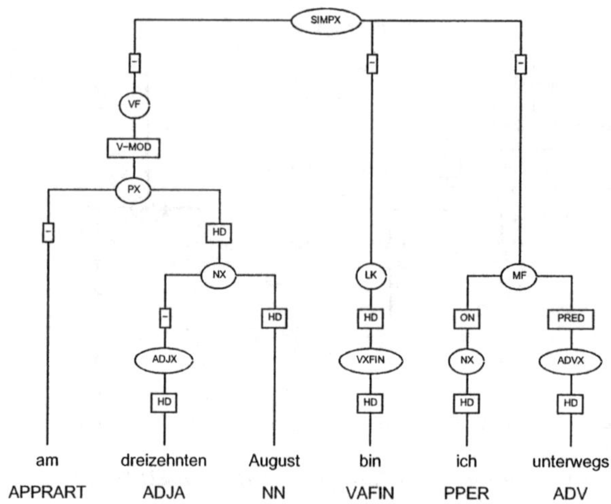

Fig. 6.10: *The gold standard for sentence (103).*

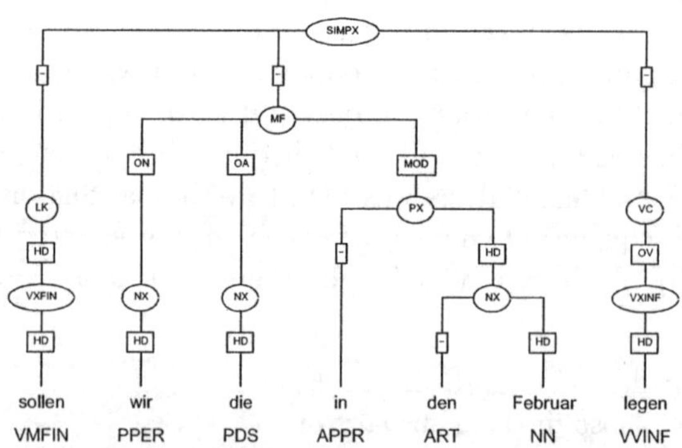

Fig. 6.11: *A sample analysis where one of the constituents received the wrong grammatical function.*

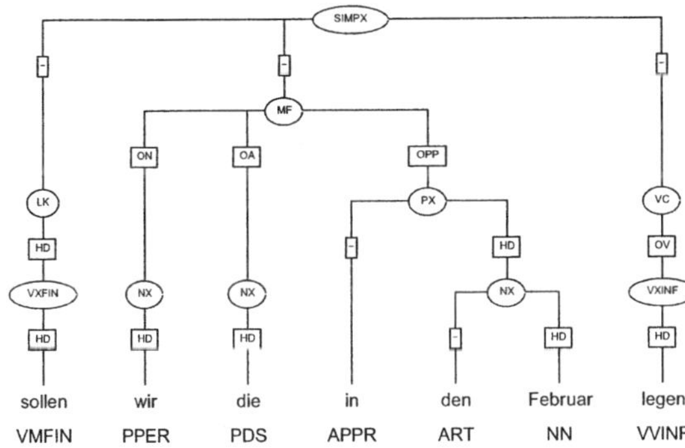

Fig. 6.12: *The gold standard for sentence (104).*

6.5.4 *Superfluous Nodes*

The parser often deletes parts of the tree structure that were retrieved from the most similar tree in order to adapt the tree to the input sentence. If the nodes to be deleted are at the end of the sentence, there is also the question of whether some of the mother nodes are superfluous. This question often cannot be answered without any knowledge of the particular annotation scheme used in the gold standard. Since the memory-based parsing module, MBP, is intended to be independent from any specific annotation scheme, the necessary information for deciding which node needs to be deleted is not available. The parser's analysis for sentence (106) contains such superfluous nodes, as shown in Figure 6.13. Here, the two ADVX nodes, node 502 and node 504 are superfluous. The correct analysis for this phrase is shown in Figure 6.14.

(106) Donnerstag abends
Thursday in the evening
'Thursday in the evening'

6.5.5 *Unrecoverable POS Tagging Errors*

The POS tagger used for the evaluation reported in this chapter, TnT (Brants, 2000), is one of the most successful POS taggers available at present. However, it still has an error rate of approximately 2%. Some of these tagging errors can be corrected by MBP if there is enough evidence for the correct analysis in the instance base. In other cases, this is not pos-

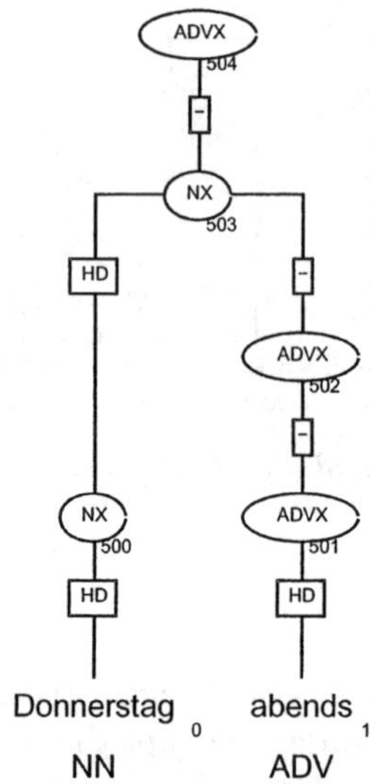

Fig. 6.13: *A sample analysis with superfluous nodes.*

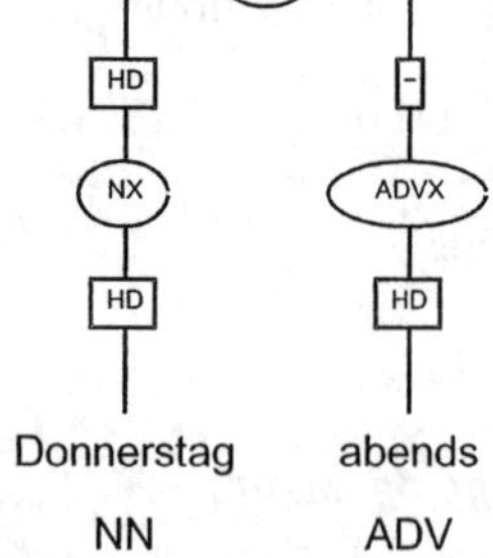

Fig. 6.14: *The gold standard for sentence (106).*

sible. An example for such a POS tagging error that leads to an error in the syntactic analysis is shown for sentence (107).

(107) ich habe hier drei auf meiner Liste stehen die alle recht
I have here three on my list stand which all pretty
zentral liegen
central lie
' I have three written on my list here which are all pretty close by'

In this sentence, the word "die" is ambiguous with regard to the tag to be assigned, possibilities being an article (ART) and a relative pronoun (PRELS), the article being the more frequent POS tag, especially in front of a substituting indefinite pronoun (PIS). Thus, the POS tagger assigned the wrong POS tag to this word. As a consequence, the chunk parser did not recognize the relative clause, and MBP could only find partial analyses (cf. Figure 6.15). The correct analysis is shown in Figure 6.16.

6.6 A Proposal for Dependency-Based Evaluation

Quantitative evaluation of parsers has traditionally centered around the PARSEVAL measures of *crossing brackets, (labeled) precision*, and *(labeled) recall* (cf. Section 6.1). However, it is well known that these measures do not always give an accurate picture of the quality of the parser's output (cf. (Manning & Schütze, 1999)), for example in cases of attachment errors (cf. Section 6.6.1). Additionally, many phenomena like negation or unary branches are ignored in the original measures in order to allow a comparison between parsers that use incompatible grammars. For this reason, research in recent years has concentrated on other types of evaluation, such as dependency-based evaluation measures (cf. for example (Lin, 1995, 1998)). We will argue here that such a dependency-based evaluation scheme is particularly suitable for partial parsers since it does not lead to disproportionately high losses in precision and recall for partial parses. Furthermore, the dependency representations are not only reliable, they are also linguistically motivated (cf. for example introductions to Dependency Grammar (Mel'čuk, 1988; Heringer, 1996)), and can be used for linguistic purposes since the treebank used for evaluation contains all the necessary dependency information.

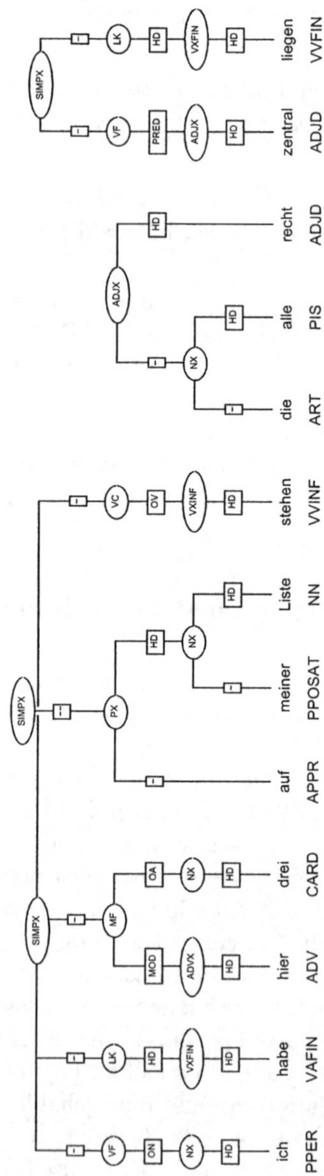

Fig. 6.15: *A sample analysis where a POS tagging error could not be corrected.*

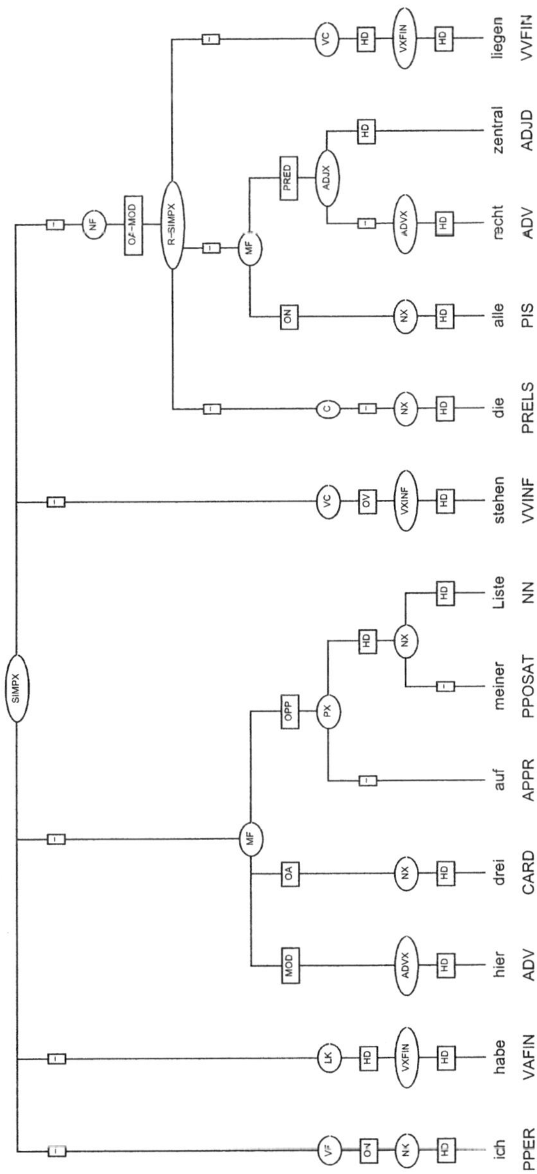

Fig. 6.16: *The gold standard for sentence (107).*

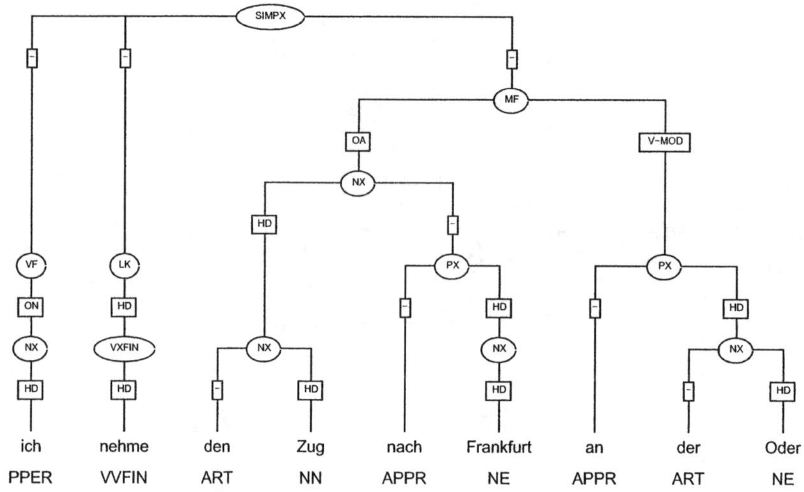

Fig. 6.17: *Wrong attachment of the prepositional phrase "an der Oder".*

6.6.1 *Deficiencies of Constituency-Based Precision and Recall*

As mentioned above, it is a well-known fact that PARSEVAL measures do not necessarily accurately evaluate the quality of a parser's output. Carroll & Briscoe (1996), for example, note that the *crossing brackets* measure is too lenient in cases of errors involving the disambiguation of arguments and adjuncts, which in some cases are not recognized as errors. The failure to attach a constituent which should be embedded n levels deep leads to n crossing errors although this constituent may not be very important to the overall structure. Manning & Schütze (1999) show that this behavior is mirrored in *precision* and *recall*, where if a constituent is attached very high in a complex right branching structure, but the parser attached it at a lower point in the structure, both precision and recall will be greatly diminished. An example of such a parsing error for sentence (108) is shown in Figure 6.17.

(108) ich nehme den Zug nach Frankfurt an der Oder
I take the train to Frankfurt on the Oder
'I will take the train to Frankfurt on the Oder'

There the prepositional phrase "an der Oder" is erroneously grouped

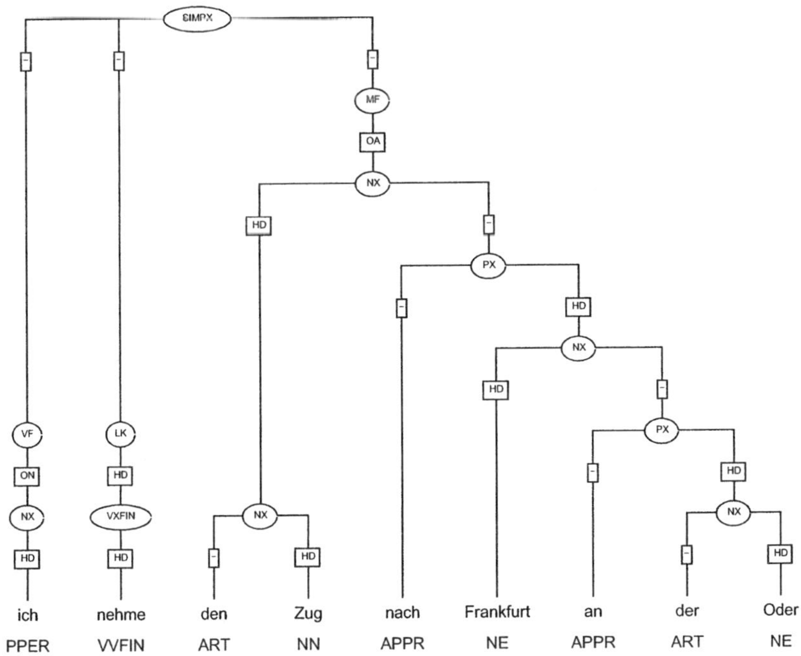

Fig. 6.18: *Correct attachment of the prepositional phrase "an der Oder".*

as an adjunct of the verb instead of being attached to the noun phrase "Frankfurt" as a postmodifier. The correct tree is shown in Figure 6.18. When using the PARSEVAL measures, the output of the parser shown in Figure 6.17 results in 10/13 = 76.92% recall[1] and 10/12 = 83.33% precision, the only error being the wrong attachment of the last prepositional phrase.

The same behavior can be observed when the parser attaches a constituent very high in a complex right branching structure instead of very low, or if the constituent is not attached at all. The latter is often the case for chunk parsers (Abney, 1991, 1996) or partial parsers (cf. for example Aït-Mokhtar & Chanod (1997)). These parsers generally aim at annotat-

[1] Contrary to the original PARSEVAL measures, we do count the root node as well , since there are different root nodes in the annotation scheme, and there are cases when a sentence in the treebank is annotated with more than one tree (for example parentheses, cf. Section 5.1.1).

ing only partial, reliably discoverable tree structures, i.e. base phrases and clausal structures. Postmodifications are generally not attached as this decision cannot be reliably taken based on very limited local context. TüSBL, the memory-based parsing algorithm presented in Chapter 5, also belongs to this group of parsers since it is designed to prefer partial analyses over uncertain ones. This strategy leads to unattached phrases, mostly at the ends of sentences, which results in high losses in precision and recall. We therefore propose to use a dependency-based evaluation as described in (Lin, 1995, 1998), where both the gold standard and the parser's output are transformed into dependencies and then compared on the basis of dependencies rather than on the basis of the constituent structure.

6.6.2 *Converting TüBa-D/S into Dependencies*

Kübler & Telljohann (2002) present an approach to convert TüBa-D/S into a dependency-based representation for evaluating TüSBL, and Ule & Kübler (2004) show that this approach can also be used for error correction in the treebank and for improving the constituency-based annotation scheme. For TüBa-D/S, the conversion of the constituent structure into dependencies is generally determined by the head/non-head distinction in the tree. The dependency relations are labeled with the functional labels of the governed constituents. Using these strategies, the tree for sentence (109) shown in Figure 6.19 is converted into the dependency structure in Figure 6.20. Here, the noun phrase "einen Bericht" is converted into one dependency relation, which denotes that the noun "Bericht" governs the article *den*.

(109) wir müssen ja noch einen Bericht abfassen über diese Reise
we need well still a report write about this journey
nach Hannover
to Hanover
'we still need to write a report on this journey to Hanover'

It is evident that the dependency structure contains two different types of dependencies: head/non-head dependencies within phrases and dependencies from the finite verb, i.e. from the head of the clause, to its complements and adjuncts, which are labeled by the grammatical functions of the governed constituents (ON, MOD, OA, OV). This is why, for example, the direct object "einen Bericht" is represented as a dependent of the modal verb "müssen" although it constitutes an argument of the embedded main verb "abfassen". However, the dependency relations among the finite verb and the (possibly multiple) non-finite verbs is explicitly annotated in

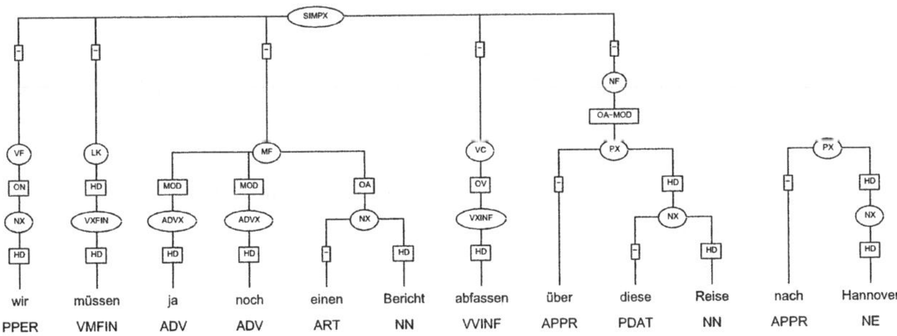

Fig. 6.19: *A tree annotated according to the TüBa-D/S treebank annotation scheme.*

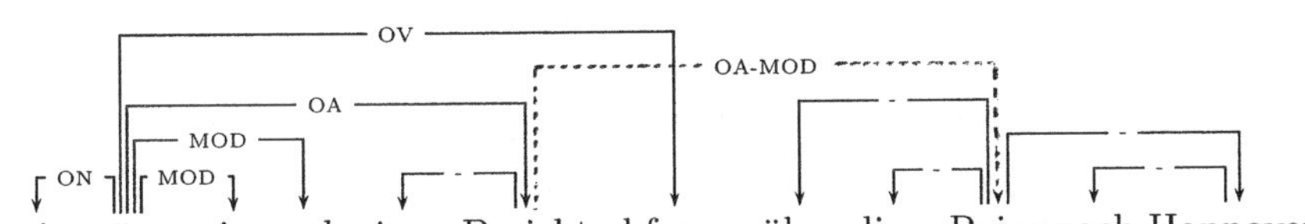

Fig. 6.20: *The dependency structure of the tree in Figure 6.19. The crossing dependency is shown as a dotted line.*

the syntactic, and therefore the dependency structure. Since information about clausal boundaries is present in the trees, even in this surface-oriented structure, the function-argument structure can be recovered.

The long-distance dependency between the direct object and its modifying prepositional phrase is modeled in the syntactic tree by the function label OA-MOD instead of by the attachment of the prepositional phrase to the direct object because the latter would have resulted in a *crossing branch*. In the dependency structure, this restriction is suspended, and the dependency is explicitly marked and results in crossing dependencies. Note that this is the only type of phrase-internal dependency that is not labeled by the head/non-head distinction but by unambiguous labels which denote their specific reference.

Since head information is present on all levels for the majority of constituents, specific decisions for determining dependency only have to be taken in the few cases when dependency relations are not clearly defined in the tree structure, i.e. for the phenomena in the following cases:

1. Conjunctions within coordinations do not depend on the head of the whole construction. Therefore, they are attached to the conjunct on their right hand side. An example of such a coordination is shown in Figure 6.21 for sentence (110), and the corresponding dependency structure in Figure 6.22. Here, the third conjunct is positioned after the verb complex and thus is assigned the label OAK.

   Similar constructions with a preposition instead of a conjunction such as in (111) are treated in the same way. In order to stress the identical syntactic status of conjuncts, all conjuncts depend on the head governing the coordination. This analysis is in contrast to Lin (1998), who relies on the *Single Head Assumption* and proposes a dependency relation between the first and the second conjunct.

   (110) das Hotel hat sogar ein Schwimmbad und ein
   the hotel has even a swimming pool and a
   Solarium dabei und einen Fitnessraum
   tanning booth [verb particle] and a fitness room
   'the hotel even has a swimming pool and a tanning booth and a fitness room'

   (111) der achte bis neunte
   the eights until ninth
   'the eighth until the ninth'

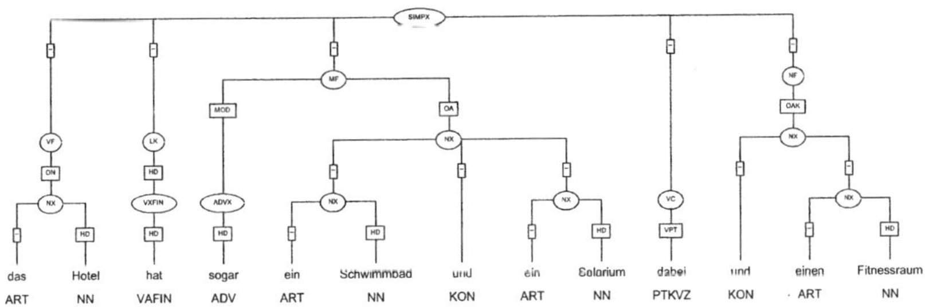

Fig. 6.21: *A complex coordination of noun phrases.*

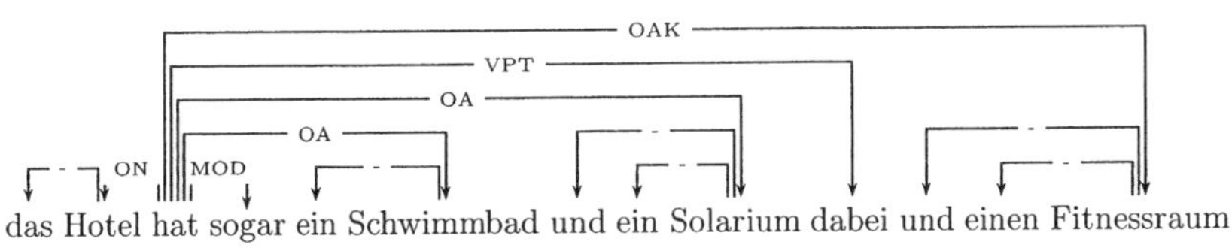

Fig. 6.22: *The dependency structure of the tree in Figure 6.21.*

2. Sentence-initial coordinative particles such as "und" (and) or "oder" (or) in the KOORD-field depend on the head of the sentence.
3. The annotation of prepositional phrases in the syntactic trees is based on the principles of Dependency Grammar (Heringer, 1996). Therefore, the noun phrase constitutes the head. For an example of the dependency structure of a prepositional phrase, see the phrase "nach Hannover" in Figure 6.20. Circumpositions and postpositions are treated similarly.
4. The single elements of proper names, split cardinal numbers, the spelling of words, and complex conjunctions in the C-field, for example "so daß" (so that), are attached on the same level carrying a non-head edge label to indicate that there is no obvious dependency relation between them. Consequently, they are treated like conjuncts in coordinations.
5. A heuristic analysis has to be applied when long-distance relations are underspecified – a MOD-MOD label (modifier of a modifier), for example, may refer to one of several modifiers in the sentence, as in sentence (112) in Figure 6.23. Here, the long-distance modifier MOD-

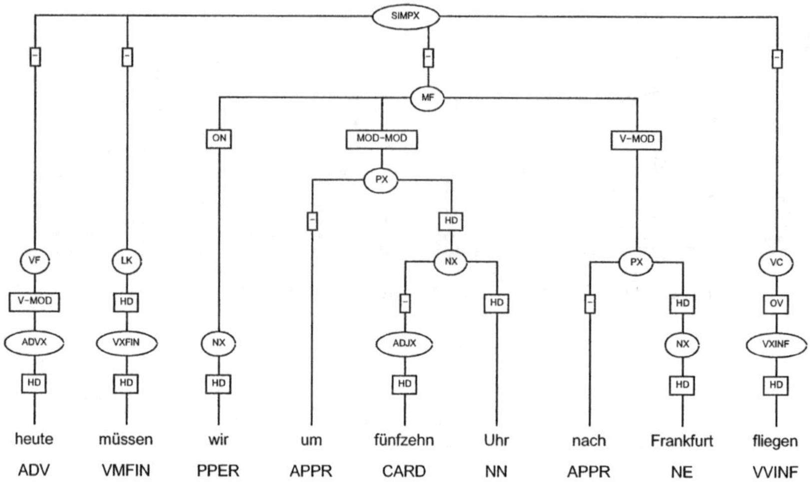

Fig. 6.23: *An ambiguous long-distance modifier: MOD-MOD.*

MOD might modify the V-MOD "heute" or the V-MOD "nach Frankfurt". A close inspection of such ambiguous sentences in TüBa-D/S revealed that in the majority of cases, the MOD-MOD label refers to the first V-MOD in the clause, or the first MOD if there is no V-MOD present. Exceptions to this rule are MOD-MODs in resumptive constructions, which generally refer to the modifier in the VF. Ambiguous OA-MODs generally refer to the closest OA in the clause. By applying these heuristics, the ambiguities are resolved in the dependency structure, as shown in Figure 6.24 for the syntactic tree in Figure 6.23.

(112) heute müssen wir um fünfzehn Uhr wieder nach Frankfurt
today need we at fifteen o'clock again to Frankfurt
fliegen
fly
'today we need to fly again to Frankfurt'

6.6.3 *Dependency-Based Parser Evaluation*

Lin (1998) proposed a procedure for converting syntactic trees from the gold standard and the parser into dependency structures. From these structures,

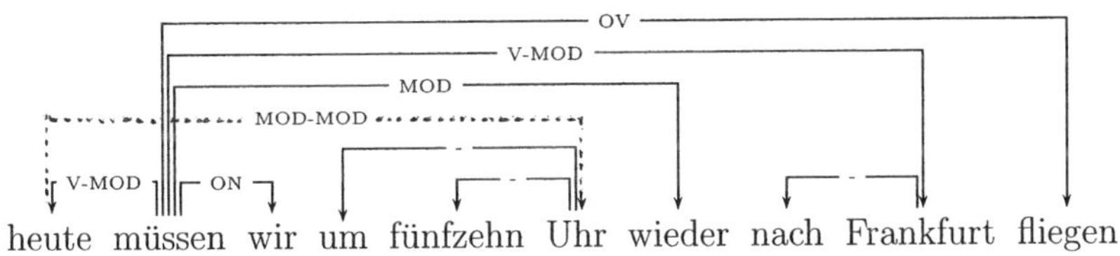

Fig. 6.24: *Resolved dependencies for ambiguous long-distance modifiers. The crossing dependency is shown as a dotted line.*

precision and recall are calculated.

A similar evaluation procedure was suggested by Bangalore et al. (1996), who first convert hierarchical phrasal constituents into chunks, and then compute the dependencies between these chunks. This is a valid approach for the Penn treebank annotation style, which assumes a completely flat annotation of complex noun phrases such as noun compounds. Parsers based on manually developed rules tend to assign more internal structure to such noun phrases, which leads to decreased precision. Reducing such phrases to flat chunks alleviates this problem of comparing these different structures. The TüBa-D/S annotations, however, assign more complex, non-trivial structures to complex noun phrases. Using the method of Bangalore et al. (1996) would therefore lead to a significant loss in information. Additionally, the flattening of phrases into chunks might introduce errors in the data in cases where conversion into chunks is not obvious, such as for the noun phrase "wichtige Konferenzen und Besprechungen" in sentence (113) shown in Figure 6.25.

(113) da haben wir noch wichtige Konferenzen und Besprechungen
then have we still important conferences and business meetings
'we still have important conferences and business meetings then'

Basili et al. (1998) developed a similar approach for Italian. But instead of parsing a sentence completely and then reducing this parse to chunks and dependencies between chunks, they apply a chunk parser combined with a module that calculates dependencies between these chunks. For this approach, the same restrictions hold as for the evaluation procedure of Bangalore et al. (1996).

The evaluation method presented in the following section is based on (Kübler & Telljohann, 2002) which in turn is based on Lin's approach (Lin, 1998). Following Lin's procedure, we first convert both the gold standard

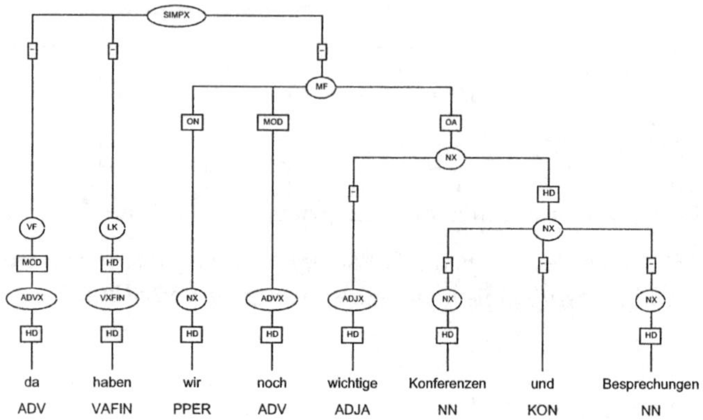

Fig. 6.25: *A complex noun phrase in the TüBa-D/S annotation scheme.*

recall	60.14%
precision	90.20%
F_1	72.16
labeled recall	56.53%
labeled precision	84.78%
F_1	67.83

Table 6.9: *The dependency-based analysis of TüSBL.*

tree and the parser's output into dependency structures and compare these by applying (labeled) precision and (labeled) recall to these dependency structures.

6.7 Dependency-Based Evaluation of TüSBL

6.7.1 *Evaluating TüSBL*

The evaluation of TüSBL based on dependencies was performed on the data that were used for the constituency-based evaluation of TüSBL presented in Section 6.4.1. The results of this dependency-based evaluation are shown in Table 6.9.

A comparison with the results of the constituency-based results in Table 6.2 shows that the dependency-based recall is considerably lower than even the constituency-based labeled recall including functional categories. Preci-

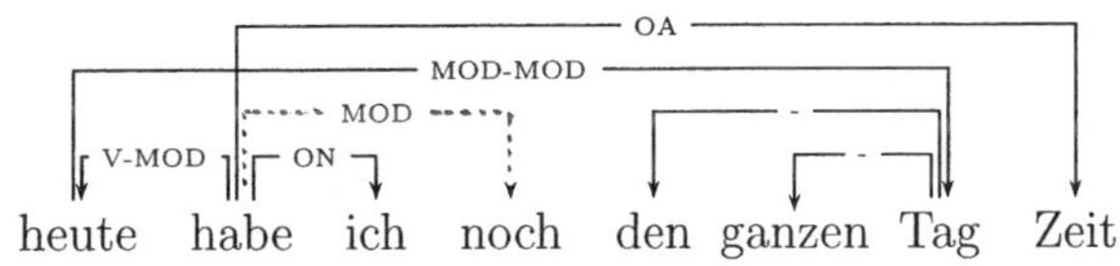

Fig. 6.26: *The dependencies for sentence (100). The dependency that the parser did not find is shown as a dotted line.*

sion and labeled precision, on the other hand are higher for the dependency-based approach than their constituency-based counterparts labeled precision for syntactic categories and labeled precision including grammatical functions.

The lower recall numbers are due to the fact that unattached words are given a higher weight since one missing dependency counts as $1/n$th in a sentence containing n dependencies. When constituents are evaluated, however, the missing constituent has an offset in several constituents covering the attached words. The higher precision rates, give a clearer picture of the quality of the grammatical functions assigned by the parser. Thus, the dependency-based evaluation gives a better indication of how useful the parser's output is for modules which rely on such an input.

6.7.2 *A Comparison of Constituency-Based and Dependency-Based Evaluation*

As described in Section 6.5, TüSBL's analyses depend heavily on the sentences in the instance base, so it is difficult to give examples of errors for specific sentences or linguistic phenomena. For this reason, we will compare the differences in dependency-based and constituency-based evaluation for error types and the examples presented in Section 6.5.

Unattached Constituents. When parsing sentence (100), TüSBL was unable to attach the adverb in the middle field. TüSBL's analysis (cf. Figure 6.3 for the tree structure) of this sentence is assigned the dependency structure in Figure 6.26, with the missing dependency shown as a dotted line. The results for different measures for the sentence are shown in Table 6.10.

	constituency-based	dependency-based
(syntactic) recall	94.74%	85.71%
(syntactic) precision	94.74%	100%
F_1	94.74	92.31
(functional) labeled recall	94.74%	85.71%
(functional) labeled precision	94.74%	100%
F_1	94.74	92.31

Table 6.10: *The comparison for sentence (100).*

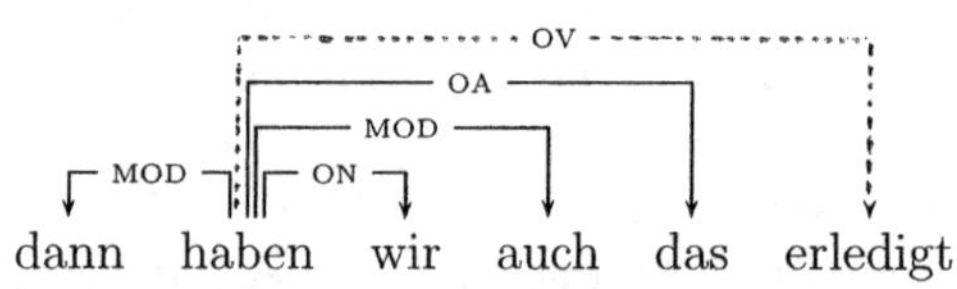

Fig. 6.27: *The dependencies for sentence (101). The dependency that the parser did not find is shown as a dotted line.*

In sentence (101), TüSBL could not attach the participle. The parser's analysis of this sentence (cf. Figure 6.5 for the tree structure) is assigned the dependency structure in Figure 6.27, with the missing dependency shown as a dotted line. The different results for the sentence are shown in Table 6.11.

For the error type of unattached constituents, dependency-based recall is generally lower since the missing dependencies represent a higher percentage of all required dependencies. Precision, on the contrary, is higher because the dependency is missing, in contrast to the incorrectly labeled constituent, and in general, it does not affect the other dependencies.

Errors as Consequences of Unattached Constituents. In sentence (102), TüSBL was unable to find an analysis for the first two chunks, an adverb and the finite verb. As a consequence, it grouped the remaining adverbs and the noun phrase into a complex noun phrase. The parser's analysis of this sentence (for the tree structure cf. Figure 6.7) is assigned the dependency structure in Figure 6.28, the correct analysis is shown in Figure 6.29, and the different results for the sentence are shown in Table

	constituency-based	dependency-based
(syntactic) recall	88.24%	80.00%
(syntactic) precision	93.75%	100%
F_1	90.91	88.89
(functional) labeled recall	82.35%	80.00%
(functional) labeled precision	87.50%	100%
F_1	84.85	88.89

Table 6.11: *The comparison for sentence (101).*

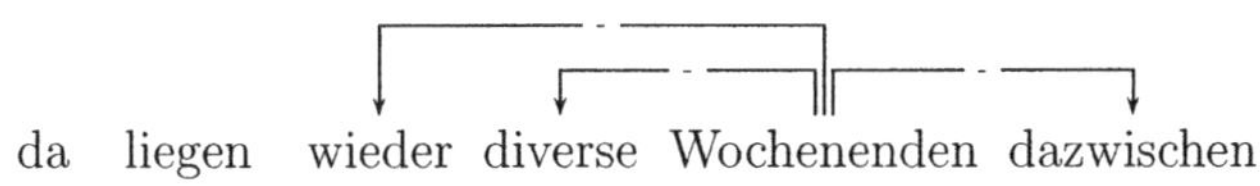

Fig. 6.28: *The dependencies for sentence (102) found by the parser.*

6.12.

In such cases where the parser's inability to find an analysis for the first constituents leads to an incorrect analysis of the remaining sentence, the dependency-based analysis shows a clearer picture of the deficiencies of the tree structure assigned to such sentences. These phenomena, however, occur very infrequently.

Incorrect Grammatical Functions. For sentence (103), TüSBL assigned wrong grammatical functions to a verbal modifier (V-MOD) and the predicate (PRED). TüSBL's analysis (cf. Figure 6.9 for the tree structure) of this sentence is assigned the dependency structure in Figure 6.30, with the incorrect grammatical functions shown in gray. The different results for the sentence are shown in Table 6.13.

For sentence (104), TüSBL analyzed the prepositional phrase as a modifier (MOD) instead of as a verbal object (OPP). TüSBL's analysis (cf. Figure 6.11 for the tree structure) of this sentence is assigned the dependency structure in Figure 6.31, the incorrect grammatical function is shown in gray. The different results for the sentence are shown in Table 6.14.

In the cases discussed here, the syntactic structure that the parser attached to the sentences is completely correct. Consequently, the syntac-

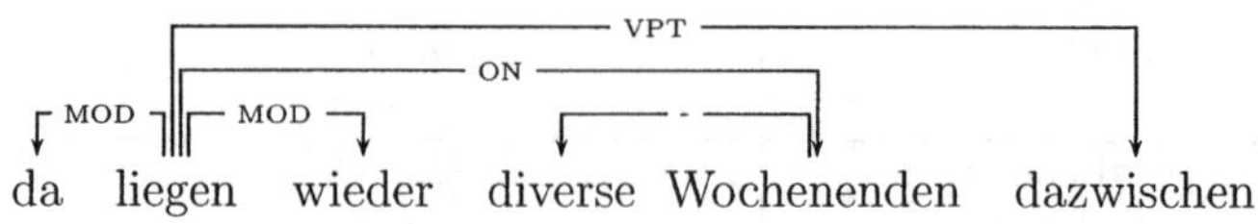

Fig. 6.29: *The correct dependencies for sentence (102).*

	constituency-based	dependency-based
(syntactic) recall	62.50%	20.00%
(syntactic) precision	76.92%	33.33%
F_1	68.97	25.00
(functional) labeled recall	37.50%	20.00%
(functional) labeled precision	46.15%	33.33%
F_1	41.38	25.00

Table 6.12: *The comparison for sentence (102).*

tically labeled recall and precision for the constituency-based evaluation and the unlabeled recall and precision in dependency-based evaluation both amount to 100%. However, if the grammatical functions are also evaluated, the dependency-based evaluation becomes stricter: now, there are fewer dependencies than constituents so that an incorrect dependency is considered more harmful.

Superfluous Nodes. TüSBL's analysis of phrase (106) contained too many nodes although the syntactic structure was, in principle, correct. This analysis (cf. Figure 6.13 for the tree structure) is assigned the dependency structure in Figure 6.32. The different results for the phrase are shown in Table 6.15.

Such cases with superfluous nodes only occur when the parser deletes parts of complex phrases – within a sentence structure, the root node is always the SIMPX node, therefore the node is part of the intended structure. From the conversion into dependencies, however, it is evident that the important information can be successfully extracted even if superfluous nodes are present in the tree structure. This is reflected in the higher numbers for dependency-based recall and precision.

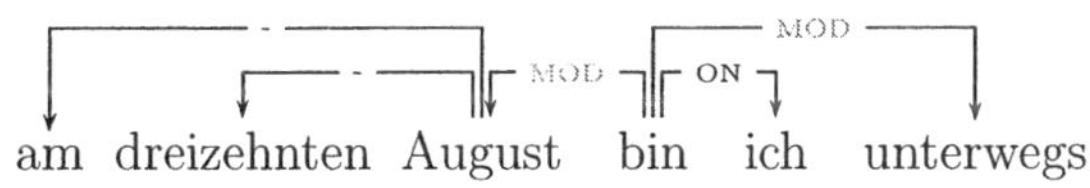

Fig. 6.30: *The dependencies for sentence (103). The incorrect grammatical functions are shown in gray.*

	constituency-based	dependency-based
(syntactic) recall	100%	100%
(syntactic) precision	100%	100%
F_1	100	100
(functional) labeled recall	87.50%	60.00%
(functional) labeled precision	88.89%	60.00%
F_1	88.19	60.00

Table 6.13: *The comparison for sentence (103).*

Unrecoverable POS Tagging Errors. For sentence (107), TüSBL was unable to correct the POS tagger's error in analyzing the relative pronoun (PRELS), which was erroneously tagged as an article (ART). TüSBL's analysis (cf. Figure 6.15 for the tree structure) of this sentence is assigned the dependency structure in Figure 6.33, with the correct analysis shown in Figure 6.34. The different results for the sentence are shown in Table 6.16.

For these types of errors, it is impossible to give a general comparison of constituency-based and dependency-based evaluation. These numbers depend on the different errors of the POS tagger and the resulting errors of the chunk parser and MBP. Thus no general tendency can be found in the comparison of the two types of evaluation.

6.8 Summary

In this chapter, we described the empirical evaluation of TüSBL. Parser evaluation is usually based on the PARSEVAL measures, of (labeled) precision and (labeled) recall. We introduced these evaluation metrics and described the test settings. After a short description of the parser's time and memory requirements, the results for the complete system as well as for single mod-

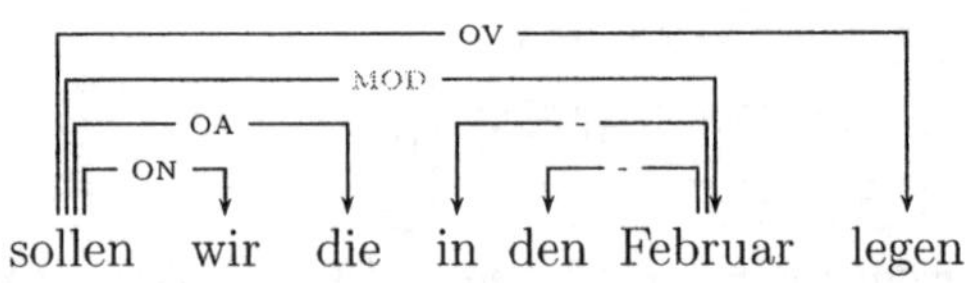

Fig. 6.31: *The dependencies for sentence (104). The incorrect grammatical function is shown in gray.*

	constituency-based	dependency-based
(syntactic) recall	100%	100%
(syntactic) precision	100%	100%
F_1	100	100
(functional) labeled recall	94.12%	83.33%
(functional) labeled precision	94.12%	83.33%
F_1	94.12	83.33

Table 6.14: *The comparison for sentence (104).*

ules of the memory-based approach were presented. The evaluation shows that TüSBL is successful in parsing spontaneous speech data, with an F_β measure of approximately 85. If just the search in the instance base is applied, both recall and precision are considerably lower as a lower percentage of sentences was found. However, the analyses found by the search in the instance base are highly reliable concerning the assignment of grammatical functions. When omission is also allowed, the coverage of the memory-based parser is increased with only a slight decrease in the reliability of the grammatical functions. The backing-off module reaches approximately the same F_β measure as the complete TüSBL system. It can, therefore, also be used as a stand-alone parser. The evaluation of the grammatical functions in the analyses of this module shows that they are less reliable than those found by searching the instance base.

Following the empirical evaluation of TüSBL, an error analysis was performed in order to find the limits of the parser in its present state as well as to find indicators for further improvement of the parsing system. The error analysis shows that the errors can be grouped into a small number of categories: unattached constituents, errors resulting from unattached

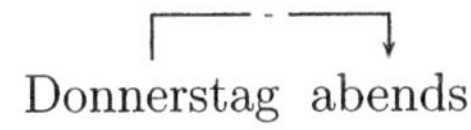

Fig. 6.32: *The dependency for phrase (106).*

	constituency-based	dependency-based
(syntactic) recall	100%	100%
(syntactic) precision	75.00%	100%
F_1	85.71	100
(functional) labeled recall	80.00%	100%
(functional) labeled precision	62.50%	100%
F_1	70.18	100

Table 6.15: *The comparison for phrase (106).*

constituents, incorrect grammatical functions, superfluous nodes, and POS tagging errors that could not be corrected by the parsing module. Of these, the first category occurs by far the most frequently.

It is well known that for some error types, the PARSEVAL measures give a skewed picture of the performance of parsers. For this reason, a dependency-based evaluation scheme was proposed. In order to evaluate a parser based on dependencies rather than on constituents, both the gold standard and the parser's output need to be converted into dependencies. The conversion algorithm for the TüBa-D/S annotation scheme was also described. Since the TüBa-D/S trees contain functional information on all levels of annotation, the conversion does not need to rely on heuristics for finding the correct governor of a word. The dependency-based evaluation of TüSBL in comparison to the constituency-based evaluation shows that recall is considerably decreased, but precision is increased. This type of evaluation thus gives a clearer picture of the parser's capabilities: the parser often cannot attach constituents for a spanning analysis, but the constituents that are attached are very reliable. In constituency-based evaluation, the picture is less clear because unattached constituents also have a negative effect on precision.

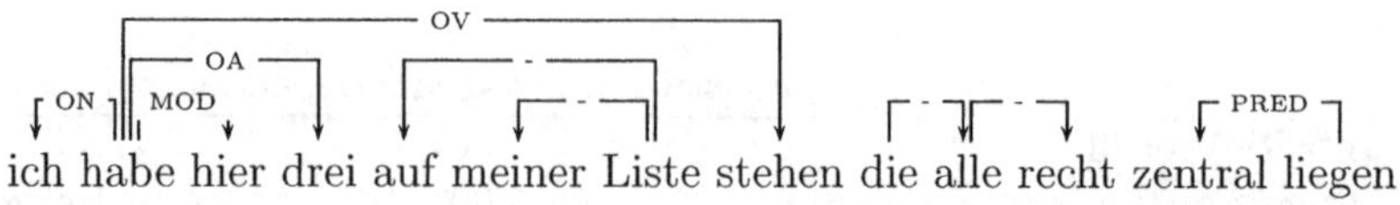

Fig. 6.33: *The dependencies for the parser's analysis of sentence (107).*

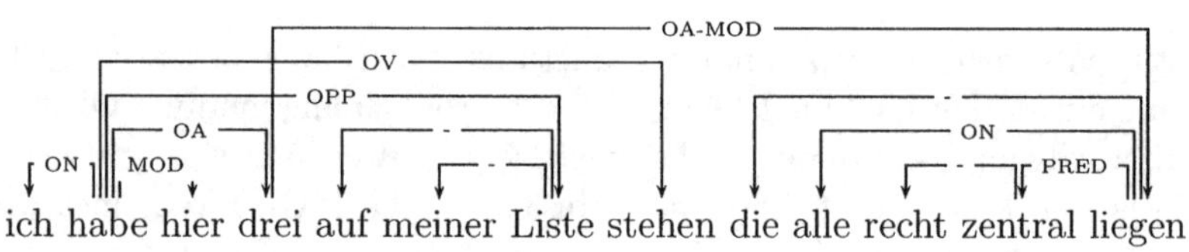

Fig. 6.34: *The correct dependencies for sentence (107).*

	constituency-based	dependency-based
(syntactic) recall	62.86%	58.33%
(syntactic) precision	66.67%	77.78%
F_1	63.34	66.67
(functional) labeled recall	62.68%	58.33%
(functional) labeled precision	63.64%	77.78%
F_1	63.34	66.67

Table 6.16: *The comparison for sentence (107).*

Chapter 7
A Comparison of Memory-Based Approaches to TüSBL

We presented the memory-based parser TüSBL in Chapter 5. TüSBL is a memory-based parser that attempts to find a complete syntactic analysis, including function-argument structure, by searching the instance base and then adapting the retrieved tree structure to the input sentence. In this section, we will compare TüSBL to some related approaches that we described in Chapters 3 and 4.

TüSBL's approach to parsing contrasts it from standard stochastic parsing approaches, which generally abstract from the complete tree structures in the training data to rules which describe local mother-daughter relations in the tree. One of the very few exceptions to parsing based on abstraction can be found in *Data-Oriented Parsing* (DOP), for which we gave an overview in Chapter 4. In DOP, the trees are not split into local rules but instead into tree fragments of varying size. TüSBL and DOP are similar in that they both preserve a more global context in the structures used in training.

TüSBL also differs from approaches to parsing within the field of *Memory-Based Learning* (for an overview of approaches in this area cf. Section 3.2). In this area, parsing is generally regarded as a pure classification task, and thus needs to be split into different subtasks, the parser consisting of a cascade of classifiers, each of which is specialized for a particular task. One such approach for finding grammatical relations is GRF, a module of the memory-based shallow parser MBSP (cf. Section 3.2).

The most similar approach to TüSBL is OCTOPUS (cf. Section 3.3), a memory-based parser that also attempts to find a parse in one step and then adapts the retrieved analysis to the input sentence. But while the underlying ideas of the application of memory-based techniques to parsing are the same, the two parsers differ in design decisions.

In the following section, we will compare the above mentioned three parsing approaches to TüSBL in order to find similarities and differences in these approaches. It would also be enlightening to compare the empirical results, but such a comparison can only be very superficial since these approaches differ either in the training and test data or in the specific task definition. For this reason, a comparison of performance based on a comparison of the evaluation metrics *precision* and *recall* would be misleading.

7.1 Comparing TüSBL and DOP

TüSBL and DOP (Bod & Scha, 1996; Bod, 1998) share a common trait that distinguishes these two parsing approaches from most others that have been developed until now: both parsers rely on trees or tree fragments that go beyond the local information present in rules. This allows both approaches to take a wider context into account when parsing non-local phenomena and thus to make more reliable decisions about such phenomena. However, the method in which this information is used is different for the two parsers: TüSBL uses the complete input sentence as well as information from the preprocessing steps in order to find the most similar tree structure and then adapts the tree to the input sentence. This approach necessitates a completely new parsing architecture. DOP, on the other hand, uses the complete trees and tree fragments that it extracts from the training data in a more conventional way, namely as rules with internal structure, i.e. a tree fragment is treated in parsing as if it were a rule $fragment\_root \rightarrow leaves$. Thus, a standard parsing algorithm can be used. The internal structure is then inserted into the final step of compiling the parse tree from the possibilities that an exhaustive search produced.

A closer look at the information that is used for parsing reveals a fundamental difference in TüSBL and DOP with regard to the role of generalization. DOP makes use of generalization since it splits trees into fragments of different size, including very local fragments of depth 1, which correspond to standard context-free rules. Since the use of larger fragments generally implies a higher probability of a derivation, the level of generalization is kept as low as possible. TüSBL, in contrast, uses generalization only if no other method succeeded in finding a similar sentence in the instance base. Generalization is only possible in the backing-off module that matches the chunk sequence of the input sentence to the chunk sequences of sentences in the instance base. Only here can fragments from different trees be combined.

The use of a higher level of generalization results in a higher coverage for DOP. TüSBL's more conservative approach to generalization should result in a higher precision for those sentences for which the parser finds an analysis in the instance base. A direct comparison of overall results, however, is not possible since the inclusion of chunk information in TüSBL's parse output distorts the picture. Additionally, the parsers have so far been evaluated on different training material – a direct comparison is made more difficult since TüSBL's performance is expected to be directly related to the amount of training data, and for DOP, scaling up to large training sets is still a difficult issue.

The level of generalization used in the two parsing approaches also gives an indication of the differences in efficiency and memory requirements. TüSBL stores only complete trees in its instance base since it generally accesses complete trees. The only exception is the search for sequences of chunks. Here, the phrases in the retrieved tree need to be replaced by phrases whose structure matches the input sentence. However, these phrases are retrieved during the parsing process from the complete tree structures. In contrast, DOP needs to store a single tree from the training data in several different versions, depending on the number of fragments that are extracted from this tree. These considerably higher storage requirements also lead to higher processing times in parsing as the search in a data base is always dependent on its size. The difference in processing times also mirrors the design decision concerning the search. TüSBL restricts itself to a heuristic search: the search in the word trie as well as the search based on POS sequences or chunk sequences only consider sentences that match in the initial sequence. Alternatively, DOP performs an exhaustive search of the search space. Only disambiguation needs to rely on heuristics. The size of the search space that is examined though, is still larger by orders of magnitude than the size of the examined search space for TüSBL.

7.2 Comparing TüSBL and MBSP

Both MBSP (Daelemans, Buchholz & Veenstra, 1999; Buchholz, 2002)[1] and TüSBL are memory-based systems in the sense that they access an instance base of training examples to assign syntactic structure and grammatical functions to an input sentence. MBSP is a cascaded memory-based parser, which first assigns POS tags and chunks to the input. This preprocessed input is then passed to GRF, the module that analyzes grammatical relations between verb chunks and non-verb chunks. TüSBL also uses POS tagging and chunk parsing information, but for TüSBL, this information is only preliminary and can be modified as soon as there is enough evidence from the instance base of complete trees.

For both parsers, the selection of the specific POS tagger and chunk parser is mainly irrelevant. Any of the available chunk parsers may be used. For MBSP, these modules need to reproduce the structure of the original annotations since these are the basis for evaluation. For TüSBL, however,

[1] We will concentrate here on the work of Buchholz (2002).

there is an additional restriction on the form of the chunk grammar: it must be capable of recognizing clauses in addition to chunks since TüSBL effects a reduction of the search space by separating input sentences according to the clause boundaries found by the chunk parser. For both MBSP and TüSBL, there is an additional preference concerning the chunk annotations. The chunks should be as close as possible to the original treebank annotations. This is not always possible since chunks are by definition non-recursive and generally do not contain postmodifiers following the head of a phrase. This poses no real difficulty for MBSP since the chunk parser which is used by Buchholz (2002) is based on a machine learning approach and will thus model the same chunk structures that have been extracted from the treebank annotations as the gold standard. For TüSBL, discrepancies between chunks and (non-recursive) phrases are generally not problematic since the chunks are replaced by the tree structure retrieved from the instance base. There is only one step in the algorithm where specific differences may cause a problem: in the backing-off step which attempts to find the chunk sequences and then replaces the corresponding phrases in the retrieved tree by phrases that model the actual chunks in the input sentence. If a chunk covers more than one phrase, the parser must be able to split the chunk accordingly. This problem, however, occurs only in very few cases and can be avoided completely when some care is applied in the design of the chunk grammar.

The main difference between TüSBL and MBSP, however, lies in the task definition: while TüSBL has as its goal the complete syntactic annotation of an input sentence, including function-argument structure, MBSP concentrates on analyzing base chunks and finding grammatical relations between such chunks. It is impossible to rank these tasks on a scale of difficulty – for both tasks, there exist different circumstances that create difficulties.

For TüSBL, the task is more broadly defined: it additionally needs to group complex phrases and fields, and it needs to determine the function-argument structure for every level. The task is made more complex by the nature of spontaneous speech, which is characterized by elliptical utterances, in which complements might be missing, by ungrammatical utterances, or by lapses in concentration, etc. This leads to atypical sentence patterns which do not generalize well. The situation is complicated even further since for German, there are no ordering regulations as there are for English. While in English, the probability of finding the subject, for example, to the left of the verb chunk is very high, the subject in a German sentence might be found with approximately the same probability to the left of the finite verb or between the finite verb and the verb complex.

A difficulty for MBSP lies in the fact that it has no access to information on clause boundaries. Thus it needs to classify each focus chunk with regard to every verb chunk in a sentence. Additionally, the system of grammatical function labels in the Penn treebank is much more fine grained than the one in TüBa-D/S. The Penn treebank, for example, distinguishes between temporal and local adjuncts, a distinction which can only be made based on the lexical heads of a phrase.

A comparison of the architectures of the two parsers reveals a more fundamental difference in the approach. For MBSP, each decision on grammatical relations between two chunks is taken independently without any access to previous decisions. It is thus possible that the parser might assign the same grammatical relation to two different chunks with regard to the same verb chunk. In contrast, TüSBL bases the decision for all grammatical functions on the complete sentence. It is thus very improbable that the same grammatical function is assigned to two different constituents. In the light of these differences, it is surprising that the recall of MBSP in comparison to precision is considerably lower, while for TüSBL, for which a drop in recall would be expected, recall and precision are much closer.

The design decisions on which TüSBL and MBSP are based, however, do not only influence the performance of the systems but also their efficiency. While TüSBL needs approximately 10 minutes for training and parsing almost 7 000 sentences, MBSP needs approximately 4 1/2 hours for training and testing on approximately 2 200 sentences[2]. This difference is, to a high degree, due to the high number of separate classifications that MBSP needs to perform for analyzing a single sentence. For TüSBL, the effort per sentence is smaller since it attempts to find the complete tree in a deterministic architecture.

7.3 Comparing TüSBL and OCTOPUS

TüSBL and OCTOPUS (Streiter, 2001*a*,*b*) are similar in their overall parsing strategy. Both parsers are based on memory-based learning without resorting to the principle of cascaded classifiers for different levels of annotation. Both parsers attempt to match the complete input sentence against

[2] We are aware that the direct comparison of these figures gives a skewed picture since Buchholz used fewer sentences for testing, but the sentences tend to be longer than those in TüBa-D/S. However, we think that the magnitude of the difference gives an indication of the actual differences.

the most similar sentences in the instance base. The tree structure retrieved from the most similar sentence in the instance base then needs to be adapted to the input sentence in a second step. Since a comparison of complete sentences leads to data sparseness problems and consequently to a comparatively low coverage of a memory-based parser, both parsers employ backing-off strategies.

But while the overall architecture is the same for both parsers, there are several important differences in the modules of the parsers. OCTOPUS, for example, uses a k-nearest neighbor approach. It retrieves the k most similar sentences from the instance base and then performs a more fine-grained search on this reduced set of sentences. TüSBL is restricted to finding a single most similar sentence. Instead of using the two-level search of OCTOPUS, TüSBL bases its comparison for similarity on different types of information: not only the sequence of words, but also their POS tags and their chunk analysis.

Where the similarity metric is concerned, TüSBL follows a more conservative approach than OCTOPUS, both for the search in the instance base and the backing-off step. While OCTOPUS bases its primary search for similar sentences on a fuzzy match based on keywords, TüSBL conducts the search in the instance base relying on the sequence of words as well as the identity of these words. Thus, it only accepts sentences that have complete sequences of words or POS tags in common. During backing-off, both parsers make use of the notion of chunks. However, OCTOPUS' strategy consists of finding the first chunk, accepting the internal structure of its syntactic analysis, replacing this chunk by its head, and performing the complete search on the shortened sentence. Since such a chunk may consist of several phrases, there is a risk that these phrases are assigned an internal structure without any reference to the main verb of the clause, while this structure may depend on the verb. TüSBL, in contrast, only accepts a sentence from the instance base as sufficiently similar if the complete sequence of chunks matches with the input sentence. Thus it is ascertained that the function-argument structure of the clause can only be decided with regard to the verb.

OCTOPUS generally relies on statistical information about pattern co-occurrences, for the keywords as well as for the definition of chunks. TüSBL on the other hand, bases its decision on linguistically motivated chunks. This difference may be due to the different languages that were used for evaluation and and which therefore also guided the development of the parsers. Since Chinese contains a high number of non-local structures, an approach based on sequential chunks seems less applicable than for German. For Chinese, the relative frequencies of patterns consisting of single words throughout the sentence might provide more information.

Both parsers use weights for the selection of the most similar sentence from the instance base. OCTOPUS assigns weights to all words in a tree structure. These weights signify the *importance* of a word for a tree structure. They are distributed equally over daughters of a node, starting with the weight of 1 for the root node, so the highest importance is given to words which are close to the root and have few sister nodes (and whose ancestors also have few sisters). TüSBL, in contrast, assigns weights that model the *cost* of omitting words, phrases, or chunks. The weights for omission in the sentences from the instance base are based on structural similarity of the trees structures. Thus, if the deletion of a word from the sentence results in major changes in the tree structure, the word will receive a high weight. This weighting method gives an indication of the word's influence on the tree structure, but such weights can only be calculated if there exists a sentence in the training data which is identical to the sentence in question except for the deleted word. If there is no such sentence without this word in the training data, the word will receive the maximal weight 1. This approach results in data sparseness problems since it is highly unlikely that all variants of a sentence can be found in the training data. The weighting scheme used for OCTOPUS is more robust in terms of coverage. It is, however, unclear whether the equal distribution of a weight over all daughter nodes is a useful measure for the importance of a word when the parser is applied to different annotation schemes.

Another difference between the two parsers concerns the treatment of words in the input sentence that could not be matched during the retrieval of the most similar sentence. OCTOPUS attaches these words to the tree structure, generally to the lowest constituent. This is only possible if the segmentation of the input into sentences is reliable. For the spontaneous speech input, for which TüSBL was mainly designed, this prerequisite does not hold. It is for this reason that TüSBL refrains from attaching such words or phrases. Since there is not enough evidence to include these fragments in the sentence, TüSBL's preference is for partial parses.

TüSBL follows the same strategy of not attaching chunks for which there is no evidence during the last step in backing-off. Instead, it converts the first chunk into the output structures and continues to parse the remaining sentence. OCTOPUS, conversely, assigns the first chunk an internal structure, reduces it to its head, and attempts to analyze the complete sentence with only the head word instead of the chunk. This step can only succeed if the instance base contains such reduced tree structures. Thus, a single tree from the training data needs to be stored in many different forms, basically covering all combinations of reduced constituents. In this respect, OCTOPUS shows a similar generalization strategy to DOP. Since a complete coverage of all different generalizations would result in an unmanageably large instance base (cf. the experience with DOP in Chapter 4), Streiter (2001*a*) restricts the number of different generalizations over one tree to approximately 20. However, it remains unclear according to which criteria these 20 generalizations are selected[3].

An important feature of both parsers is the adaptation of selected tree structures to the input sentence. Here, TüSBL again prefers more conservative methods: TüSBL only allows the deletion of parts of the tree structures if a longer sentence was retrieved or if words or phrases were omitted during the search. OCTOPUS allows more widespread changes to the tree structure. If there is a mismatch between a word and the respective POS tag from the instance base, either the POS tag and the semantic role of the word are modified, or a complete sub-sequence of the sentence is reparsed. This means that the parser no longer has access to the complete sentence as a context which might result in less reliable results.

The comparison of the two memory-based parsers shows that TüSBL restricts itself to more reliable search and adaptation strategies. If there is not enough evidence for attaching a constituent to a clause structure, TüSBL prefers partial analyses. OCTOPUS, on the other hand, attempts to find analyses spanning complete sentences by allowing more severe changes in the tree structure, which should result in a higher coverage. A comparison of differences in recall and precision of both parsers might give a clearer picture, but unfortunately, Streiter (2001*a*) only presents the F_β measure with no separate values for precision and recall.

[3] The higher storage requirements also influence the parser's efficiency. Streiter (2001*a*) reports a mean processing time of 0.12 seconds per sentence, i.e. 8.3 sentences per second. TüSBL processes slightly more than 58 sentences per second. These figures, however, cannot be compared reliably since the parsers were evaluated on different data and on different machines. Additionally, OCTOPUS was implemented in PERL, while TüSBL is written in C.

7.4 Summary

In this chapter, a short comparison of four of the major approaches to memory-based (partial) parsing were compared. Since the parsers either differ in their task description or in the data sets on which they were evaluated, or in both, a comparison of the empirical results can only show tendencies. The comparison shows that memory-based approaches are well suited to parsing but that the optimal design of such a parser depends on the task as well as on the characteristics of the data to be covered.

DOP, which employs the most extensive search, reaches the highest performance (but also see the restrictions of such a comparison described above), although it lacks efficiency and scalability to large training sets. MBSP is optimized to recognize grammatical relations for English, TüSBL gives syntactic analyses including function-argument structure for German spontaneous speech, and OCTOPUS is optimized for Chinese newspaper sentences. It seems that the most important feature of a language, which necessitates the most differences in the memory-based parsing architecture, is the degree of configurationality. The higher the freedom in word (or phrase) order, the more complex the changes are in the respective syntax trees.

Chapter 8
Conclusion and Future Directions

Although syntactic parsing is one of the areas that has been approached very early on in the history of NLP, it is still far from being a solved problem. The major problem with standard probabilistic parsers is that the probabilities generally model only a very local context in the already existing tree fragment, while the information which is needed to disambiguate specific attachment ambiguities might require a wider context. Thus, recent approaches attempt to include as much information as possible without having to estimate too many parameters. Estimating a large number of parameters is difficult since the number of parameters correlates with the size of the annotated training data that is needed.

In this book, we presented parsing approaches that employ the machine learning paradigm *memory-based learning*, which has been successfully applied to problems in NLP in general as well as in parsing, as we have shown in Chapter 3. Memory-based learning is based on the assumption that decisions are taken by relying on previous experiences. This bias is helpful in the analysis of subregularities and exceptions, which constitute frequent phenomena in the syntactic analysis of sentences and which generally pose a problem for statistical approaches to parsing. Memory-based learning, however, is generally defined as classification, i.e. as the choice of a specific class from a set of classes. This assumption does not translate smoothly to the problem of parsing. For this reason, a number of adaptations of the original memory-based learning algorithm were presented.

Apart from giving an introduction to the machine learning paradigm of memory-based learning and an extensive overview of the literature in the area of applying memory-based learning to parsing, including DOP, we also presented a novel approach to parsing spontaneous speech which accesses the problem from a different direction. Instead of starting with the least possible amount of information and adding as much information as is possible or necessary, our parser, TüSBL, attempts to include all readily available information for the decision on the syntactic analysis for a sentence. By readily available information we mean the types of information that are either present in the sentence to be analyzed, i.e. the sequence of words, or that can be acquired efficiently by standard methodology without any major effort. The types of information which can be presently acquired without major effort are POS tagging and chunk parsing information. For both methodologies, there exist very efficient off-the-shelf implementations, and in the case of the POS tagger, enough training data.

The use of the sequence of all words as well as POS tags and chunk parses is a consequence of a parsing approach which attempts to decide on the complete tree structure in a single step. This decision is difficult in the best of circumstances, and it requires the use of all available information. Since the different types of information would translate into a large set of parameters, a probabilistic method is not an ideal approach. For this reason, memory-based learning was chosen as the underlying methodology. The evaluation of this parser and its comparison to other memory-based parsers show the validity of the general approach. Further research is needed to show whether this parser can also be successfully applied to the syntactic annotation of other text types, annotation schemes, or domains.

All memory-based approaches to parsing can be grouped into two classes: one class of approaches concentrates on exploiting the inventory provided by memory-based learning from its original form to its fullest. In such approaches, the treatment of interdependent decisions and of long-distance relations concentrates on optimizing the architecture of single specialized classifiers, and the selection of the features and parameters used in the classifiers. These approaches share the advantage that they use a standard implementation, which can be adapted to new domains or to new languages without any implementation efforts. As demonstrated in Section 5.2, however, parsing is a complex task which needs to model an interaction of many more decisions, many more types of information, and wider context than are generally required of other tasks in NLP. For this reason, other approaches to parsing in the memory-based paradigm concentrate on the modification of the original MBL algorithm to adapt it to the problems specific to parsing. A comparison of these approaches shows two main tendencies: the stress on linear information and the use of larger syntactic fragments. Both tendencies can also be found in other parsing paradigms (cf. for example (Kathol, 2000; Charniak, 2001).

Linear information is often lost in probabilistic parsers during the abstraction of the training data in the assumption that the internal structure of a phrase is independent of its exact location in the sentence. The high accuracy of Memory-Based Sequence Learning (cf. Section 3.2.1), as well as recent empirical studies of word order (cf. (Kurz, 2000) for example), suggest that this is only partially true, and a more thorough investigation of how sequence information can be used in parsing without losing too much flexibility in ordering constituents may be fruitful.

The use of tree fragments larger than rewrite rules in parsing counteracts the independence assumption in grouping constituents. These fragments allow the inclusion of information about a larger context in parsing, which has been shown to improve results in DOP (cf. Chapter 4). However, the use of larger structures leads to a significantly higher processing load since the number of combinations of fragments of different size grows exponentially. It is thus necessary to investigate methods that allow the use of such larger structures without overly increasing the processing load.

The memory-based parser presented in Chapter 5 is a first attempt at using the two main adaptations described above without sacrificing efficiency. The approach is especially tailored towards processing spontaneous speech. In other domains, the insistence on following the linear order of words or parts of speech will cause data sparseness problems of a higher magnitude than for speech data. Consequently, future work in this area needs to address the problem of including more information on the parsing process, while at the same time keeping the flexibility in ordering constituents, which is necessary for parsing unseen events not present in the limited training data.

In conclusion, memory-based parsing was shown to be successful for the task of syntactic parsing. The empirical tests prove that the bias of memory-based parsing is well-suited to this task. As shown above, the problems that can be identified for this paradigm are the same as those in other parsing paradigms. The already existing modifications of memory-based learning show that the approach is flexible enough to be further adapted for an optimized parsing architecture.

Appendix A
The Stuttgart-Tübingen Tagset

POS =	description	examples
ADJA	attributive adjective	*[das] große [Haus]*
ADJD	adverbial or predicative adjective	*[er fährt] schnell [er ist] schnell*
ADV	adverb	*schon, bald, doch*
APPR	preposition; left circumposition	*in [der Stadt], ohne [mich]*
APPRART	preposition + article	*im [Haus], zur [Sache]*
APPO	postposition	*[ihm] zufolge, [der Sache] wegen*
APZR	right circumposition	*[von jetzt] an*
ART	definite or indefinite article	*der, die, das, ein, eine*
CARD	cardinal number	*zwei [Männer], [im Jahre] 1994*
FM	foreign language material	*[Er hat das mit "] A big fish [" übersetzt]*
ITJ	interjection	*mhm, ach, tja*
KOUI	subordinating conjunction with "zu" and infinitive	*um [zu leben], anstatt [zu fragen]*
KOUS	subordinating conjunction with clause	*weil, daß, damit, wenn, ob*
KON	coordinating conjunction	*und, oder, aber*
KOKOM	particle of comparison, no clause	*als, wie*
NN	noun	*Tisch, Herr, [das] Reisen*
NE	proper noun	*Hans, Hamburg, HSV*
PDS	substituting demonstrative pronoun	*dieser, jener*
PDAT	attributive demonstrative pronoun	*jener [Mensch]*
PIS	substituting indefinite pronoun	*keiner, viele, man, niemand*
PIAT	attributive indefinite pronoun without determiner	*kein [Mensch], irgendein [Glas]*
PIDAT	attributive indefinite	*[ein] wenig [Wasser],*

POS =	description	examples
	pronoun with determiner	*[die] beiden [Brüder]*
PPER	irreflexive personal pronoun	*ich, er, ihm, mich, dir*
PPOSS	substituting possessive pronoun	*meins, deiner*
PPOSAT	attributive possessive pronoun	*mein [Buch], deine [Mutter]*
	relative pronoun	
PRELS	substituting	*[der Hund,] der*
PRELAT	attributive relative pronoun	*[der Mann ,] dessen [Hund]*
PRF	reflexive personal pronoun	*sich, einander, dich, mir*
PWS	substituting interrogative pronoun	*wer, was*
PWAT	attributive interrogative pronoun	*welche [Farbe], wessen [Hut]*
PWAV	adverbial interrogative or relative pronoun	*warum, wo, wann, worüber, wobei*
PAV	pronominally used preposition	*dafür, dabei, deswegen, trotzdem*
PTKZU	"zu" with infinitive	*zu [gehen]*
PTKNEG	negation	*nicht*
PTKVZ	separated verb particle	*[er kommt] an, [er fährt] rad*
PTKANT	answer particle	*ja, nein, danke, bitte*
PTKA	particle with adjective or adverb	*am [schönsten], zu [schnell]*
TRUNC	truncated word - first part	*An– [und Abreise]*
VVFIN	finite main verb	*[du] gehst, [wir] kommen [an]*
VVIMP	imperative, main verb	*komm [!]*
VVINF	infinitive, main	*gehen, ankommen*
VVIZU	infinitive with "zu", main	*anzukommen, loszulassen*
VVPP	perfect participle, main	*gegangen, angekommen*
VAFIN	finite verb, aux	*[du] bist, [wir] werden*
VAIMP	imperative, aux	*sei [ruhig !]*
VAINF	infinitive, aux	*werden, sein*
VAPP	perfect participle, aux	*gewesen*
VMFIN	finite verb, modal	*dürfen*
VMINF	infinitive, modal	*wollen*

POS =	description	examples
VMPP	perfect participle, modal	*[er hat] gekonnt*
XY	non-word containing special characters	*D2XW3*
$,	comma	,
$.	sentence-final punctuation	. ? ! ; :
$(	sentence -internal punctuation	– [ ] ( )

For the use in TüBa-D/S and in TüSBL, there were two minor adaptations from the original tagset (Schiller et al., 1995, pp. 7 – 8): instead of the POS tag "PAV", the tag "PROP" (for: pronominal adverb) was used. And an additional POS tag "BS" for single characters in spellings was introduced.

Appendix B
The TüBa-D/S Inventory of Syntactic Categories and Grammatical Functions

Phrase Node Labels	
NX	noun phrase
PX	prepositional phrase
ADVX	adverbial phrase
ADJX	adjectival phrase
VXFIN	finite verb phrase
VXINF	infinite verb phrase
DP	determiner phrase (e.g. *gar keine*)
Topological Field Node Labels	
LV	resumptive construction (Linksversetzung)
VF	initial field (Vorfeld)
LK	left sentence bracket (Linke (Satz-)Klammer)
MF	middle field (Mittelfeld)
VC	verb complex (Verbkomplex)
NF	final field (Nachfeld)
C	complementizer field (C-Feld)
KOORD	field for coordinative particles
PARORD	field for coordinative particles
FKOORD	coordination consisting of conjuncts of fields
Field Conjunct Node Labels	
LKM, LKMVC, LKMVCN, LKMN, LKVCN, LKN, MVC, MVCN, MN, VCN, CM, CMVC	combinations of fields - node labels are derived by concatenation of conjunct field labels (V = VF, M = MF, N = NF) e.g. LKM = LK + MF
Root Node Labels	
SIMPX	simplex clause
R-SIMPX	relative clause
P-SIMPX	paratactic construction of simplex clauses
DM	discourse marker

The syntactic categories in TüBa-D/S (Stegmann et al., 2000, p. 20).

Edge Labels denoting Head	
HD	head
-	non-head
Complement Edge Labels	
ON	nominative object
OD	dative object
OA	accusative object
OS	sentential object
OPP	prepositional object
OADVP	adverbial object
OADJP	adjectival object
PRED	predicate
OV	verbal object
FOPP	optional prepositional object
VPT	separable verb prefix
APP	apposition
Modifier Edge Labels	
MOD	ambiguous modifier
ON-MOD, OA-MOD, OD-MOD, MOD-MOD, V-MOD, OPP-MOD, PRED-MOD, FOPP-MOD	modifiers modifying complements or modifiers e.g. V-MOD = modifier of the verb
Edge Labels in Split-up Coordinations	
ONK, ODK, OAK, OPPK, FOPPK, OADJPK, PREDK, MODK, OA-MODK, V-MODK, OPP-MODK, PREDMODK, MOD-MODK	second conjunct in split-up coordinations e.g. ONK = second conjunct of a nominative object (subject)
Secondary Edge Labels	
ref1	first verbal object in VC selected by a verbal object

The grammatical function labels in TüBa-D/S (Stegmann et al., 2000, p. 21).

References

Abney, Steven. 1991. "Parsing by Chunks". Robert Berwick, Steven Abney & Caroll Tenney, eds. *Principle-Based Parsing.* Dordrecht: Kluwer Academic Publishers. 257–278.

Abney, Steven. 1996. "Partial Parsing via Finite-State Cascades". John Carroll, ed. *ESSLLI Workshop on Robust Parsing.* Prague, Czech Republic. 8–15.

Aha, David, Dennis Kibler & Marc K. Albert. 1991. "Instance-Based Learning Algorithms". *Machine Learning* 6.37–66.

Aha, David W. 1991. "Incremental Constructive Induction: An Instance-Based Approach". *Proceedings of the 8th International Workshop on Machine Learning.* Evanston, IL. Morgan Kaufmann. 117–121.

Aha, David W. 1998. "Feature Weighting for Lazy Learning Algorithms". H. Liu & H. Motoda, eds. *Feature Extraction, Construction, and Selection: A Data Mining Perspective.* Boston, London: Kluwer Academic Publishers.

Aha, David W. & Robert L. Goldstone. 1990. "Learning Attribute Relevance in Context in Instance-Based Learning Algorithms". *Proceedings of the 12th Annual Conference of the Cognitive Science Society.* Hillsdale, NJ. Lawrence Erlbaum. 141–148.

Aha, David W. & Robert L. Goldstone. 1992. "Concept Learning and Flexible Weighting". *Proceedings of the 14th Annual Conference of the Cognitive Science Society.* Hillsdale, NJ. Lawrence Erlbaum. 534–539.

Aït-Mokhtar, Salah & Jean-Pierre Chanod. 1997. "Incremental Finite-State Parsing". *Proceedings of the 5th Conference on Applied Natural Language Processing, ANLP '97.* Washington, D.C. 72–79.

Argamon, Shlomo, Ido Dagan & Yuval Krymolowski. 1998. "A Memory-Based Approach to Learning Shallow Natural Language Patterns". *Proceedings of the 36th Annual Meeting of the Association for Computational Linguistics and the 17th International Conference on Computational Linguistics, COLING/ACL 1998.* Montreal, Canada. 67–73.

Argamon, Shlomo, Ido Dagan & Yuval Krymolowski. 1999. "A Memory-Based Approach to Learning Shallow Natural Language Patterns". *Journal of Experimental and Theoretical AI* 11.369–390. Special Issue on Memory-Based Language Processing.

Baar, Thomas & Mario Lenz. 1996. *Fallbasiertes Schließen - Eine kurze Übersicht.* Institut für Informatik, LFG KI, Humboldt-Universität zu Berlin.
URL: *http://www.informatik.hu-berlin.de/Institut/struktur/ki/forschung/FBS/index.html*

Baker, James K. 1979. "Trainable Grammars for Speech Recognition". *Proceedings of the Spring Conference of the Acoustic Society of America.* Boston, MA. 547–550.

Bangalore, Srinivas, Christine Doran, Beth Ann Hockey & Aravind Joshi. 1996. "An Approach to Robust Partial Parsing and Evaluation Metrics". John Carroll, ed. *ESSLLI Workshop on Robust Parsing.* Prague, Czech Republic. 70–82.

Banko, Michele & Eric Brill. 2001*a*. "Mitigating the Paucity-of-Data Problem: Exploring the Effect of Training Corpus Size on Classifier Performance for Natural Language Processing". *Proceedings of HLT 2001, First International Conference on Human Language Technology Research.* San Diego, CA. 253–257.

Banko, Michele & Eric Brill. 2001*b*. "Scaling to Very Very Large Corpora for Natural Language Disambiguation". *Proceedings of the 39th Annual Meeting of the Association for Computational Linguistics and the 10th Conference of the European Chapter of the Association for Computational Linguistics, ACL/EACL 2001.* Toulouse, France. 26–33.

Basili, Roberto, Maria Teresa Pazienza & Fabio Massimo Zanzotto. 1998. "Evaluating a Robust Parser for Italian Language". *Proceedings of the International Conference on Language Resources and Evaluation, LREC 1998.* Granada, Spain.

Bies, Ann, Mark Ferguson, Karen Katz & Robert MacIntyre. 1995. *Bracketing Guidelines for Treebank II Style Penn Treebank Project.* University of Pennsylvania.
URL: *ftp://ftp.cis.upenn.edu/pub/treebank/doc/manual/*

Black, Ezra, Frederick Jelinek, John Lafferty, David Magerman, Robert Mercer & Salim Roukos. 1992. "Towards History-Based Grammars: Using Richer Models for Probabilistic Parsing". *Proceedings of the DARPA Speech and Natural Language Workshop.* Harriman, NY. 31–37.

Black, Ezra, Steven Abney, Dan Flickinger, Claudia Gdaniec, Ralph Grishman, Philip Harrison, Donald Hindle, Robert Ingria, Frederick Jelinek, Judith Klavans, Mark Liberman, Mitchell Marcus, Salim Roukos, Beatrice Santorini & Tomek Strzalkowski. 1991. "A Procedure for Quantitatively Comparing the Syntactic Coverage of English Grammars". *Pro-*

ceedings of the DARPA Speech and Natural Language Workshop 1991. Pacific Grove, CA. 306–311.

Bod, Rens. 1992. "A Computational Model of Language Performance". *Proceedings of the 14th International Conference on Computational Linguistics, COLING 92.* Nantes, France.

Bod, Rens. 1998. *Beyond Grammar: An Experience-Based Theory of Language.* Stanford, CA: CSLI Publications.

Bod, Rens. 2000*a*. *Do All Fragments Count.* Technical Report COMP-11-12. Institute for Logic, Language and Computation, University of Amsterdam.
URL: *http://xxx.lanl.gov/ps/cs.CL/0011404*

Bod, Rens. 2000*b*. "Parsing with the Shortest Derivation". *Proceedings of the 18th International Conference on Computational Linguistics COLING 2000.* Saarbrücken, Germany.

Bod, Rens & Remko Scha. 1996. *Data-Oriented Language Processing: An Overview.* Technical Report LP-96-13. Institute for Logic, Language and Computation, University of Amsterdam.

Bod, Rens & Ron Kaplan. 1998. "A Probabilistic Corpus-Driven Model for Lexical-Functional Grammar". *Proceedings of the 36th Annual Meeting of the Association for Computational Linguistics and the 17th International Conference on Computational Linguistics, COLING/ACL 1998.* Montreal, Canada. 145–151.

Bod, Rens & Ronald Kaplan. 2003. "A DOP Model for Lexical-Functional Grammar". Rens Bod, Remko Scha & Khalil Sima'an, eds. *Data-Oriented Parsing.* Stanford, CA: CSLI Publications. Chapter 12, 211–232.

Bonnema, Remko & Remko Scha. 2003. "Reconsidering the Probability Model for Data-Oriented Parsing". Rens Bod, Remko Scha & Khalil Sima'an, eds. *Data-Oriented Parsing.* Stanford, CA: CSLI Publications. Chapter 3, 25–41.

Bonnema, Remko, Rens Bod & Remko Scha. 1997. "A DOP Model for Semantic Interpretation". *Proceedings of the 35th Annual Meeting of the Association for Computational Linguistics and the 8th Conference of the European Chapter of the Association for Computational Linguistics, ACL/EACL'97.* Madrid, Spain. 159–167.

Brants, Thorsten. 1997. *The NeGra Export Format for Annotated Corpora.* Universität des Saarlandes, Computational Linguistics. Saarbrücken, Germany.

Brants, Thorsten. 1998. *TnT–A Statistical Part-of-Speech Tagger.* Universität des Saarlandes, Computational Linguistics. Saarbrücken, Ger-

many.
URL: *http://www.coli.uni-sb.de/~thorsten/tnt/*

Brants, Thorsten. 1999*a*. "Cascaded Markov Models". *Proceedings of EACL '99, Ninth Conference of the European Chapter of the Association for Computational Linguistics.* Bergen, Norway. 118–125.

Brants, Thorsten. 1999*b*. *Tagging and Parsing with Cascaded Markov Models.* Vol. 6 of *Saarbrücken Dissertations in Computational Linguistics and Language Technology.* DFKI, Universität des Saarlandes.

Brants, Thorsten. 2000. "TnT–A Statistical Part-of-Speech Tagger". *Proceedings of the 6th Conference on Applied Natural Language Processing, ANLP-2000.* Seattle, WA. 224–231.

Brants, Thorsten & Wojciech Skut. 1998. "Automation of Treebank Annotation". *Proceedings of the Joint Conference on New Methods in Natural Language Processing and Computational Language Learning, NeMLaP3/CoNLL98.* Sydney, Australia. 49–57.

Brill, Eric. 1993. *A Corpus-Based Approach to Transformation-Based Learning.* PhD thesis. University of Pennsylvania.

Buchholz, Sabine. 1998. "Distinguishing Complements from Adjuncts Using Memory-Based Learning". *Proceedings of the ESSLLI-98 Workshop on Automated Acquisition of Syntax and Parsing.* Saarbrücken, Germany. 41–48.

Buchholz, Sabine. 2002. *Memory-Based Grammatical Relation Finding.* PhD thesis. University of Tilburg, The Netherlands.

Buchholz, Sabine, Jorn Veenstra & Walter Daelemans. 1999. "Cascaded Grammatical Relation Assignment". *Proceedings of the Joint SIGDAT Conference on Empirical Methods in NLP and Very Large Corpora, EMNLP/VLC-99.* University of Maryland, College Park, MD. 239–246.

Bunt, Harry. 1996. "Formal Tools for Describing and Processing Discontinuous Constituency Structure". Harry Bunt & Arthur van Horck, eds. *Discontinuous Constituency.* Berlin: Mouton de Gruyter. 63–83.

Cain, Thomas, Michael J. Pazzani & Glenn Silverstein. 1991. "Using Domain Knowledge to Influence Similarity Judgement". *Proceedings of the Case-Based Reasoning Workshop.* Washington, D.C. 191–202.

Cardie, Claire. 1993. "Using Decision Trees to Improve Case-Based Learning". *Proceedings of the 10th International Conference on Machine Learning.* Amherst, MA. Morgan Kaufmann. 25–32.

Cardie, Claire & Nicholas Howe. 1997. "Improving Minority Class Prediction Using Case-Specific Feature Weights". *Proceedings of the 14th International Conference on Machine Learning.* Nashville, TN. Morgan Kaufmann. 57–65.

Carroll, John & Ted Briscoe. 1996. "Apportioning Development Effort in a Probabilistic LR Parsing System Through Evaluation". *Proceedings of the ACL/SIGDAT Conference on Empirical Methods in Natural Language Processing.* University of Pennsylvania, Philadelphia, PA. 92–100.

Carroll, John, Ted Briscoe & Antonio Sanfilippo. 1998. "Parser Evaluation: a Survey and a New Proposal". *Proceedings of the 1st International Conference on Language Resources and Evaluation LREC 1998.* Granada, Spain. 447–454.

Chappelier, Jean-Cédric & Martin Rajman. 1998. "A generalized CYK Algorithm for Parsing Stochastic CFG". *Proceedings of Tabulation in Parsing and Deduction (TAPD'98).* Paris, France. 133–137.

Charniak, Eugene. 2000. "A Maximum-Entropy-Inspired Parser". *Proceedings of the 1st Conference of the North American Chapter of the Association for Computational Linguistics and the 6th Conference on Applied Natural Language Processing, ANLP/NAACL'2000.* Seattle, WA. 132–139.

Charniak, Eugene. 2001. "Immediate Head Parsing for Language Models". *Proceedings of the 39th Annual Meeting of the ACL and the 10th Conference of the European Chapter of the ACL, ACL/EACL 2001.* Toulouse, France. 116–123.

Chen, Keh-Jiann, Chi-Ching Luo, Zhao-Ming Gao, Ming-Chung Chang, Feng-Yi Chen & Chao-Jan Chen. 1999. "The CKIP Chinese Treebank". *Journées ATALA sur les Corpus Annotés sur la Syntaxe.* TALANA, Paris VII, France.

Christianini, Nello & John Shawe-Taylor. 2000. *An Introduction to Support Vector Machines and Other Kernel-Based Learning Methods.* Cambridge: Cambridge University Press.

Church, Kenneth & Robert Mercer. 1993. "Introduction to the Special Issue on Computational Linguistics Using Very Large Corpora". *Computational Linguistics* 19:1.1–24.

Collins, Michael. 1999. *Head-Driven Statistical Models for Natural Language Parsing.* PhD thesis. University of Pennsylvania.

Cost, Scott & Steven Salzberg. 1993. "A Weighted Nearest Neighbor Algorithm for Learning with Symbolic Features". *Machine Learning* 10:1.57–78.

Cover, Thomas M. & Joy A. Thomas. 1991. *Elements of Information Theory.* New York: John Wiley.

Daelemans, Walter & Antal van den Bosch. 1992. "Generalization Performance of Backpropagation Learning on a Syllabification Task". *Proceedings of TWLT3: Connectionism and Natural Language Processing.*

Enschede, The Netherlands. 27–37.

Daelemans, Walter, Antal van den Bosch & Jakub Zavrel. 1997. "A Feature-Relevance Heuristic for Indexing and Compressing Large Case Bases". *Proceedings of the Ninth European Conference on Machine Learning.* Prague, Czech Republic.

Daelemans, Walter, Antal van den Bosch & Jakub Zavrel. 1999. "Forgetting Exceptions is Harmful in Language Learning". *Machine Learning* 34.11–43. Special Issue on Natural Language Learning.

Daelemans, Walter, Antal van den Bosch & Ton Weijters. 1996. "IGTree: Using Trees for Compression and Classification in Lazy Learning Algorithms". *Artificial Intelligence Review* 11.407–423.

Daelemans, Walter, Jakub Zavrel, Ko van der Sloot & Antal van den Bosch. 2001. *TiMBL: Tilburg Memory Based Learner– version 4.1–Reference Guide.* Technical Report ILK 01-04. Induction of Linguistic Knowledge, Computational Linguistics, Tilburg University.
URL: *http://ilk.kub.nl/downloads/pub/papers/ilk.0104.ps.gz*

Daelemans, Walter, Jakub Zavrel, Ko van der Sloot & Antal van den Bosch. 2002. *TiMBL: Tilburg Memory Based Learner– version 4.2–Reference Guide.* Technical Report ILK 02-01. Induction of Linguistic Knowledge, Computational Linguistics, Tilburg University.
URL: *http://ilk.kub.nl/downloads/pub/papers/ilk.0201.ps*

Daelemans, Walter, Jakub Zavrel, Peter Berck & Steven Gillis. 1996. "MBT: A Memory-Based Part of Speech Tagger-Generator". Eva Ejerhed & Ido Dagan, eds. *Proceedings of the 4th Workshop on Very Large Corpora.* Copenhagen, Denmark. 14–27.

Daelemans, Walter, Sabine Buchholz & Jorn Veenstra. 1999. "Memory-Based Shallow Parsing". *Proceedings of Computational Natural Language Learning, CoNLL-99.* Bergen, Norway. 53–60.

Daelemans, Walter, Steven Gillis, Gert Durieux & Antal van den Bosch. 1993. "Learnability and Markedness in Data-Driven Acquisition of Stress". T. Mark Ellison & James M. Scobbie, eds. *Computational Phonology.* Vol. 8. Edinburgh Working Papers in Cognitive Science. 157–178.

Daelemans, Walter & Véronique Hoste. 2002. "Evaluation of Machine Learning Methods for Natural Language Processing". *Proceedings of the 3rd International Conference on Language Resources and Evaluation (LREC 2002).* Las Palmas, Gran Canaria. 755–760.

Daelemans, Walter, Véronique Hoste, Fien De Meulder & Bart Naudts. 2003. "Combined Optimization of Feature Selection and Algorithm Parameter Interaction in Machine Learning of Language". *Proceedings of the 14th European Conference on Machine Learning (ECML-2003).* Vol. 2837 of *Lecture Notes in Computer Science.* Cavtat-Dubrovnik, Croatia. Berlin: Springer. 84–95.

Dagan, Ido, Lillian Lee & Fernando Pereira. 1997. "Similarity-Based Models of Word Cooccurrence Probabilities". *Proceedings of the 35th Annual Meeting of the ACL.* Somerset, NJ. 56–63.

Dagan, Ido & Yuval Krymolowski. 2003. "Compositional Memory-Based Partial Parsing". Rens Bod, Remko Scha & Khalil Sima'an, eds. *Data-Oriented Parsing.* Stanford, CA: CSLI Publications. Chapter 10, 169–188.

De Pauw, Guy. 2000. "Aspects of Pattern-Matching in Data-Oriented Parsing". *Proceedings of the 18th International Conference on Computational Linguistics COLING 2000.* Saarbrücken, Germany.
URL: *http://xxx.lanl.gov/ps/cs.CL/0008014*

De Pauw, Guy. 2002. *An Agent-Based Evolutionary Computing Approach to Memory-Based Syntactic Parsing of Natural Language.* PhD thesis. Department of Germanic Languages, University of Antwerp.

De Pauw, Guy. 2003. "An Approximation of DOP Through Memory Based Learning". Rens Bod, Remko Scha & Khalil Sima'an, eds. *Data-Oriented Parsing.* Stanford, CA: CSLI Publications. Chapter 9, 147–167.

Drach, Erich. 1937. *Grundgedanken der Deutschen Satzlehre.* Frankfurt/M.: Diesterweg.

Dudani, Sahibsingh. 1976. "The Distance-Weighted k-Nearest Neighbor Rule". *IEEE transactions on Systems, Man, and Cybernetics* SMC-6.325–327.

Erdmann, Oskar. 1886. *Grundzüge der deutschen Syntax nach ihrer geschichtlichen Entwicklung dargestellt.* Stuttgart: Verlag der Cotta'schen Buchhandlung. Erste Abteilung.

Escudero, Gerard, Lluìs Márquez & German Rigau. 2000. "Naive Bayes and Exemplar-Based Approaches to Word Sense Disambiguation Revisited". *Proceedings of the 14th European Conference on Artificial Intelligence, ECAI'2000.* Berlin, Germany. 421–425.

Everitt, Brian. 1981. *Cluster Analysis.* London: Heinmann.

Feller, William. 1968. *An Introduction to Probability Theory and Its Applications.* New York, NY: John Wiley.

Friedman, Jerome H. 1994. *Flexible Metric Nearest Neighbor Classification.* Technical report. Stanford University.
URL: *http://www-stat.stanford.edu/~jhf*

Good, I.J. 1953. "The Population Frequencies of Species and the Estimation of Population Parameters". *Biometrika* 40.237–264.

Goodman, Joshua. 1996*a*. "Efficient Algorithms for Parsing the DOP Model". *Proceedings of the Conference on Empirical Methods in Natural Language Processing.* Philadelphia, PA.

Goodman, Joshua. 1996*b*. "Parsing Algorithms and Metrics". *Proceedings of the 34th Annual Meeting of the ACL.* Santa Cruz, CA. 177–183.

Goodman, Joshua. 1998. *Parsing Inside-Out.* PhD thesis. Harvard University. Cambridge, MA.

Goodman, Joshua. 2003. "Efficient Parsing of DOP with PCFG-Reductions". Rens Bod, Remko Scha & Khalil Sima'an, eds. *Data-Oriented Parsing.* Stanford, CA: CSLI Publications. Chapter 8, 125–146.

Hearne, Mary & Andy Way. 2004. "Data-Oriented Parsing and the Penn Chinese Treebank". *Proceedings of The First International Joint Conference on Natural Language Processing.* Hainan Island, China.

Heringer, Hans Jürgen. 1996. *Deutsche Syntax Dependentiell.* Tübingen: Stauffenburg-Verlag.

Herling, Simon Heinrich Adolf. 1821. "Über die Topik der deutschen Sprache". *Abhandlungen des frankfurterischen Gelehrtenvereins für deutsche Sprache.* Frankfurt/M. 296–362, 394. Drittes Stück.

Hinrichs, Erhard W., Julia Bartels, Yasuhiro Kawata, Valia Kordoni & Heike Telljohann. 2000*a*. "The Tübingen Treebanks for Spoken German, English, and Japanese". Wolfgang Wahlster, ed. *Verbmobil: Foundations of Speech-to-Speech Translation.* Berlin: Springer. 550–574.

Hinrichs, Erhard W., Julia Bartels, Yasuhiro Kawata, Valia Kordoni & Heike Telljohann. 2000*b*. "The Verbmobil Treebanks". *Proceedings of KONVENS 2000, 5. Konferenz zur Verarbeitung natürlicher Sprache.* Ilmenau, Germany. 107–112.

Hinrichs, Erhard W., Sandra Kübler, Valia Kordoni & Frank H. Müller. 2000. "Robust Chunk Parsing for Spontaneous Speech". Wolfgang Wahlster, ed. *Verbmobil: Foundations of Speech-to-Speech Translation.* Artificial Intelligence. Berlin: Springer Verlag. 163–182.

Höhle, Tilman. 1986. "Der Begriff "Mittelfeld", Anmerkungen über die Theorie der topologischen Felder". *Akten des Siebten Internationalen Germanistenkongresses 1985.* Göttingen, Germany. 329–340.

Jelinek, Frederick. 1997. *Statistical Methods for Speech Recognition.* Cambridge, MA: MIT Press.

Jelinek, Frederick, John Lafferty & Robert Mercer. 1990. *Basic Methods of Probabilistic Context Free Parsing.* Technical Report IBM RC 16374, #72684. IBM. Yorktown Heights, NY.

Johnson, Mark. 2002. "The DOP Estimation Method Is Biased and Inconsistent". *Computational Linguistics* 28:1.71–76.

Joshi, Aravind. 1987. "An Introduction to Tree Adjoining Grammars". A. Manaster-Ramer, ed. *Mathematics of Language.* Amsterdam: John Benjamins. 87–115.

Kaplan, Ronald & Joan Bresnan. 1982. "Lexical Functional Grammar: A Formal System for Grammatical Representation". Joan Bresnan, ed. *The Mental Representation of Grammatical Relations.* Cambridge, MA: MIT Press. 173–281.

Kathol, Andreas. 2000. *Linear Syntax.* Oxford Univesity Press.

Katz, Slava M. 1987. "Estimation of Probabilities from Sparse Data for the Language Model Component of a Speech Recognizer". *IEEE Transactions on Acoustics, Speech and Signal Processing* 35:3.400–401.

Kiefer, Bernd, Hans-Ulrich Krieger & Mark-Jan Nederhof. 2000. "Efficient and Robust Parsing of Word Hypotheses Graphs". Wolfgang Wahlster, ed. *Verbmobil: Foundations of Speech-to-Speech Translation.* Artificial Intelligence. Berlin: Springer Verlag. 280–295.

Kolodner, Janet. 1993. *Case-Based Reasoning.* San Mateo, CA: Morgan Kaufmann.

Kool, Anne, Jakub Zavrel & Walter Daelemans. 2000. "Simultaneous Feature Selection and Parameter Optimization for Memory-Based Natural Language Processing". *Proceedings of the 10th BENELEARN Meeting.* Tilburg, The Netherlands. 93–100.

Kool, Anne, Walter Daelemans & Jakub Zavrel. 2000. "Genetic Algorithms for Feature Relevance Assignement in Memory-Based Processing". *Proceedings of the 4th Conference on Computational Natural Language Learning (CoNLL-00) and of the Second Learning Language in Logic (LLL-00) Workshop.* Lisbon, Portugal. 103–106.

Kordoni, Valia. 2000. *Stylebook for the English Treebank in VERBMOBIL.* Technical Report 241. Verbmobil.
URL: *http://verbmobil.dfki.de/cgi-bin/verbmobil/htbin/doc-access.cgi*

Krymolowski, Yuval & Ido Dagan. 2000. "Incorporating Compositional Evidence in Memory-Based Partial Parsing". *Proceedings of the 38th Annual Meeting of the Association for Computational Linguistics, ACL 2000.* Hong Kong.

Kübler, Sandra. 2001. "Braucht Nominalphrasenerkennung linguistisches Wissen?". Henning Lobin, ed. *Proceedings der GLDV-Frühjahrstagung.* Gießen, Germany. 225–233.

Kübler, Sandra. 2002. *Memory-Based Parsing of a German Corpus.* PhD thesis. Seminar für Sprachwissenschaft, Universität Tübingen. Version of 3rd Nov. 2002.

Kübler, Sandra. 2003. "Parsing Without Grammar – Using Complete Trees Instead". *Proceedings of the International Conference on Recent Advances in Natural Language Processing, RANLP 2003.* Borovets, Bulgaria.

Kübler, Sandra & Erhard W. Hinrichs. 2000. "Robustes Chunkparsing mit variabler Analysetiefe". *Proceedings of KONVENS 2000, 5. Konferenz zur Verarbeitung natürlicher Sprache.* Ilmenau, Germany. 121–126.

Kübler, Sandra & Erhard W. Hinrichs. 2001*a*. "From Chunks to Function-Argument Structure: A Similarity-Based Approach". *Proceedings of the 39th Annual Meeting of the ACL and the 10th Conference of the European Chapter of the ACL, ACL/EACL 2001.* Toulouse, France. 338–345.

Kübler, Sandra & Erhard W. Hinrichs. 2001*b*. "TüSBL: A Similarity-Based Chunk Parser for Robust Syntactic Processing". *Proceedings of the 1st International Human Language Technology Conference, HLT-2001.* San Diego, CA. 356–361.

Kübler, Sandra & Heike Telljohann. 2002. "Towards a Dependency-Based Evaluation for Partial Parsing". *Proceedings of the LREC-Workshop Beyond PARSEVAL–Towards Improved Evaluation Measures for Parsing Systems.* Las Palmas, Gran Canaria. 9–16.

Kurz, Daniela. 2000. "A Statistical Account on Word Order Variation in German". *Proceedings of the Workshop on Linguistically Interpreted Corpora LINC-2000.* Luxembourg. 35–41.

Langley, Pat & Wayne Iba. 1993. "Average-Case Analysis of a Nearest Neighbor Algorithm". *Proceedings of the 13th International Joint Conference on Artificial Intelligence (IJCAI-93).* Chambery, France. Morgan Kaufmann. 889–894.

Lin, Dekang. 1995. "A Dependency-Based Method for Evaluating Broad-Coverage Parsers". *Proceedings of the 14th International Joint Conference on Artificial Intelligence, IJCAI-95.* Montreal, Canada. 1420–1425.

Lin, Dekang. 1998. "A Depedency-Based Method for Evaluating Broad-Coverage Parsers". *Natural Language Engineering* 4:2.97–114.

Manning, Christopher D. & Hinrich Schütze. 1999. *Foundations of Statistical Natural Language Processing.* Cambridge, MA: MIT Press.

Marcus, Mitchell, Beatrice Santorini & Mary Ann Marcinkiewicz. 1993. "Building a Large Annotated Corpus of English: The Penn Treebank". *Computational Linguistics* 19:2.313–330.

Marcus, Mitchell, Grace Kim, Mary Ann Marcinkiewicz, Robert MacIntyre,

Ann Bies, Mark Ferguson, Karen Katz & Britta Schasberger. 1994. "The Penn Treebank: Annotating Predicate Argument Structure". *Proceedings of the ARPA Human Language Technology Workshop, HLT 94*. Plainsboro, NJ.

McArthur, Tom, ed. 1992. *The Oxford Companion to the English Language*. Oxford: Oxford University Press.

Mel'čuk, Igor A. 1988. *Dependency Syntax: Theory and Practise*. SUNY Series in Linguistics. Albany, NY: State University of New York Press.

Mitchell, Melanie. 1996. *An Introduction to Genetic Algorithms*. Cambridge, MA: MIT Press.

Mitchell, Tom. 1997. *Machine Learning*. Boston, MA: McGraw-Hill.

Mitchell, Tom, Richard Keller & Smadar Kedar-Cabelli. 1986. "Explanation-Based Learning: A Unifying View". *Machine Learning* 1.47–80.

Mooney, Raymond J. 1996. "Comparative Experiments on Disambiguating Word Senses: An Illustration of the Role of Bias in Machine Learning". *Proceedings of the 1st Conference on Empirical Methods in Natural Language Processing EMNLP*. Philadelphia, PA. 82–91.

Motwani, Rajeev & P. Ragavan. 1995. *Randomized Algorithms*. Cambridge: Cambridge University Press.

Murphy, P.M. & David W. Aha. 1994. *UCI Repository of Machine Learning Databases [Machine-Readable Data Repository]*. Technical report. University of California, Irvine.

Naumann, Sven & Hagen Langer. 1994. *Parsing: Eine Einführung in die maschinelle Analyse natürlicher Sprache*. Stuttgart: Teubner.

Neumann, Günter. 2003. "A Data-Driven Approach to Head-Driven Phrase Structure Grammar". Rens Bod, Remko Scha & Khalil Sima'an, eds. *Data-Oriented Parsing*. Stanford, CA: CSLI Publications. Chapter 13, 233–251.

Nosofsky, Robert M. 1986. "Attention, Similarity, and the Identification-Categorization Relationship". *Journal of Experimental Psychology: General* 15.39–57.

Nosofsky, Robert M. 1987. "Attention and Learning Processes in the Identification and Categorization of Integral Stimuli". *Journal of Experimental Psychology: Learning, Memory, and Cognition* 13.87–108.

Pinker, Steven. 1979. "Formal Models of Language Learning". *Cognition* 7.217–283.

Plaehn, Oliver. 1998. *Annotate Bedienungsanleitung*. Universität des Saarlandes, Sonderforschungsbereich 378, Projekt C3. Saarbrücken, Germany.

Plaehn, Oliver. 1999. *Probabilistic Parsing with Discontinuous Phrase Structure Grammar*. Master's thesis. Department of Computational

Linguistics, University of the Saarland. Saarbrücken, Germany.

Pollard, Carl & Ivan Sag. 1994. *Head-Driven Phrase Structure Grammar*. Studies in Contemporary Linguistics. Chicago, IL: University of Chicago Press.

Quinlan, John Ross. 1986. "Induction of Decision Trees". *Machine Learning* 1.81–206.

Quinlan, John Ross. 1993. *C4.5: Programs for Machine Learning*. San Mateo, CA: Morgan Kaufmann.

Ramshaw, Lance A. & Mitchell P. Marcus. 1995. "Text Chunking Using Transformation-Based Learning". *Proceedings of the ACL 3rd Workshop on Very Large Corpora*. Cambridge, MA. 82–94.

Reis, Marga. 1980. "On Justifying Topological Frames: 'Positional Field' and the Order of Nonverbal Constituents in German". *DRLAV: Revue de Linguistique* 22/23.59–85.

Riesbeck, Christopher K. & Roger S. Schank. 1989. *Inside Case Based Reasoning*. Hillsdale, NJ: Lawrence Erlbaum.

Ruland, Tobias N. 2001. *Ein hybrider Ansatz zur Strukturanalyse gesprochener Spontansprache*. Vol. DISKI 247 of *Dissertationen zur Künstlichen Intelligenz*. Berlin: Akademische Verlagsgesellschaft.

Rumelhart, David E., Bernard Widrow & Michael Lehr. 1994. "The Basic Ideas in Neural Networks". *Communications of the ACM* 37:3.87–92.

Rumelhart, David E., James L. McClelland & the PDP Research Group. 1986. *Parallel Distributed Processing: Explorations in the Microstructure of Cognition*. Cambridge, MA: MIT Press.

Salzberg, Steven. 1990. *Learning with Nested Generalized Exemplars*. Boston, MA: Kluwer Academic Publishers.

Salzberg, Steven. 1991. "A Hyperractangular Learning Method". *Machine Learning* 6.251–276.

Sampson, Geoffrey. 1993. "The SUSANNE Corpus". *ICAME Journal* 17.125 - 127.

Santorini, Beatrice. 1990. "Part-Of-Speech Tagging Guidelines for the Penn Treebank Project". Department of Computer and Information Science, University of Pennsylvania, 3rd Revision, 2nd Printing.
URL: *ftp://ftp.cis.upenn.edu/pub/treebank/doc/tagguide.ps.gz*

Santorini, Beatrice. 1991. "Bracketing Guidelines for the Penn Treebank Project". Department of Computer and Information Science, University of Pennsylvania.
URL: *ftp://ftp.cis.upenn.edu/pub/treebank/doc/old-bktguide.ps.gz*

Scha, Remko, Rens Bod & Khalil Sima'an. 1999. "Memory-Based Syntactic Analysis". *Journal of Experimental and Theoretical Artificial Intel-*

ligence 11.409–440. Special Issue on Memory-Based Language Processing.

Schiller, Anne, Simone Teufel & Christine Thielen. 1995. *Guidelines für das Tagging deutscher Textkorpora mit STTS*. Technical report. Universität Stuttgart and Universität Tübingen.
URL: *http://www.sfs.nphil.uni-tuebingen.de/Elwis/stts/stts.html*

Shannon, Claude E. 1948. "A Mathematical Theory of Communication". *Bell Systems Technology Journal* 27.379–423.

Sima'an, Khalil. 2003. "Computational Complexity of Disambiguation under DOP1". Rens Bod, Remko Scha & Khalil Sima'an, eds. *Data-Oriented Parsing*. Stanford, CA: CSLI Publications. Chapter 5, 63–81.

Simon, Herbert. 1984. "Why Should Machines Learn?". Ryszard Michalski, Jaime Carbonell & Tom Mitchell, eds. *Machine Learning: An Artificial Intelligence Approach*. New York: Springer. 25–38.

Skut, Wojciech, Thorsten Brants, Brigitte Krenn & Hans Uszkoreit. 1998. "A Linguistically Interpreted Corpus of German Newspaper Texts". *ESSLLI Workshop on Recent Advances in Corpus Annotation*. Saarbrücken, Germany.

Stanfill, Craig & David L. Waltz. 1986. "Towards Memory-Based Reasoning". *Communications of the ACM* 29:12.1213–1228.

Stegmann, Rosmary, Heike Telljohann & Erhard W. Hinrichs. 2000. *Stylebook for the German Treebank in* VERBMOBIL. Technical Report 239. Verbmobil.
URL: *http://verbmobil.dfki.de/cgi-bin/verbmobil/htbin/doc-access.cgi*

Streiter, Oliver. 2001*a*. "Memory-Based Parsing: Enhancing Recursive Top-down Fuzzy Match with Bottom-Up Chunking". *19th International Conference on Computer Processing of Oriental Languages, ICCPOS 2001*. Seoul, South Korea.

Streiter, Oliver. 2001*b*. "Recursive Top-Down Fuzzy Match, New Perspectives on Memory-Based Parsing". *Proceedings of the 15th Pacific Asia Conference on Language, Information and Computation, PACLIC 2001*. Hong Kong.

Streiter, Oliver. 2002. "Abduction, Induction and Memorizing in Corpus-Based Parsing". Erhard W. Hinrichs & Sandra Kübler, eds. *Proceedings of the ESSLLI Workshop on Machine Learning Approaches to Computational Linguistics*. Trento, Italy.

Thielen, Christine & Anne Schiller. 1994. "Ein kleines und erweitertes Tagset fürs Deutsche". Helmut Feldweg & Erhard Hinrichs, eds. *Lexikon & Text*. Tübingen: Niemeyer. 215–226.

Tjong Kim Sang, Erik F. 2000. "Noun Phrase Recognition by System Combination". *Proceedings of the 1st Conference of the North American Chapter of the Association for Computational Linguistics and the 6th Conference on Applied Natural Language Processing, ANLP-NAACL 2000.* Seattle, WA. Morgan Kaufmann.

Tjong Kim Sang, Erik F. 2001. "Transforming a Chunker to a Parser". Walter Daelemans, Khalil Sima'an, Jorn Veenstra & Jakub Zavrel, eds. *Computational Linguistics in the Netherlands 2000.* Amsterdam: Rodopi. 177–188.

Tjong Kim Sang, Erik F. & Jorn Veenstra. 1999. "Representing Text Chunks". *Proceedings of EACL '99, Ninth Conference of the European Chapter of the Association for Computational Linguistics.* Bergen, Norway. 173–179.

Tjong Kim Sang, Erik & Sabine Buchholz. 2000. "Introduction to the CoNLL Shared task: Chunking". *Proceedings of CoNLL and LLL 2000.* Lisbon, Portugal. 127–132.

Tjong Kim Sang, Erik, Walter Daelemans, Hervé Déjean, Rob Koeling, Yuval Krymolowski, Vasin Punyakanok & Dan Roth. 2000. "Applying System Combination to Base Noun Phrase Identification". *Proceedings of the 18th International Conference on Computational Linguistics COLING 2000.* Saarbrücken, Germany. 857–863.

Ule, Tylman & Sandra Kübler. 2004. "From Constituent Structure to Dependencies, and Back". *Proceedings of the International Conference on Linguistic Evidence.* Tübingen, Germany.

van den Bosch, Antal. 2002. "Expanding k-NN Analogy with Instance Families". R. Skousen, D. Lonsdale & D. Parkinson, eds. *Analogical Modeling: An Exemplar-Based Approach to Language.* Amsterdam: John Benjamins. 209–224.

van den Bosch, Antal & Sabine Buchholz. 2002. "Shallow Parsing on the Basis of Words Only: A Case Study". *Proceedings of the 40th Meeting of the Association for Computational Linguistics (ACL'02).* Pittsburgh, PA. 433–440.

van den Bosch, Antal & Walter Daelemans. 1993. "Data-Oriented Methods for Grapheme-to-Phoneme Conversion". *Proceedings of the 6th Conference of the European Chapter of the ACL.* Utrecht, The Netherlands. 45–53.

van Zaanen, Menno. 2000*a*. "ABL: Alignment-Based Learning". *Proceedings of the 18th International Conference on Computational Linguistics (COLING).* Saarbrücken, Germany.

van Zaanen, Menno. 2000*b*. "Bootstrapping Syntax and Recursion Using Alignment-Based Learning". Pat Langley, ed. *Proceedings of the*

Seventeenth International Conference on Machine Learning. Morgan Kaufmann Publishers. 1063–1070.

van Zaanen, Menno. 2003. "Alignment-Based Learning Versus Data-Oriented Parsing". Rens Bod, Remko Scha & Khalil Sima'an, eds. *Data-Oriented Parsing*. Stanford, CA: CSLI Publications. Chapter 20, 385–403.

Veenstra, Jorn. 1998. "Fast NP Chunking Using Memory-Based Learning Techniques". F. Verdenius & W. van den Broek, eds. *Proceedings of BENELEARN-98*. Wageningen, The Netherlands. 71–79.

Veenstra, Jorn & Antal van den Bosch. 2000. "Single-Classifier Memory-Based Phrase Chunking". *Proceedings of the 4th Conference on Computational Language Learning (CoNLL-2000) and the Second Learning Language in Logic Workshop (LLL-2000)*. Lisbon, Portugal. 157–159.

Veenstra, Jorn, Antal van den Bosch, Sabine Buchholz, Walter Daelemans & Jakub Zavrel. 2000. "Memory-Based Word Sense Disambiguation". *Computers and the Humanities, Special Issue on Senseval, Word Sense Disambiguations* 34:1/2.171–177.

Viterbi, A. 1967. "Error Bounds for Convolutional Codes and an Asymptotically Optimum Decoding Algorithm". *IEEE Transactions on Information Theory* IT-13.260–269.

Weischedel, Ralph, Marie Meteer, Richard Schwartz, Lance Ramshaw & Jeff Palmucci. 1993. "Coping with Ambiguity and Unknown Words through Probabilistic Models". *Computational Linguistics* 19:2.359–382.

Weiss, Sholom M. & Casimir A. Kulikowski. 1991. *Computer Systems that Learn: Classification and Prediction Methods from Statistics, Neural Nets, Machine Learning, and Expert Systems*. San Mateo, CA: Morgan Kaufmann.

Wettschereck, Dietrich. 1994. *A Study of Distance-Based Machine Learning Algorithms*. PhD thesis. Department of Computer Science, Oregon State University. Corvallis, OR.

Wettschereck, Dietrich, David W. Aha & Takao Mohri. 1997. "A Review and Empirical Evaluation of Feature Weighting Methods for a Class of Lazy Learning Algorithms". *Artificial Intelligence Review* 11.273–314.

Wettschereck, Dietrich & Thomas G. Dietterich. 1995. "An Experimental Comparison of the Nearest-Neighbor and Nearest-Hyperrectangle Algorithms". *Machine Learning* 19.1–25.

Yeh, Alexander. 2000. "More Accurate Tests for the Statistical Significance of Result Differences". *Proceedings of the 18th International Conference on Computational Linguistics COLING 2000*. Saarbrücken, Germany. 947–953.

Zavrel, Jakub & Walter Daelemans. 1997*a*. "Memory-Based Learning: Using Similarity for Smoothing". *Proceedings of the 35th Annual Meeting of the Association of Computational Linguistics and the 8th Conference of the European Chapter of the ACL*. Madrid, Spain. 436–443.

Zavrel, Jakub & Walter Daelemans. 1997*b*. "Recent Advances in Memory-Based Part-of-Speech Tagging". *VI Simposio Internacional de Comunicacion Social*. Santiago de Cuba. 590–597.

Zell, Andreas. 1994. *Simulation neuronaler Netze*. Bonn: Addison-Wesley.

Index of Subjects and Terms

In the *London Oriental and African Language Library* the following titles have been published thus far or are scheduled for publication:

1 **BUNT, Harry and William BLACK (eds.):** Abduction, Belief and Context in Dialogue. Studies in computational pragmatics. 2000. vii, 471 pp.

2 **BOURIGAULT, Didier, Christian JACQUEMIN and Marie-Claude L'HOMME (eds.):** Recent Advances in Computational Terminology. 2001. xviii, 380 pp.

3 **MANI, Inderjeet:** Automatic Summarization. 2001. xii, 286 pp.

4 **MERLO, Paola and Suzanne STEVENSON (eds.):** The Lexical Basis of Sentence Processing. Formal, computational and experimental issues. 2002. viii, 363 pp.

5 **JACKSON, Peter and Isabelle MOULINIER:** Natural Language Processing for Online Applications. Text retrieval, extraction and categorization. 2002. x, 226 pp.

6 **ANDROUTSOPOULOS, Ion:** Exploring Time, Tense and Aspect in Natural Language Database Interfaces. 2002. x, 307 pp.

7 **KÜBLER, Sandra:** Memory-Based Parsing. 2004. viii, 294 pp.